14.99

W9-BBZ-431

BREAKFAST with FRIENDS

BREAKFAST with FRIENDS

Seasonal Menus to Celebrate the Morning

ELIZABETH ALSTON

WINGS BOOKS

New York • Avenel, New Jersey

This 1995 edition is published by Wings Books, distributed by Random House Value Publishing, Inc., 40 Engelhard Avenue, Avenel, New Jersey 07001, by arrangement with the author.

Random House
New York • Toronto • London • Sydney • Auckland

Printed and bound in the United States of America

Library of Congress Cataloging-in-Publication Data
Alston, Elizabeth.
Breakfast with friends : seasonal menus to celebrate the morning /
Elizabeth Alston.
p. cm.—(Wings great cookbooks)
Originally published: New York : McGraw-Hill, c1989.
Includes index.
ISBN 0-517-14788-2
1. Breakfasts. 2. Brunches. 3. Menus. I. Title. II. Series.
TX733.A37 1995   95-23445
641.5'2—dc20   CIP

8 7 6 5 4 3 2 1

For
Richard Lansing, my favorite friend
to have breakfast with

Acknowledgments

I could not have produced this book without the help of Miriam Rubin and Marinella Cancio. Miriam, a food writer and superb chef, turned many of the thoughts and tastes in my head into wonderful reality, and contributed many of her own. As a side effect of long weekend hours spent working out recipes together, you will also find several recipes from Miriam's family.

Marinella, word processing whiz in the *Woman's Day* food department, spent many of her own hours turning my heavily edited pages into beautiful, legible ones.

I'd also like to thank Ellen Levine, editor-in-chief of *Woman's Day*, for her support; Ellen Greene, my associate at *Woman's Day*, Celia Misicka, whose office I used as a weekend kitchen, and other members of the food staff who took my borrowing their equipment with grace; Susan Pomerantz and Ann Clark, food consultants and caterers both, for help with the Wedding Breakfast; Margaret Ribaroff, for inspiration and support; and finally, artist Sally Sturman who for a third book has made me look good.

ELIZABETH ALSTON

Contents

INTRODUCTION
1

SPRING

To Greet the Groundhog   5

Valentine's Day   9

Mardi Gras   12

Come See the First
Blossoms   18

An Early-Morning Picnic   21

Easter for Adults and
Children   24

For Mother, with Love   30

Graduation Day Breakfast   33

SUMMER

Memorial Day   39

For Dad, with Love, Too   42

Weekend Breakfast on the
Porch   45

Breakfast with a Southwestern
Flavor   49

Fourth of July Steak
Breakfast   54

Light Breakfast for a
Hot Day   59

Happy Birthday!   62

A Breakfast Smorgasbord   65

Lazy August Breakfast   69

FALL

Back-to-School Breakfast
Party   75

Portable Breakfast for a
Fall Outing   78

Breakfast from the Oven   81

Celebrate Rosh Hashana   84

Come Help—Raise Our
New Roof, Plant Bulbs,
Rake Leaves   89

Hearty Breakfast for
Columbus Day   92

A New England Breakfast   95

Breakfast Treats for Pumpkin
Pickers   101

Hearty Fare for a Country
Weekend   104

Thanksgiving Day   108

W I N T E R

Come Trim the Tree   *115*

Christmas Morning Feast   *120*

Hogmanay—A Scottish
New Year   *126*

After the Ball   *131*

Pre-ski Energy Input   *134*

Breakfast with a Southern
Flair   *137*

Make-ahead Breakfast   *141*

For a Cold Country
Morning   *144*

B I G
B A S H E S

Breakfast for a Crowd   *151*

Successful Big Bashes:
Advice from a Pro   *153*

A Wedding Breakfast   *154*

B R E A K F A S T
F O R
H E A L T H-
C O N S C I O U S
F R I E N D S

Great Grains   *167*

Recipes for Special Diet
Needs   *174*

B R E A K F A S T
B A S I C S

Measuring Ingredients   *183*

A Few Words About
Utensils   *185*

Breakfast Fruit   *186*

Eggs   *190*

Breakfast Meats   *195*

Breakfast Beverages   *199*

I N D E X
205

Introduction

Breakfast is absolutely my favorite time to have guests. True, I'm a morning person, and that may be part of it, but consider some of the advantages of inviting friends for breakfast:

- Everyone is at their most relaxed. On weekend mornings, Monday seems far away.
- Everyone is hungry. Whatever you serve will be happily devoured. Since most people eat cold cereal for breakfast, if anything at all, they are absolutely delighted to be presented with hot oatmeal or even the simplest bacon and eggs.
- You won't spend the entire day cleaning, cooking, and worrying yourself into a degree of high tension.
- Friends can bring their children. You can enjoy the children while your guests enjoy eating without having to worry about the baby sitter's time or cost. (If several young children are expected, it may be worth hiring a baby sitter.)
- Breakfast generally does not strain your dish collection, or for that matter, the dish washer.
- There's no need to feel you should offer wine or spirits.
- Casual clothes are in order.
- After your friends have enjoyed themselves and left, you still have a good part of the day to spend doing whatever else you want to do.

Having convinced you, I hope, that breakfast is the smartest, as well as the newest, time to entertain, you may wonder just what time breakfast is.

That depends on you and what else you've planned for the day. Breakfast before an antiquing trip is bound to be early, as is a birthday breakfast for children. Breakfast after church—a favorite with many people—dictates itself, as does breakfast before or after sports, whether you are watching or actively participating. I'd say breakfast can be anytime from pre-dawn (after an evening spent dancing) to about twelve noon. But there again, suit yourself.

Whatever hour you decide on, and whatever the time of year, you'll find a menu to match in this book. With few exceptions (one being the Mardi Gras Breakfast), the breakfasts are simple and include comforting foods such as baked eggs, frizzled ham, oatmeal, and pancakes, along with fresh and dried fruits and cinnamon-spiced coffee cakes. Most of the recipes come complete with menus, so you don't have to worry about what to serve with what. To streamline preparation, each menu has a step-by-step Game Plan. You can practically prepare breakfast with your eyes closed.

Each menu also has another time-saving feature: a Shopping Guide. Before you leave home, do a quick pantry check with the Shopping Guide in hand, to see what staples you already have. When you are in the store, you'll find the foods in the Shopping Guide grouped as they usually are in most supermarkets, and in the best order for shopping. First are nonperishables: baking needs such as flour, sugar, and spices; dried fruits and nuts; preserves and oils. Then come breads and perishables—fresh fruits, vegetables, and herbs—followed by frozen foods and refrigerated meats such as bacon, ham, and sausage. Lastly (just before you head for the checkout counter) stop at the dairy case for milk, butter, eggs, and cheese.

Starting with Groundhog Day, the menus celebrate the seasons and occasions of the passing year. There are breakfasts for Memorial Day and Fourth of July; for a child's birthday and a graduation; for Mother's Day and Father's Day (with some recipes written for children to make with adult supervision). Get Thanksgiving Day off to a good start with a hearty breakfast and keep everyone happy until turkey time. Invite friends to help decorate the Christmas tree and serve a special breakfast of seasonal foods. Invite a tall, dark stranger to a Scottish breakfast on New Year's Day. Have a breakfast party on the porch in summer, before a roaring fire in winter. If you're ambitious, you can even stage a real wedding breakfast. All the menus have been planned and the recipes tested to make everything as comfortable, relaxed, and enjoyable for you as possible. So pour yourself a cup of coffee, and enjoy.

ELIZABETH ALSTON

To Greet the Groundhog

Upon the friendly groundhog, you will recall, falls the responsibility for signaling the status of spring. Each February 2nd, he blinks a sleepy eye and, unable to stand his stuffy burrow for another second, emerges for a breath of fresh air. Should the sun be shining, casting a shadow that frightens the groundhog back into his hole, six more wicked, wintry weeks are supposedly in store. If no shadow tags our cabin-fever sufferer, he'll stay out to explore the world a while—the sign (so the legend goes) of an early spring. As a weather forecaster, the groundhog is probably no more accurate than all the computers in Kansas, but he certainly is a lot more fun.

What better excuse for a breakfast than to second-guess the groundhog and toast the coming of spring? And what better way to start than with a fresh mixture of orange juice and strawberries, a true herald of spring, now starting to blossom and fruit in the southern part of California. Meanwhile, in Canada and New England, the maple sap is just beginning its annual spring rise, making maple syrup on sunny yellow pancakes entirely appropriate.

M E N U

FOR 6

*STRAWBERRY-ORANGE
JUICE

*CORNMEAL GRIDDLE
CAKES

*BROWN-SUGAR SYRUP
OR
MAPLE SYRUP

DOUBLE-SMOKED BACON

*LEMON-CHOCOLATE CHIP
MUFFINS

*RECIPE FOLLOWS

GAME PLAN

UP TO 2 WEEKS AHEAD YOU MAY:

◆ Make Brown-Sugar Syrup.
◆ Make Lemon-Chocolate Chip Muffin batter; freeze in muffin pans lined with foil baking cups. When frozen, remove from the pans and store in a plastic bag or container. To bake, return to pans and bake without thawing.

THE DAY BEFORE YOU MAY:

◆ Measure dry ingredients for Cornmeal Griddle Cakes; mix well; cover; leave at room temperature.
◆ Pour liquid ingredients for griddle cakes into a 1-quart measure. Add eggs, but do not beat. Cover; refrigerate.
◆ Squeeze lemon juice for finishing muffins.
◆ Prepare Strawberry-Orange Juice.

◆ ABOUT 1 TO 1¼ HOURS BEFORE SERVING:
◆ Cook bacon in 350°F. oven (see page 195); drain on paper towels.
◆ Squeeze oranges if serving fresh juice.
◆ Turn oven to 375°F. Bake muffins (if frozen, do not thaw). Remove from oven; add topping.
◆ Turn oven to 200°F.

LAST MINUTE:

◆ Complete griddle cake batter; make griddle cakes; keep
continued

Strawberry-Orange Juice

1 pint fresh strawberries
1½ quarts freshly-squeezed or refrigerated orange juice, or 1 12-ounce container frozen orange juice concentrate (see note)

Granulated sugar, if needed

Rinse and drain berries; remove hulls. Put berries in blender or food processor with 2 cups of juice. Process until smooth.

Pour juice into large pitcher. Add remaining orange juice. Stir; taste. If too tart, stir in a little granulated sugar and taste again.

Cover and refrigerate until serving. *Makes 8 cups.*

NOTE: Put frozen concentrate into blender or food processor along with 1 juice can of water. Add berries and process until smooth. Pour into pitcher; add 2 more juice cans of water. Stir, taste, and sweeten if you wish. *Makes 8 cups.*

Cornmeal Griddle Cakes

When you're making pancakes, always make the first pancake a test. If the batter is too thick to spread on the griddle, thin it with a very small amount of additional milk. Serve the pancakes with either Brown-Sugar Syrup (recipe follows) or with maple syrup.

2 cups yellow cornmeal
1 cup all-purpose flour
1 tablespoon brown or white sugar
1 teaspoon salt
1 teaspoon baking soda
1 teaspoon baking powder
2 cups buttermilk or plain yogurt
½ cup milk
¼ cup light olive or vegetable oil
2 large eggs
Oil for the griddle

Mix cornmeal, flour, sugar, salt, baking soda, and baking powder in a large bowl.

Add buttermilk, milk, oil, and eggs. Beat briskly with a wooden spoon just until well mixed; batter will be thick.

Heat griddle or large nonstick skillet over high heat. Reduce heat to moderate and oil griddle very lightly. For each pancake, pour a scant ¼ cup batter onto griddle; cook 3 to 4 minutes, until lightly browned on the underside but still moist on top. Turn pancakes over and cook until browned on bottom. *Makes about 24 to 26 griddle cakes.*

Brown-Sugar Syrup

1 pound light brown sugar   *1 cup water*

Mix sugar and water in a medium-sized saucepan. Bring to a boil over moderate heat, stirring once or twice to help sugar dissolve. Boil 5 minutes. Remove from heat. Serve warm. Store in refrigerator. *Makes 2 cups.*

NOTE: If syrup is stored for several weeks, sugar crystals may form in bottom of container. Stand jar of syrup (uncovered) in a small pan of water and heat over moderately-low heat until crystals dissolve. You can also microwave the syrup (without the pan of water) in a microwave-safe jar, 1 or 2 minutes at a time, until crystals dissolve.

Lemon-Chocolate Chip Muffins

Serve these muffins hot or warm.

1 medium-sized lemon, well scrubbed and wiped dry
8 tablespoons (1 stick) unsalted butter, at room temperature
1 cup plus 4 teaspoons granulated sugar
2 large eggs
1 teaspoon baking soda
2 cups all-purpose flour
1 cup buttermilk or plain yogurt
¾ cup (5 ounces) semisweet chocolate chips
¼ cup freshly-squeezed lemon juice

Heat oven to 375°F. Grease muffin cups, or use foil or paper baking cups.

Finely grate the lemon peel. Try to remove as little white pith as possible.

Beat butter and 1 cup sugar with an electric mixer until pale and creamy. Beat in eggs, one at a time. Stir in baking soda and grated peel.

Fold in half the flour, then half the yogurt. Repeat, then fold in chocolate chips.

Scoop batter into muffin cups. Bake 20 to 25 minutes, or until browned.

Remove from oven. Spoon lemon juice over the hot muffins until used up. Sprinkle with remaining 4 teaspoons sugar. Let stand 5 more minutes before removing from pans. *Makes 12 regular muffins.*

FOOD PROCESSOR METHOD: Thinly peel lemon with a vegetable peeler. Put peel and 1 cup sugar in the food processor. Process 3 to 4
continued

SHOPPING GUIDE

3 cups all-purpose flour
2 cups yellow cornmeal
¾ cup (5 ounces) semisweet chocolate chips
1¼ cups granulated sugar
1 pound light brown sugar plus 1 tablespoon brown or white sugar
1 teaspoon baking powder
2 teaspoons baking soda
Foil or paper baking cups for muffins
Maple syrup
¼ cup light olive or vegetable oil

3 lemons
12 juice oranges; or 1½ quarts refrigerated orange juice; or 1 12-ounce container frozen orange juice concentrate
1 pint fresh strawberries

Double-smoked bacon, 2 or 3 slices per person

½ cup milk
3 cups (1½ pints) buttermilk or plain yogurt
8 tablespoons (1 stick) unsalted butter, plus butter to spread on pancakes
4 large eggs

(Coffee? Tea? Add what you need.)

BUTTER AND MARGARINE

Recipes in this book call for stick butter. You may use the same amount of stick margarine or a butter/margarine blend instead. Do not substitute whipped or tub or "light" butter or margarine; air and/or liquid added to these products make baking results difficult to predict.

minutes until peel is finely chopped and sugar looks quite damp. Add butter and process until creamy, about 1 minute. Add eggs, one at a time, processing until each is well mixed. Scrape down sides. Add yogurt and baking soda; process to mix; scrape down sides. Sprinkle flour over butter mixture. Turn on/off 3 or 4 times, just until flour is incorporated. Add chocolate chips. Turn on/off once or twice to distribute chips. Continue as above.

Valentine's Day

Ah, a tricky menu indeed to decide on. The occasion calls for delectable fare, yes, but something neither time-consuming nor complicated. What good is it if the bearer of breakfast to bed arrives distracted, hurried, and not in the mood of the day at all? An omelet, then, is a perfect choice. The impressive look and luxurious flavor belie the ease of preparation. This one is lavishly filled with sautéed mushrooms. But the omelet is also delicious left unfilled, topped with the dill sour cream and a generous spoonful of red salmon caviar.

No matter which flavor you choose, directions are given for making two individual omelets because they look prettier and each takes less than one minute. If you insist on making one large omelet, you can use a skillet that is seven to eight inches across the bottom, both for cooking the mushrooms and making the omelet.

The muffin recipe makes just four. You can organize all the ingredients the night before, or you can make the batter completely and freeze it in the muffin cups. In the morning, bake the muffins without thawing.

M E N U

FOR 2

MIMOSAS

OR

FRESHLY-SQUEEZED ORANGE OR GRAPEFRUIT JUICE

*MUSHROOM OMELET WITH DILL SOUR CREAM

BUTTERED TOAST
OR
ENGLISH MUFFINS

*MARMALADE MUFFINS FOR TWO

*RECIPE FOLLOWS

GAME PLAN

THE DAY BEFORE YOU MAY:

◆ Make Marmalade Muffins batter; freeze unbaked in foil-lined muffin cups. (Or, mix dry ingredients in one bowl, cover, and leave at room temperature. In another bowl, mix egg, sour cream, and vanilla; cover and refrigerate.)

◆ Wipe mushrooms clean with damp paper towel (do not rinse mushrooms if preparing a day ahead).

◆ Squeeze oranges or grapefruit; cover juice and refrigerate.

◆ Chill Champagne if serving Mimosas (see page 155).

ABOUT 1¼ HOURS BEFORE SERVING:

◆ Heat oven to 375°F. and complete muffin batter. Whisk butter into liquid ingredients and fold into dry mixture. As soon as oven is heated, put muffins in to bake. (If frozen, do not thaw.) After muffins are baked, turn oven off.

◆ Slice mushrooms and cook.

◆ Prepare omelet mixture.

LAST MINUTE:

◆ Put plates in oven to warm; toast bread or English muffins and spread with butter.

◆ Make omelets.

Mushroom Omelet with Dill Sour Cream

If you make one large omelet, see note at end.

8 ounces mushrooms

2 tablespoons plus 1 or 2 teaspoons unsalted butter

Salt and freshly-ground pepper

1 tablespoon snipped fresh dill or (as last resort) ½ teaspoon dried dillweed

3 tablespoons sour cream

4 large eggs

4 tablespoons water

Put mushrooms in a strainer, rinse quickly with cold water, and dry with paper towel. If stems seem tough, cut a thin slice off the end. Slice mushrooms.

Choose a skillet 7 to 8 inches across the bottom. In it, melt 2 tablespoons butter over moderately-high heat. Add mushrooms (pan will be very full), and cook 3 to 4 minutes, stirring and tossing mushrooms almost constantly with two wooden spoons, until lightly browned but still firm (volume will be greatly reduced). Remove pan from heat; sprinkle mushrooms lightly with salt, pepper, and a pinch of dill.

Mix sour cream with remaining dill and season with salt and pepper.

Break two eggs into a bowl; season with salt and pepper and add 2 tablespoons water. Beat with a fork until well broken up.

Have ready two warm plates and a slotted spoon to remove mushrooms from skillet. Now make the omelets, which will take no longer than one minute each.

Choose a nonstick skillet 6 to 7 inches across the bottom. In it, melt 1 teaspoon butter over moderately-high heat. When skillet is hot, pour in egg mixture; it will immediately start to set around the edge. With back of fork touching bottom of pan, draw cooked egg mixture from outside edge toward the center, allowing the still-liquid egg to flow toward the outside edge (tip and tilt pan a little to help egg along). When egg mixture is almost completely set, but still moist on top, spoon half the mushroom filling onto side of omelet farthest from handle. Grasp handle from underneath and tip it up; as you tip, lift side of omelet nearest the handle with a pancake turner and fold it over the mushroom filling. Tip pan until omelet slides out onto one of the warm plates.

Make a second omelet with remaining eggs, butter, and filling.

Spoon dill sour cream over each omelet and serve at once. *Makes 2 servings.*

NOTE: If using one large skillet, scrape cooked mushrooms into a bowl. Wipe out pan. Make omelet in pan using all 4 eggs at once. Use a slotted spoon to remove cooked mushrooms from bowl, leaving behind any liquid.

Marmalade Muffins for Two

Orange marmalade, or any intensely flavored preserve such as raspberry or apricot, is excellent baked inside these muffins. The recipe makes just four and, if you don't mind muffins that are wider than they are high, you don't even need muffin pans: spoon the batter into foil baking cups set on a metal baking pan. You can even bake them in a toaster-oven.

¾ cup all-purpose flour
½ teaspoon baking powder
⅛ teaspoon baking soda
⅛ teaspoon salt
1 large egg
¼ cup granulated sugar

¼ cup sour cream
2 tablespoons unsalted butter, melted
¼ teaspoon vanilla extract (optional)
¼ cup orange marmalade or red raspberry, black currant, or apricot preserves

Heat oven to 375°F. Line four muffin cups with foil baking cups or place the foil baking cups directly on a baking pan.

Put flour, baking powder, baking soda, and salt in a medium-sized bowl; stir to mix well.

Break egg into a small bowl. Add sugar, sour cream, butter, and vanilla; whisk with a fork to blend well. Pour into flour mixture and fold in with a rubber spatula just until ingredients are blended.

Spoon 1 tablespoon batter into each muffin cup. Top with 2 teaspoons preserves, then with remaining batter.

Bake 18 to 22 minutes, until lightly browned and springy to the touch. Remove from oven and let cool in pan at least 10 minutes. Remove from pan; serve warm. *Makes 4 muffins.*

SHOPPING GUIDE

¾ cup all-purpose flour
¼ cup granulated sugar
½ teaspoon baking powder
⅛ teaspoon baking soda
¼ cup orange marmalade or red raspberry, black currant, or apricot preserves
¼ teaspoon vanilla extract (optional)
Foil baking cups for muffins

3 to 5 juice oranges or 2 grapefruit
8 ounces fresh mushrooms
Fresh dill (enough for 1 tablespoon, snipped) or ½ teaspoon dried dillweed

½ cup sour cream
4 tablespoons (½ stick) plus 1 or 2 teaspoons unsalted butter
5 large eggs

(Coffee? Tea? Add what you need. Also Champagne; bread or English muffins for toasting; and butter for the table.)

Mardi Gras

New Orleans is full of parades for at least two weeks before Lent begins, and the Sunday before Fat Tuesday is a popular time to have friends for breakfast or brunch. On the big day itself everyone leaves home early to ensure getting a good place along the parade route. Besides, says New Orleans native, food writer John DeMers, "on Mardi Gras no one does much eating, just a whole lot of drinking."

With that in mind, I've planned a hearty, pre-Mardi Gras feast. Grits and grillades (as they say in New Orleans) means a hearty beef or veal stew (grillades) served with garlicky cheese grits to complement the gravy. Eggs Sardou is a favorite not only in many of those famous New Orleans bruncheries, but in private homes as well. I was amazed (and very impressed) to find that energetic New Orleans home cooks often start by cleaning and cooking whole fresh artichokes for the artichoke hearts this dish usually calls for, as well as poaching eggs and making hollandaise sauce. I've devised a casserole version that, if I might brag on it, is just as rich and delicious as the original, but much simpler to make and serve.

Milk Punch

Serve this traditional New Orleans favorite in large stemmed glasses or punch cups. Warning! It goes down real easy.

2 tablespoons granulated sugar
6 cups milk
½ cup bourbon
¼ cup crème de cacao (optional)

Ice cubes
About ⅛ teaspoon nutmeg, freshly-
grated or from a jar

Mix sugar and 1 cup milk in a large serving pitcher. Add remaining milk, bourbon, and crème de cacao. Stir to blend. Serve at once, or cover and chill.

Put three or four ice cubes in each glass. Fill with Milk Punch and top with a little grated nutmeg. *Makes about 7 cups, 14 ½-cup servings.*

NUTMEG

For best flavor buy whole nutmegs. Put one nutmeg and a small fine grater next to the pitcher and glasses. Grate a very little nutmeg over each serving. Once you've discovered how delicious fresh nutmeg is and how easy to grate (you can even just scrape the nutmeg with a small knife) you'll never buy ready-ground again.

Melon and Berry Platter

I think the flavor of an orange-fleshed melon, such as cantaloupe, tastes best with berries, but base your choice on which melons look best at the supermarket. You can serve peeled melon wedges with berries spooned over them, but for a party I think it is nice to cut the peeled melon into bite-size chunks and arrange the fruit either in individual serving bowls or on a large platter from which guests can serve themselves.

2 large cantaloupe melons
2 or 3 pints fresh strawberries and/or
raspberries or blueberries

Mint sprigs for garnish

Seed and peel melons (see page 186) and cut into bite-size chunks, cover, and refrigerate.

Shortly before serving, pick over and rinse berries. Hull strawberries. If strawberries are very large, halve or slice them.

Arrange melon chunks in bowls or on platter. Scatter berries over melon. Garnish with mint sprigs. *Makes 8 to 10 servings.*

GAME PLAN

UP TO 2 MONTHS AHEAD YOU MAY:
- Bake Blackberry Jam Coffee Cake; cool, cover tightly, and freeze.

UP TO 3 DAYS AHEAD YOU MAY:
- Make Grillades.

THE DAY BEFORE:
- Mix Milk Punch in pitcher; cover and refrigerate.
- Make Garlic Cheese Grits; put in baking dish; cover and refrigerate.
- Hard-cook eggs; peel and refrigerate in bowl of cold water.
- Prepare artichoke layer of Casserole Eggs Sardou; refrigerate in baking dish.
- Organize Sauce Sardou ingredients.
- Peel and cut up melons; refrigerate.
- Transfer coffee cake from freezer to refrigerator.

UP TO 2 HOURS BEFORE SERVING:
- Remove grits from refrigerator; uncover; leave at room temperature.
- Remove and discard any hardened fat from surface of Grillades. Leave Grillades at room temperature.
- Prepare Sauce Sardou; assemble Casserole Eggs Sardou.
- Heat oven to 350°F. Put in grits and Casserole Eggs Sardou.

continued

Grillades

This very thick, rich stew is a breakfast and brunch favorite in New Orleans. I make it with beef, rather than the more traditional veal, because beef is more readily available. After trimming, you should have a little more than three pounds of meat.

4 pounds lean, boneless beef chuck roast or steak cut about 1-inch thick, or boneless veal stew meat
¾ teaspoon salt
¾ teaspoon freshly-ground pepper
¾ cup all-purpose flour
¼ cup vegetable oil
1 cup chopped onion
1 cup diced celery
1 cup diced green bell pepper
1 cup sliced scallions
4 teaspoons minced fresh garlic (about 6 cloves)
½ teaspoon dried thyme leaves
1 28-ounce can tomatoes, crushed lightly with hands
1 13- to 14-ounce can beef broth
½ cup dry red wine
3 tablespoons tomato paste
2 Turkish bay leaves

Heat oven to 375°F. Trim fat from meat and cut meat into strips about ¼-inch thick and 3-inches long, cutting across the grain where possible. Sprinkle meat with salt and pepper.

Put flour on a sheet of wax paper. Toss meat in flour, a few pieces at a time, and place on another sheet of wax paper. Save remaining flour.

Heat ¼ cup oil in a large heavy skillet over high heat. Brown meat in small batches and put browned pieces in a bowl. Add more oil to skillet as needed.

Heat ¼ cup oil in a 6- to 8-quart rangetop-to-oven casserole over moderate heat. Add onion, celery, green pepper, scallions, and garlic. Cook about 10 minutes, stirring often, until vegetables are tender. Stir in thyme; cook 30 seconds. Reduce heat to low and stir in flour left over from coating meat; cook 3 to 4 minutes, stirring frequently.

Add remaining ingredients and browned meat (including any juices). Stir well and bring to a boil. Boil 5 minutes, then cover and bake 1 hour and 10 to 20 minutes, or until meat is very tender. Discard bay leaves. *Makes 10 or more servings.*

Garlic Cheese Grits

6 cups water	½ teaspoon minced fresh garlic
1½ cups quick grits	½ teaspoon freshly-ground pepper
1½ teaspoons salt	¼ teaspoon hot-pepper sauce
4 tablespoons (½ stick) unsalted butter	8 ounces sharp or extra-sharp cheddar cheese, shredded (2 cups)
2 large eggs	

Heat oven to 350°F. Bring water to a boil in a large heavy saucepan over moderately-high heat. Stir in grits and salt and bring to a boil. Reduce heat to low and simmer 5 minutes, stirring occasionally.

Remove from heat. Put butter on top of grits. Cover and let stand 5 minutes. Uncover, stir, and cool 5 more minutes, stirring 2 or 3 times.

Beat in eggs, garlic, pepper, and hot-pepper sauce. When thoroughly mixed, beat in 1½ cups of cheese. Spread mixture in a well-buttered baking dish about 13 × 9 × 2 inches. Sprinkle with remaining cheese.

Bake 30 minutes (40 minutes, if chilled) until hot and bubbly. *Makes 10 to 12 servings.*

GAME PLAN *cont'd*

- ◆ If you have oven space, heat Grillades, covered, at 350°F. Otherwise, cover and heat slowly on rangetop.
- ◆ Rinse berries. Arrange fruit plates or platter.
- ◆ Uncover eggs; continue baking.
- ◆ Cut coffee cake into serving pieces; loosely cover pan with foil.
- ◆ Serve fruit and punch.
- ◆ Remove eggs and grits from oven, turn oven to 250°F.
- ◆ Put coffee cake in to heat for 15 to 20 minutes.

GRATING AND SHREDDING

A four-sided grater has many uses around the kitchen. If you need to buy one, choose a good-quality, stainless steel grater that will last a long time and not rust.

When a recipe calls for grating an ingredient, use one of the sides that looks as if the holes were made by a tin punch. Ingredients such as fresh ginger, hard cheeses, or citrus peels are often grated. When a recipe calls for shredding an ingredient such as cheese, use a side that has v-shaped cuts.

SHOPPING GUIDE

4½ cups all-purpose flour
1½ cups quick grits
1 cup light brown sugar
2 tablespoons granulated sugar
2 teaspoons baking powder
½ teaspoon baking soda

2 Turkish bay leaves
1¾ teaspoons ground cinnamon
1⅛ teaspoons nutmeg, freshly-grated or from a jar
½ to 1 teaspoon dried thyme leaves
¼ teaspoon hot-pepper sauce
1 13- to 14-ounce can beef broth
1 13- to 14-ounce can chicken broth
¾ cup vegetable oil
1 28-ounce can tomatoes
3 tablespoons tomato paste
½ cup blackberry jam

2 large cantaloupe melons
2 or 3 pints fresh strawberries and/or raspberries or blueberries
3 lemons
2 stalks celery (1 cup diced)
2 medium-sized onions (2 cups chopped)
1 green bell pepper (1 cup diced)
2 bunches scallions (2 cups sliced)
1 or 2 heads garlic (6½ teaspoons minced)
Fresh thyme leaves (enough for 1 tablespoon chopped) or an additional ½ teaspoon dried thyme
Mint sprigs for garnish
1 10-ounce package frozen chopped spinach

continued

Casserole Eggs Sardou

ARTICHOKE LAYER

4 tablespoons (½ stick) unsalted butter
1 cup finely chopped onion
1 cup sliced scallions
2 teaspoons minced fresh garlic
1 10-ounce package frozen chopped spinach, thawed and squeezed dry

2 9-ounce packages frozen artichoke hearts
½ teaspoon salt
¼ teaspoon freshly-ground pepper
12 hard-cooked eggs, peeled (see page 193)

SAUCE SARDOU

5 tablespoons unsalted butter
¼ cup all-purpose flour
1½ cups heavy cream
1 13- to 14-ounce can chicken broth
½ cup freshly-grated Parmesan cheese
5 tablespoons freshly-squeezed lemon juice

1 tablespoon chopped fresh thyme leaves or ½ teaspoon dried thyme
½ teaspoon salt
¼ teaspoon freshly-ground pepper

Artichoke layer. Melt butter in a 4- to 5-quart pot over moderate heat. Stir in onion, scallions, and garlic. Cover and cook 5 minutes, stirring once, until onion is tender. Stir in spinach, artichoke hearts, and ¼ cup of the chicken broth called for in the sauce. Cover and cook 10 to 12 minutes, until artichokes are tender; season with salt and pepper. Spread evenly in a baking dish about 13 × 9 × 2 inches. Slice hard-cooked eggs with a knife or egg slicer. Arrange on top of artichoke mixture without spreading slices out too much. Heat oven to 350°F.

Sauce. Wash and dry the pot. In it, melt 3 tablespoons butter over moderate heat. Stir in flour and cook, stirring constantly, for 2 minutes. Pour in cream and remaining chicken broth. Whisk well; cover and remove from heat; let stand 1 minute. Put back over moderate heat and bring to a boil, stirring with a wooden spoon, until sauce begins to thicken. Reduce heat to low and simmer 2 minutes, stirring constantly. Remove from heat and let cool 5 minutes. Add cheese, remaining 2 tablespoons butter, lemon juice, thyme, salt, and pepper. Stir well. Spoon or pour over eggs. Cover dish with foil and bake 25 minutes until heated through. Uncover and bake 10 to 15 minutes longer, until bubbling. *Makes 10 to 12 servings.*

Blackberry Jam Coffee Cake

TOPPING
- ⅔ cup all-purpose flour
- ¼ cup packed light brown sugar
- 4 tablespoons (½ stick) unsalted butter, at room temperature
- ¾ teaspoon ground cinnamon

BATTER
- 2½ cups all-purpose flour
- 2 teaspoons baking powder
- 1 teaspoon ground cinnamon
- 1 teaspoon nutmeg, freshly-grated or from a jar
- ½ teaspoon baking soda
- ½ teaspoon salt
- 12 tablespoons (1½ sticks) unsalted butter, melted and cooled
- ¾ cup packed light brown sugar
- 3 large eggs
- 1 cup buttermilk or plain yogurt
- 1 teaspoon freshly-grated lemon peel
- ½ cup blackberry jam

Topping. Put all ingredients into a small bowl and work with fingertips until mixture looks like coarse crumbs.

Batter. Heat oven to 350°F. Butter a 13 × 9 × 2-inch baking pan. Put flour, baking powder, cinnamon, nutmeg, baking soda, and salt in a large bowl. Stir to mix well.

Put butter and sugar in a medium-sized bowl. Whisk until smooth. Whisk in eggs, buttermilk, and lemon peel. Pour over flour mixture. Stir just until dry ingredients are moistened. (Batter may be slightly lumpy.)

Scrape batter into prepared pan. Spoon jam on top of batter and swirl gently through batter with a rubber spatula, spreading batter to edge of pan. Sprinkle with topping.

Bake 25 to 35 minutes, until topping is lightly browned. Cake will feel firm to the touch, and a toothpick inserted in the center will come out clean.

Place pan on wire rack to cool. Cut into 12 pieces and transfer to a plate. *Makes 12 servings.*

SHOPPING GUIDE *cont'd*

2 9-ounce packages frozen artichoke hearts

4 pounds lean, boneless beef chuck roast or steak about 1 inch thick; or boneless veal stew meat

6 cups milk (1½ quarts)
1 cup (½ pint) buttermilk or plain yogurt
1½ cups (¾ pint) heavy cream
32 tablespoons (4 sticks) unsalted butter
17 large eggs
8 ounces sharp or extra-sharp cheddar cheese (2 cups shredded)
½ cup (2 ounces) freshly-grated Parmesan cheese

½ cup bourbon
¼ cup crème de cacao (optional)
½ cup dry red wine

(Coffee? Coffee with Chicory (see page 200)? Tea? Add what you need.)

Come See the First Blossoms

M E N U

FOR 6

*MELON AND ORANGE
BOWL

*EGGS SCRAMBLED WITH
SMOKED SALMON AND
POTATOES

BAGELS, CREAM CHEESES,
BUTTER, AND PRESERVES

*RECIPE FOLLOWS

The first snowdrops, almond blossoms, or magnolias—depending on where you live—are always good reason for a breakfast celebration. The weather may not permit you to plan this event too far ahead, but that simply heightens the anticipation.

Eggs Scrambled with Smoked Salmon and Potatoes is a specialty of many well-known New York delis such as Barney Greengrass and the Carnegie Delicatessen. But you don't have to be in New York to enjoy it. This wonderful combination of mild potatoes and creamy eggs pointed up with slightly salty salmon is easy to make at home. Boil, slice, and brown the potatoes before your friends arrive; add the eggs and scramble them just before serving. Although you don't need the most expensive smoked salmon to make this dish successfully, you do need good-quality salmon, preferably sliced to your order.

Melon and Orange Bowl

1 *tablespoon honey*
1 *tablespoon freshly-squeezed lime juice*
4 *medium-sized navel oranges*

3 to 3½ *pounds honeydew melon*
   Lime slices or chopped fresh
      mint for garnish

Mix honey and lime juice in a large mixing or serving bowl.

Peel oranges with a serrated knife (see page 186). Working over the bowl, cut out each orange section, letting it drop into the bowl. When you have nothing left but a handful of membrane, squeeze it over the bowl and discard it.

Seed and peel melon (see page 186). Cut melon into thin wedges or bite-size chunks and add to oranges. Mix gently. Cover and chill until ready to serve. Ladle into bowls and garnish with lime slices or chopped mint. *Makes 6 servings.*

BAGELS

Ring-shaped bread rolls, with a chewy crust and firm crumb, bagels are unique —and uniquely Jewish. To make them, yeast dough is formed into ring-shaped rolls which are then boiled for a few minutes in slightly sweetened water. Before baking, the bagels are brushed with beaten egg or egg white, which gives them their characteristic shiny glaze.

Bagels are sold plain, sprinkled with sesame or poppy seeds, or with browned onion. There are also egg bagels, rye, whole-wheat, sourdough, and pumpernickel bagels. Comparatively new on the scene are cinnamon-raisin bagels.

A favorite way to eat bagels is to cut them in half, spread the bottom thickly with cream cheese, replace the top, and munch away. (Some people like to serve bagels warm, or to toast halved bagels before applying the cream cheese.) For lox and bagels, top the cream cheese with a slice or two of lox (a salty smoked salmon). This makes a most delicious breakfast, lunch, or snack.

Bagels are now available across the country. If you can't buy them fresh, look in the freezer case (fresh bagels freeze well, too). Try them. Their chewy texture is a delightful change from the standard too-soft bread.

GAME PLAN

THE DAY BEFORE YOU MAY:
- Start fruit bowl. Seed and peel honeydew melon; wrap and chill.
- Peel and section oranges. Mix with honey and lemon in bowl. Wrap garnish separately.
- Boil and slice potatoes.
- Slice onions; wrap tightly. (You may also cook potatoes and onions in skillet.)
- Cut salmon into 1-inch pieces.

UP TO 2 HOURS BEFORE SERVING:
- Cut up melon; mix with oranges; add garnish.

ABOUT 1 HOUR BEFORE SERVING:
- Cook onions and potatoes in skillet.
- Snip chives.
- Break eggs into bowl; add milk; beat.
- Let bagels, cream cheeses, and butter come to room temperature.
- Serve fruit.

LAST MINUTE:
- Scramble eggs with salmon and potatoes.

SHOPPING GUIDE

1 tablespoon honey

2 or 3 kinds of preserves to serve with bagels (damson plum, apricot, strawberry)

3 tablespoons pure olive or vegetable oil

1 or 2 limes (for garnish and 1 tablespoon juice)

4 medium-sized navel oranges

3 to 3½ pounds honeydew melon

1 to 1¼ pounds red or white thin-skinned potatoes ("new" potatoes)

2 or 3 onions (1½ cups sliced)

1 bunch chives (2 tablespoons snipped) or 1 bunch scallions (¼ cup sliced)

Mint for garnish

2 tablespoons milk

2 tablespoons unsalted butter (plus butter for bagels)

12 large eggs

Cream cheese for bagels, plain and chive

4 ounces sliced mild smoked salmon (Norwegian or Alaskan is good)

At least 1 dozen assorted bagels or English muffins

(Coffee? Tea? Add what you need.)

Eggs Scrambled with Smoked Salmon and Potatoes

1 to 1¼ pounds red or white thin-skinned potatoes

4 ounces sliced mild smoked salmon

3 tablespoons pure olive or vegetable oil

2 tablespoons unsalted butter

1½ cups sliced onions

12 large eggs

2 tablespoons milk
Freshly-ground pepper

2 tablespoons snipped fresh chives or ¼ cup sliced scallion greens

Scrub the potatoes (don't peel) and cook them in boiling water or in a microwave oven until tender when pierced. Drain, cool, halve lengthwise, and slice thinly. You should have about 3½ cups sliced potatoes.

Cut salmon into 1-inch pieces.

Heat oil and butter in a large heavy skillet (nonstick is great) over moderate heat. When butter is melted add onions and cook about 5 minutes, until softened, stirring occasionally.

Add potatoes and cook about 10 minutes, turning frequently with a spatula, until onions and potatoes are lightly browned. (Add another tablespoon of oil if pan seems dry.)

Break eggs into a large bowl. Add milk and pepper. Beat with a fork or wire whisk until well broken up. Whisk in about half the chives.

Shortly before serving, add smoked salmon to potatoes. Reduce heat to low and toss gently just until salmon is heated through.

Add eggs. Cook, stirring slowly and not too much (see page 193) until eggs are creamy soft and almost as firm as you like them. Sprinkle with remaining chives or scallions. Spoon onto plates. *Makes 6 servings.*

An Early-Morning Picnic

Invite close friends to watch the sunrise, go fishing, or bird-watching—anything to be out of doors and reveling in the first signs of spring. Pack a simple breakfast of foods everyone can keep going back to as the morning progresses and the mood strikes. Gingerbread may seem an unusual foil for cheese, but in fact it is a very old idea, along the same lines as apple pie and cheese. If you wish, you can be a little more adventurous in your choice of cheeses. Try Jarlsberg from Norway, or cumin-studded Leyden from Holland. A creamy Havarti is good, too. The muffin batter can be made ahead and frozen in the muffin cups, ready to pop into the oven and bake (without thawing) on the morning of departure. Keep the muffins warm in a small insulated bag—the kind you usually use to keep food cold. If the morning is cool, a thermos of vegetable soup and some crackers are nice additions, besides, hunger always seems to strike harder when one is out of doors and far from even the tiniest coffee shop.

M E N U

FOR 4

*HOT SPICED APPLE JUICE

*GINGERBREAD DATE MUFFINS

MONTEREY JACK OR CHEDDAR CHEESE

HARD-COOKED EGGS

NUTS

GRAPES

*RECIPE FOLLOWS

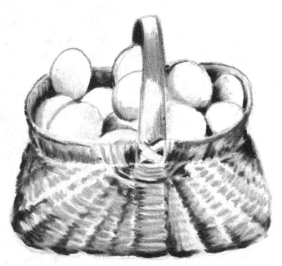

GAME PLAN

UP TO 1 WEEK AHEAD YOU
MAY:
- Make muffin batter; freeze in foil baking cups.

THE DAY BEFORE:
- Make Hot Spiced Apple Juice; refrigerate.
- Hard-cook eggs; cool in cold water and peel. Refrigerate in plastic bag or container.
- Cube and wrap cheese.
- Pack nuts (any kind, in or out of shell; pack nutcracker if in shell).
- Check picnic kit for cups, napkins, and utensils.

ABOUT 1 HOUR BEFORE
DEPARTURE:
- Bake muffins (if frozen, do not thaw).
- Rinse grapes; snip into smaller bunches; pack in paper towels in plastic container.
- Heat spiced apple juice; pour into heated thermos.

Hot Spiced Apple Juice

Make juice a day ahead for best flavor. Before setting off, reheat and pack in thermos flasks or jugs.

Thermos containers hold the heat best if heated before filling. Fill them with boiling water, cover, and let stand at least 5 minutes or until you're ready to fill them with hot juice.

1 quart apple juice
¼ cup orange juice
2 tablespoons packed brown sugar (or use white)
4 thin slices lemon, seeded and halved

2 cinnamon sticks (each 2 to 3 inches long) or ¼ teaspoon ground cinnamon
2 whole cloves or ⅛ teaspoon ground cloves

Stir all ingredients in a large stainless steel or enameled saucepan. Cover and bring to a boil over moderate heat. Remove from heat and let stand 10 minutes. Remove whole spices, if used; serve juice or pour into heated thermos flasks. Or refrigerate overnight and reheat in the morning, removing flavorings then. *Makes just over 1 quart, 4 servings.*

Gingerbread Date Muffins

2 cups all-purpose flour
1½ teaspoons baking powder
½ teaspoon baking soda
1½ teaspoons ground ginger
1 teaspoon ground cinnamon
½ teaspoon nutmeg, freshly-grated or
    from a jar
¼ teaspoon ground cloves
¼ teaspoon salt

1 large egg
¾ cup milk
½ cup light or dark molasses
2 tablespoons granulated sugar
½ cup (3 ounces) finely chopped
    dates
4 tablespoons (½ stick) unsalted
    butter, melted

Heat oven to 400°F. Grease twelve nonstick muffin cups or line muffin cups with foil or paper baking cups.

Put flour, baking powder, baking soda, spices, and salt into a large bowl. Stir to mix thoroughly.

Beat egg with a fork in a medium-sized bowl. Add milk, molasses, sugar, dates, and butter. Mix well with fork. Pour over dry ingredients. Stir with a wooden spoon or rubber spatula just until dry ingredients are well mixed in.

Scoop batter into muffin cups. Bake in center of oven 20 to 25 minutes, until muffins spring back when touched in the center with a finger. Let muffins cool 5 to 10 minutes in the pan. *Makes 12 muffins.*

CHOPPING DATES

Dates are notoriously sticky and difficult to chop with a knife. Try this for ease: Lightly oil kitchen scissor blades (or spray lightly with cooking spray). Snip dates lengthwise in 3 or 4 pieces; hold pieces together gently and snip across in ¼-inch or smaller pieces. Scissors are also good for cutting other dried fruits such as apricots, apples, and prunes.

SHOPPING GUIDE

2 cups all-purpose flour
2 tablespoons granulated sugar
2 tablespoons brown sugar (or
    use white)
1½ teaspoons baking powder
½ teaspoon baking soda
1½ teaspoons ground ginger
1 teaspoon ground cinnamon
2 cinnamon sticks (2 to 3 inches
    long) or an additional ¼ tea-
    spoon ground cinnamon
½ teaspoon nutmeg, freshly-
    grated or from a jar
¼ teaspoon ground cloves
2 whole cloves or ⅛ teaspoon
    ground cloves
Foil or paper baking cups for
    muffins
½ cup light or dark molasses
½ cup (3 ounces) pitted dates
1 quart apple juice
¼ cup orange juice

1½ to 2 pounds red or green
    seedless grapes
1 lemon

¾ cup milk
4 tablespoons (½ stick) unsalted
    butter
5 large eggs
1 pound Monterey Jack or
    cheddar cheese

Nuts for munching

(Coffee? Tea? Add what you
    need. Check number of ther-
    mos flasks or insulated coffee
    jugs on hand.)

Easter for Adults and Children

M E N U

FOR 10

*STRAWBERRIES IN
RHUBARB SAUCE WITH
FRESH CREAM

BAKED COUNTRY HAM

SELECTION OF MUSTARDS

*DEVILISH EGG BUNNIES

*EASTER BREADS:
CHICKENS, BUNNIES, AND
ITALIAN EGG BRAID

*UNORTHODOX PASKHA

*RECIPE FOLLOWS

Young children love to help in the kitchen, and if you don't have children of your own, I hope you'll be able to borrow two or three to help make (and eat) the Devilish Egg Bunnies and the Chicken and Bunny Breads. There's lots of room for individual artistic expression and fun in both recipes.

Just about everything in this menu can be made ahead. If you go to church and bring guests home with you, there need not be much delay before breakfast is served.

Very young children may not like the tart flavor of rhubarb. If you think that is a possibility, buy extra strawberries, the smallest you can find. At the last minute, rinse them, but leave the green hulls on. Give each child a small spoonful of confectioners' sugar on a plate or in a bowl. The children can pick up the berries by the hulls and dip them into the sugar before eating. (Keep an eye on the children; if there's a lot of giggling someone may swallow the sugar "the wrong way" and have a coughing fit.)

Instead of a baked country ham you may prefer ham steaks or even thin slices of ham quickly frizzled in a skillet. This choice is yours.

Strawberries in Rhubarb Sauce

This is a wonderful mixture that truly says spring. Serve with fresh cream.

1½ to 2 pounds fresh or frozen
    rhubarb
½ cup strawberry jam or red
    currant jelly

½ cup granulated sugar
6 cups fresh strawberries (about
    2 pints)

Wash fresh rhubarb, discard leaves, and cut into 1-inch lengths (you should have about 6 cups). Stir up jam and put it in the bottom of a large, heavy-bottomed stainless steel or enameled skillet or saucepan. Add rhubarb and sprinkle with ¼ cup sugar.

Cover pan and place over moderate heat. Check after 8 to 10 minutes; you want the rhubarb to cook very slowly in the jam and to break up as little as possible. Cook about 15 minutes until rhubarb is tender, shaking pan or stirring fruit gently 2 or 3 times. Remove from heat. Let cool in pan or transfer to serving bowl. Chill.

Up to 2 hours before serving, rinse and hull berries. Leave tiny ones whole, quarter larger ones. Put into a bowl; sprinkle with ¼ cup sugar. Let stand 10 minutes. Gently fold berries into rhubarb. Leave at room temperature. *Makes 10 servings.*

GAME PLAN

UP TO 1 WEEK AHEAD YOU MAY:
◆ Bake breads and freeze (omit hard-cooked eggs from braid).

THE DAY BEFORE:
◆ Make Unorthodox Paskha.
◆ Hard-cook eggs for Devilish Egg Bunnies.
◆ Cook rhubarb and chill.

THE DAY BEFORE YOU MAY ALSO:
◆ Complete egg bunnies.

ABOUT 2 HOURS BEFORE SERVING:
◆ Heat ham if not serving at room temperature (see page 196).
◆ Remove breads from freezer; let come to room temperature.
◆ Add berries to rhubarb.

UP TO 1 HOUR BEFORE SERVING:
◆ Arrange egg bunnies on platter; breads in baskets.
◆ Garnish paskha.

SHOPPING GUIDE

5¼ cups all-purpose flour

1½ cups granulated sugar

¼ cup (1½ ounces) blanched almonds

¼ cup (1½ ounces) golden raisins

2 envelopes active dry yeast

1 14-ounce can sweetened condensed milk (not evaporated milk)

⅓ cup nonfat dry milk (optional)

5½ teaspoons vanilla extract

½ cup strawberry jam or red currant jelly

½ cup mayonnaise

2 teaspoons Dijon mustard, plus 1 or more mustards to serve with ham

1½ to 2 pounds fresh or frozen rhubarb

2 pints fresh strawberries

Ham, your choice (see page 196)

1 tablespoon milk

½ to 1 pint heavy cream (to serve with fruit)

8 tablespoons (1 stick) unsalted butter

21 or 22 large eggs

1 8-ounce package cream cheese

3 7½-ounce packages farmer cheese, or about 22 ounces pot cheese

continued

Devilish Egg Bunnies

This idea came from *Sunset* magazine. Each bunny will have its own unfailingly adorable personality. Make the egg yolk mixture in a plastic food storage bag with a zip-type closure and then squeeze it from the bag into the whites. Sounds weird but it cuts cleanup and time spent hunting for a decorating bag. Invite children to help make these eggs.

15 *hard-cooked eggs (see page 193)*
½ *cup mayonnaise*
2 *teaspoons Dijon mustard*
½ *teaspoon salt*
¼ *teaspoon freshly-ground pepper*

For ears: 3 or 4 small Belgian endives or 6 slender carrot sticks about 2 inches long
For eyes: tiny pieces of ripe olive, pickle, pimiento, or capers

Cut eggs in half lengthwise. Scoop yolks into a 1-gallon plastic food storage bag with zip-type closure. Add the mayonnaise, mustard, salt, and pepper.

Close the bag and squish contents with fingers until thoroughly mixed and lump-free.

If any of the egg whites are messy around the rim, wipe them clean with a damp paper towel. Line up whites on another damp paper towel to keep them from sliding about.

Work all the filling down to one corner of the bag. Make a hole by snipping a small triangle off that corner. Twist bag above filling (to prevent it from bursting out the top) and then squeeze some of the filling through the hole into each egg white. (Neatness is not really important.)

Separate endive leaves, cutting thick stem off bottom as necessary. Stick two tiny inside leaves into filled egg for ears. Cut additional ears from the larger leaves. Make eyes with tiny pieces of olive, pickle, pimiento, or capers.

Arrange on a serving plate; cover loosely and chill up to 4 hours. Or store up to 1 day in a plastic container in the refrigerator. *Makes 30 bunnies.*

Easter Breads: Chickens, Bunnies, and Italian Egg Braid

You can make three shapes from one batch of this dough. Or, if you prefer, shape all the dough into chickens or bunnies or into two braids. Use an electric mixer that has a dough hook or flex your muscles and follow the hand method below.

> 1 cup very warm water (105° to 115°F.)
> 2 envelopes active dry yeast
> ½ cup granulated sugar
> ⅓ cup instant nonfat dry milk (optional)
> 5 to 5¼ cups all-purpose flour
> 8 tablespoons (1 stick) unsalted butter, at room temperature
> 2 large eggs
> 1½ teaspoons vanilla extract
> 1 teaspoon salt
> Homemade Vanilla Pearl Sugar (recipe follows)

> For chickens and bunnies: Zante currants; sliced almonds or pumpkin seeds
> Eggwash (1 batch does all breads): Beat 1 egg with 1 tablespoon milk
> For 1 egg braid: 3 or 4 unpeeled hard-cooked eggs, natural or dyed

SHOPPING GUIDE cont'd

1 1-gallon food freezer bag with zip-type closure
To decorate Devilish Egg Bunnies: 3 or 4 small Belgian endives; 1 or 2 carrots; 2 or 3 ripe olives, a little pickle, pimiento, or a few capers for bunnies' eyes.
To decorate chicken and bunny breads: about ¼ cup Zante currants and about ¼ to ½ cup pumpkin seeds or sliced almonds for wings and tails.
To garnish paskha: jelly beans; edible fresh flowers.

(Coffee? Tea? Add what you need, plus butter for the table.)

Mix water, yeast, and the ½ cup sugar in large mixer bowl. Let stand 2 minutes. Stir in the dry milk if you are using it (it makes dough slightly richer).

Add about half of the flour, the butter, eggs, vanilla, and salt. Mix on low speed, then beat on medium speed about 2 minutes.

At low speed, add as much of remaining flour as needed to make a soft dough that leaves sides of bowl. Switch to dough hook; knead dough 7 to 8 minutes.

Scrape dough into a greased bowl; turn dough once to bring greased side up. Cover bowl with plastic wrap and put in a warm place for about 1½ hours or until double in volume.

While dough rises, make the Vanilla Pearl Sugar so that it can dry.

When dough has risen sufficiently, attack it with a clenched fist and punch all the air bubbles out of it. Turn dough onto a board. Cut off half; use for Italian Egg Braid. Cut remaining dough in half again; use half each for chickens and bunnies. Keep dough covered with a cloth while not actually working with it; punch dough down again if one piece rises again while you're shaping another.

HAND METHOD: Melt butter; let cool slightly. Mix water, yeast, and sugar in a large bowl. Let stand 2 minutes; stir in dry milk, if you are using it. Add about half of the flour, the butter, eggs, vanilla, and salt. Stir with a wooden spoon to form a batter, then beat with a spoon

continued

for about 2 minutes. Stir in as much of remaining flour as needed to make a soft dough that leaves sides of bowl. Turn out dough onto a lightly floured surface (use some of remaining flour) and knead dough by hand for 8 to 10 minutes, until smooth and elastic. Put dough into a greased bowl and continue as above.

CHICKENS AND BUNNIES: Put a couple of tablespoons of flour near you on the work surface. Dip the cutters in the flour before and while using them to prevent dough from sticking.

To make Easter Chickens, grease one or more cookie sheets. Roll dough ¼-inch thick. Cut out with floured chicken-shaped cutter (mine is about 2¾ inches high) and transfer to cookie sheets. Insert currants for eyes. Stick in a few almond slices or pumpkin seeds to highlight wings. Cover dough loosely with plastic wrap and let rise in a warm place until double in volume, about 20 minutes. *Makes about 22 chickens.*

To make Easter Bunnies, grease one or more cookie sheets. Roll dough ¼-inch thick on unfloured surface (not so easy; dough puts up a fight). Using floured plain cutters, cut out an equal number of 2½-inch rounds for bodies and 2-inch rounds for heads. Arrange on cookie sheet with head and body just touching. Reroll scraps and cut out more heads and bodies. For ears, roll out scraps and cut long diamond shapes with a knife. Shape each ear slightly with fingers and tuck ends just under the head. Shape small balls for tails from the last scraps of dough.

Press currants firmly in place for eyes. Cover dough loosely with plastic wrap and let rise in a warm place until double in volume, about 20 minutes. *Makes about 20 bunnies.*

To bake chickens and bunnies, heat oven to 350°F. Brush risen dough with Eggwash and sprinkle with Homemade Vanilla Pearl Sugar (see recipe below). Bake breads until browned on bottom and golden on top. Chickens take 10 to 15 minutes, bunnies 18 to 25 minutes. Cool breads on a rack.

ITALIAN EGG BRAID: Grease a cookie sheet. Cut dough into thirds. Using palms of hands, roll each piece into a 20-inch rope. Put the three ropes side by side on cookie sheet, pinching ropes together at one end (other ends will dangle over). Braid the ropes, tucking in the hard-cooked eggs and braiding around them. Tuck in ends and pinch together.

Cover dough loosely with plastic wrap and let rise in a warm place until double in volume, 30 to 40 minutes.

Heat oven to 350°F. Brush dough with some of the Eggwash and sprinkle with some of the Homemade Vanilla Pearl Sugar (see recipe below). Bake 30 to 35 minutes, until loaf is golden brown and sounds hollow when tapped on the bottom.

HOMEMADE VANILLA PEARL SUGAR

In Scandinavia, cooks often sprinkle pearl sugar on sweet breads, and you can easily buy it there. Pearl sugar is hard to find here, but it's easy to make. Adding vanilla makes the sugar less white, but it greatly improves the flavor.

½ cup granulated sugar   *2 teaspoons vanilla extract*

Put sugar in a pie plate or shallow dish. Sprinkle with vanilla. Work with fingers until sugar is evenly moistened.

Spread sugar out on plate and leave to dry in a warm, dry place 30 minutes or longer. Store in an airtight container. *Makes about ½ cup.*

Unorthodox Paskha

Traditional for Russian Orthodox Easter celebrations, paskha is something like cheesecake without a crust. This version is divine, but it is unorthodox in method because the sieving, the egg custard, the molding, and the draining called for in most recipes have been eliminated. With this recipe, make the paskha a day ahead so that it has time to firm. Just before serving, decorate the surface with jelly beans in the shape of the Orthodox cross, and perhaps lemon or mint leaves and edible fresh flowers such as violets or pansies (see page 189). Spoon the paskha onto small plates; eat with spoon or fork.

1 *14-ounce can sweetened condensed milk (not evaporated milk)*
1 *8-ounce package cream cheese, at room temperature*
2 *teaspoons vanilla extract*
3 *7½-ounce packages farmer cheese, or about 22 ounces pot cheese, at room temperature*

¼ cup (1½ ounces) golden raisins
¼ cup (1½ ounces) finely chopped blanched almonds (optional)

Put condensed milk, cream cheese, and vanilla into a large bowl. Beat about 5 minutes with an electric mixer, scraping sides several times, until mixture is fairly smooth.

Add farmer cheese; beat until well blended. Mixture will have a grainy look.

At low speed, stir in raisins and almonds. Scrape mixture into serving bowl. Cover and chill at least 12 hours, until paskha has firmed somewhat. Keeps at least a week. *Makes about 10 to 15 servings.*

For Mother, with Love

M E N U

FOR 4

*STRAWBERRY SMASH

*CINNAMON-RAISIN
FRENCH TOAST BAKED IN
THE OVEN

APPLE SYRUP OR HONEY

*FRIZZLED HAM OR
CANADIAN BACON

*RECIPE FOLLOWS

With just a little help, children can easily manage this simple breakfast and make Mother's Day a truly special occasion. With that thought in mind, I've written these recipes especially for children to use. Knives and heat are involved, so be sure an adult is with the children at all times. Of course, if Mother is the only adult present, she may have to help prepare her own special breakfast. But that can be fun—and certainly less nerve-wracking than lying in bed anticipating the crash of a dish or a cry that sends her heading for the bandages.

The apple syrup that's served with the French toast is simply frozen apple juice concentrate that's been allowed to thaw. If you've always cooked French toast on the rangetop in a skillet, you will enjoy the ease of the baking method. You can bake at least eight slices of bread at once on a jelly-roll pan and there's no turning needed. Be sure to freeze any leftover French toast. One slice heats in about twenty-five seconds in a microwave oven, making a great before-school breakfast that children can enjoy getting for themselves.

Strawberry Smash

1 pint fresh strawberries
1 8-ounce container strawberry yogurt

Granulated sugar, if you need it

Put strawberries into a clean bowl of cold water. Move them about very gently with your fingers for a few seconds. Lift them onto a sheet of paper towel to drain.

Take off the green hulls. You can pull them out with your fingers or, if you have a huller (a small tweezer-like tool) use that. If there's a lot of white at the top of each berry, cut it and the hull off with a small knife.

Slice all the berries. Put about half the slices into four serving glasses or bowls.

Put remaining berries on a plate and mash (smash) them with a fork until they are well broken up. Stir up the strawberry yogurt and put it into a small bowl. Add the smashed berries; stir, then taste. If mixture is not sweet enough, add about 1 teaspoon sugar and taste again.

Spoon the strawberry sauce over the berries in the bowls. *Makes 4 servings.*

Cinnamon-Raisin French Toast Baked in the Oven

Serve the French toast with either apple syrup or honey.

2 tablespoons unsalted butter
2 large eggs
½ cup milk
1 tablespoon confectioners' sugar

½ teaspoon ground cinnamon
½ teaspoon vanilla extract
8 slices cinnamon-raisin bread
Confectioners' sugar

Look inside the oven and make sure one shelf is just about in the middle. Close the door and turn the oven on, setting the control at 425°F. The oven will heat while you get the French toast ready.

Get out a jelly-roll pan. That's a flat pan, about 15 × 10 inches, with sides about ½-inch high.

Look at the marks on the butter wrapper and cut off 2 separate tablespoons. Cut one into little pieces and put them on the pan; cut the other into very little pieces and leave them on the butter wrapper.

Get out a medium-sized bowl. Break the eggs one at a time into the bowl and throw away the shells. Add the milk, the 1 tablespoon confectioners' sugar, the cinnamon, and the vanilla to the eggs. With a fork, rotary beater, or wire whisk beat the egg mixture until it is an even yellow color and slightly frothy.

continued

THE NIGHT BEFORE:
- Check that you have all the ingredients and equipment you need.
- Take the container of frozen apple juice concentrate from the freezer and put it in the refrigerator to thaw.
- Choose a tray to serve breakfast on; also plates, glasses, cups, and tools.

ABOUT 1 HOUR BEFORE SERVING:
- Heat oven to 425°F.
- Take butter out to soften.
- See that coffee or tea is organized.
- Get the French toast ready to bake and into the oven.
- Make Strawberry Smash.
- Pour apple juice concentrate into a little jug for serving.
- While French toast bakes, fry ham or Canadian bacon.

LAST MINUTE:
- Put French toast on plates leaving space for the bacon or ham. Sprinkle toast with confectioners' sugar.
- Put ham or Canadian bacon on plate beside the French toast.
- Carry to Mother.
- Make a second trip with coffee or tea.
- After breakfast, clean up! Mother will think that's the best present of all.

B R E A K F A S T

SHOPPING GUIDE

3 tablespoons confectioners'
    sugar
Granulated sugar in case you
    need it
½ teaspoon ground cinnamon
½ teaspoon vanilla extract
Honey to serve with the French
    toast (½ pound should be
    plenty)

8 slices cinnamon-raisin bread

1 pint fresh strawberries
1 12-ounce container frozen
    apple juice concentrate

2 or 3 slices boiled ham (or
    baked ham from the deli
    counter) per person. You can
    also use 2 or 3 slices Cana-
    dian bacon, but ham is a bet-
    ter buy (see page 196).

½ cup milk
1 8-ounce container strawberry
    yogurt
4 tablespoons (½ stick) unsalted
    butter
2 large eggs

The butter you put on the baking pan should be soft by now. Spread it all over the bottom of the pan with your fingertips.

Cut the slices of bread in half. Have the bowl of egg mixture near the buttered baking pan. Pick up one piece of bread at a time, dip both sides into the egg mixture, and place the bread flat on the buttered baking pan.

When you've finished dipping, wash your hands. Take the little pieces of butter and spread or sprinkle them over the surfaces of the dipped bread.

Ask an adult to help you put the pan into the oven. Put the pan on the shelf so that it isn't touching the walls of the oven.

Set a timer for 12 minutes. When it rings, check the French toast. If it seems rather pale, set the timer for 3 more minutes then check again. When ready, the French toast should have a nice brown color that makes you want to eat it.

Ask an adult to take the pan of French toast out of the oven and put it on a heatproof countertop. You can help to carefully lift the pieces of French toast onto the serving plates with a pancake turner. Sift a little confectioners' sugar over the toast—some sugar will fall on the plate and that's fine. *Makes 4 servings.*

Frizzled Ham or Canadian Bacon

Butter
Sliced fully-cooked ham or Canadian
    bacon (allow 2 or 3 slices per
    person)

Heat a large skillet over moderately-high heat. Add 1 tablespoon butter. When melted and bubbling, add a single layer of bacon or ham. Cook ham 1 to 1½ minutes per side, just until tinged with brown; cook Canadian bacon 2 to 3 minutes on each side, turning once.

Remove from pan and cook remaining meat, adding a little more butter if needed.

Graduation Day Breakfast

M E N U

FOR 12

*BAKED APPLES AND
APRICOTS

*FRESH SALMON HASH

*BAKED EGGS

*PARMESAN CHIVE BISCUITS

*RECIPE FOLLOWS

Reward hard work and achievement with an elegant breakfast honoring the graduates in your inner circle and starting this important day on a memorable note.

If you can't get really good fresh salmon, try the Homemade Corned Beef Hash on page 96. If you want to add a coffee cake, make the Walnut Cinnamon-Chocolate Coffee Cake on page 136.

While the hash does require last minute attention, most of the rest of the menu can be organized ahead. Make the Baked Apples and Apricots the day before; reheat them shortly before serving (a microwave oven works well here). The Parmesan Chive Biscuits can be frozen unbaked, then baked without thawing. Baking eggs in muffin cups is a very easy and efficient way to cook several eggs at one time. It's a trick I learned years ago from friends who had packed up city life to go grow wild blueberries in Maine. In their old farmhouse, breakfast guests were welcomed with huge mounds of freshly cooked sausage, baked eggs, and, of course, blueberry muffins.

GAME PLAN

UP TO 1 WEEK AHEAD YOU
MAY:
◆ Make Parmesan Chive Bis-
cuits; freeze unbaked.

THE DAY BEFORE:
◆ Make Baked Apples and Apricots; cool, cover, and refrigerate.
◆ Chop shallots or scallions;
cover tightly and refrigerate.
◆ Cut, but don't cook, salmon.

ABOUT 1½ TO 2 HOURS
BEFORE SERVING
◆ Boil potatoes for Fresh
Salmon Hash; cut into
chunks.
◆ Heat oven to 350°F. Heat
apples and apricots about 20
minutes. Cover and keep
warm until ready to serve.
◆ Turn oven to 450°F. Place
frozen biscuits (don't thaw)
on a cookie sheet and bake.
◆ Turn oven to 325°F.
◆ Break eggs into muffin cups.

LAST MINUTE:
◆ Cook salmon and continue to
make hash.
◆ Bake eggs.

Baked Apples and Apricots

½ cup apple juice
1 11-ounce package dried apricots
5 pounds (about 12 large) Granny
  Smith apples

1 cup packed light brown sugar
8 tablespoons (1 stick) unsalted
  butter, cut into small pieces
¼ cup freshly-squeezed lemon juice

Measure apple juice in a 1-quart or larger measuring cup. Add apricots, press them down into the liquid, and let soak while you cut up the apples.

Peel, halve, and core apples; cut them into ½- to 1-inch chunks. Heat oven to 375°F. about half way through preparing apples.

Divide apricots and liquid between two 2½- to 3-quart baking dishes. Divide apples and remaining ingredients between the two dishes. Mix well.

Bake 50 to 60 minutes, stirring every 15 minutes or so, until apples are very soft and have begun to look translucent.

Serve warm. May be covered and refrigerated overnight and reheated before serving. *Makes 12 to 15 servings.*

Fresh Salmon Hash

1¾ to 2 pounds red or white thin-
    skinned potatoes, scrubbed
    Water
1 tablespoon distilled white
    vinegar or fresh lemon
    juice
1½ teaspoons salt
1 clove garlic, peeled
2 pounds skinned and boned
    fresh salmon fillet, cut into
    ¾-inch chunks
8 tablespoons pure olive oil
4 tablespoons (½ stick)
    unsalted butter

¾ cup chopped shallots or white
    part of scallions
1 medium-sized red bell pepper,
    diced
2 cups frozen corn kernels
¾ teaspoon freshly-ground
    pepper
½ cup chopped fresh cilantro
    (coriander or Chinese
    parsley) or flat-leaf
    parsley

In a heavy 4- to 5-quart pot cook potatoes in boiling water until tender. Drain in a colander. When cool enough to handle, cut into ½-inch chunks (no need to peel).

While potatoes cool, rinse pot. Pour in 3 cups water; add the vinegar, ½ teaspoon salt, and garlic clove. Bring to a boil over high heat. Reduce heat to moderately-low and simmer 5 minutes. Add salmon and stir gently with a rubber spatula. Remove pot from heat; cover and let stand 4 minutes. Carefully pour contents into colander; discard garlic clove.

Choose two heavy skillets, each 8 to 10 inches across the bottom. (Cast iron or nonstick work well.) Add 3 tablespoons pure olive oil to each and heat over moderately-high heat.

Add 2 tablespoons butter to each skillet. When melted add half the potatoes and shallots to each. Reduce heat to moderately-low. Cook 10 to 15 minutes, stirring frequently, until potatoes are nicely browned. Add red pepper and cook 5 to 8 minutes longer, until tender. Stir in corn and cook 3 minutes, stirring once.

Add 1 tablespoon more olive oil to each skillet. Add salmon, remaining 1 teaspoon salt, and the pepper. Cook 5 to 7 minutes, stirring gently and frequently, until salmon is hot and lightly browned in places. Remove from heat, stir in cilantro or parsley, and serve. *Makes 12 servings.*

Baked Eggs

Use a nonstick or well-seasoned iron muffin pan.

Soft butter	*Water*
12 large eggs	*Salt and freshly-ground pepper*

Heat oven to 325°F. Heavily butter twelve nonstick muffin cups. One by one, break each egg into a custard cup or other small dish and slide it into a muffin cup. Do not break eggs directly into muffin cups because if you break a yolk, it is almost impossible to remove the egg without tipping out all the other eggs you've already put in. (Should you disregard my warning and the inevitable happens, try removing the broken egg with a bulb baster.)

Spoon 1 teaspoon water over each egg and sprinkle lightly with salt and pepper.

Bake 13 to 15 minutes, or until whites are set and yolks still soft. Remove from oven. Run the tip of a rubber spatula around each egg, lift out gently, and place on top of each serving of hash. *Makes 12 servings.*

SHOPPING GUIDE

3¼ cups all-purpose flour
1 cup light brown sugar
4 teaspoons baking power
1 11-ounce package dried apricots
½ cup pure olive oil
½ cup apple juice
1 tablespoon distilled white vinegar or fresh lemon juice

5 pounds (about 12 large) Granny Smith apples
2 lemons
1¾ to 2 pounds red or white thin-skinned potatoes ("new" potatoes)
4 ounces shallots or 2 bunches scallions (¾ cup chopped)
1 medium-sized red bell pepper
1 bunch chives (enough for 3 tablespoons snipped)
1 bunch cilantro (also known as coriander or Chinese parsley) or flat-leaf parsley (enough for ½ cup chopped)
1 clove garlic

1 10-ounce package frozen corn kernels (2 cups)

2 pounds skinned and boned fresh salmon fillet

1¼ cups milk
24 tablespoons (3 sticks) unsalted butter
12 large eggs
½ cup (2 ounces) freshly-grated Parmesan cheese

(Coffee? Tea? Other beverages this age group may prefer? Add what you need, also butter for the table.)

Parmesan Chive Biscuits

3 cups all-purpose flour
½ cup freshly-grated Parmesan cheese
3 tablespoons snipped fresh chives
4 teaspoons baking powder
½ teaspoon salt

½ teaspoon freshly-ground pepper
8 tablespoons (1 stick) cold unsalted
    butter, cut into small pieces
1¼ cups milk

Heat oven to 450°F. Put flour into a large bowl. Add cheese, chives, baking powder, salt, and pepper. Stir to mix well.

Add butter and cut in with a pastry blender or rub in with your fingers until fine granules form.

Pour in milk. Stir with a fork until a soft dough forms.

Sprinkle work surface with flour. Turn dough out onto surface and give it 10 to 12 kneads. Sprinkle with a little more flour if very sticky.

With fingers or a lightly floured rolling pin, pat or roll dough to an 11-inch circle (about ½-inch thick). Cut out biscuits with a 2½-inch cutter dipped in flour. Put biscuits on an ungreased cookie sheet. Reroll scraps and cut out more biscuits.

Bake 10 to 12 minutes, until light golden brown. Transfer to a wire rack and cover loosely with a cotton or linen kitchen towel. Cool at least 15 minutes before serving. *Makes 19 to 22 biscuits.*

SUMMER

Memorial Day

```
   M   E   N   U
        FOR 10

FRESH FRUITS OF MAY

*EGGS WITH SAUSAGE,
PEPPERS, AND POTATOES

*CHERRY-ALMOND
  COFFEE CAKE


 *RECIPE FOLLOWS
```

Memorial Day heralds the start of summer plea-sures. I love the extra hours of daylight, walking in the park, and shopping at the Greenmarket (farmers' market) for the first local vegetables and summer berries. If well managed, summer weekends in the city can mean country pleasures, without the highway hassles neces-sary to get there. At the end of May it is already hot in some parts of the country, still surprisingly cool in oth-ers. Whatever the temperature, and wherever you are—city, country, beach, or lakeside—invite good friends to celebrate summer with a breakfast that's sure to please.

May is such an in-between-seasons time for fruit that I'm leaving you to select the best from your market. Pineapples are in good supply, as are California straw-berries. The top mango season is just beginning and the first Texas cantaloupes are on their way. You may even see early cherries and peaches, but they may not have full flavor or sweetness yet. True, oranges and grapefruit are still plentiful, but you may feel they are too reminis-cent of winter for a herald-the-summer breakfast. Choose the best fruit to peel, slice, and arrange prettily on a platter. You'll find instructions for preparing indi-vidual fruits throughout this book; consult the index by fruit name.

Two good alternatives to a fresh fruit platter are Strawberry-Orange Juice, page 6, or Strawberries in Rhubarb Sauce, page 25.

GAME PLAN

UP TO 2 MONTHS AHEAD YOU
MAY:

◆ Bake and freeze coffee cake.

THE DAY BEFORE YOU MAY:

◆ Peel and slice fruits except
delicate fruits such as strawberries.

◆ Cut potatoes for Eggs with
Sausage, Peppers, and Potatoes into chunks and cook.

◆ Grate cheese; slice onion;
cut up peppers. Wrap each
separately.

◆ Remove sausage from casings.

◆ Transfer coffee cake from
freezer to refrigerator.

ABOUT 1 HOUR BEFORE
SERVING:

◆ Arrange fruits on platter.

◆ Heat oven to 250°F.

◆ Cook sausage, peppers, and
potatoes.

LAST MINUTE:

◆ Add eggs to sausage mixture;
scramble.

◆ Heat coffee cake in oven for
10 to 15 minutes, while eggs
are served.

Eggs with Sausage, Peppers, and Potatoes

You can use two smaller skillets instead of one large one.

1 pound red or white thin-skinned potatoes, scrubbed	1 small green bell pepper
2 tablespoons pure olive or vegetable oil	1 cup sliced onion
1 pound sweet Italian sausage, removed from casings	20 large eggs
1 small red bell pepper	⅓ cup freshly-grated Parmesan cheese
	1 teaspoon salt
	1 teaspoon freshly-ground pepper

Cut unpeeled potatoes into ½-inch chunks (you should have about 3 cups) and put into a medium-sized saucepan. Cover with water and bring to a boil over high heat. Reduce heat to moderately-low, cover pan, and cook 6 to 8 minutes, until tender. Drain.

Meanwhile, get out a heavy skillet at least 12 inches across the bottom and 2 to 3 inches deep, put over moderate heat, and add oil. Crumble in sausage and cook about 5 minutes, until chunks are nearly cooked through.

Halve peppers; pull out seeds and stems. Cut peppers into ½-inch pieces. Add to skillet along with onion and drained potatoes. Cook 15 to 18 minutes, stirring several times, until sausage and potatoes are lightly browned. Pan will seem very full at first, but mixture will gradually cook down. Add another tablespoon of oil if pan gets very dry. While vegetables cook, break eggs into a large bowl.

Shortly before serving, add Parmesan, salt, and pepper to eggs. Beat with a wire whisk or electric mixer until well broken up. Pour into skillet and scramble until eggs are creamy soft and almost as firm as you like them (see page 193). Spoon onto plates and serve. *Makes 10 servings.*

Cherry-Almond Coffee Cake

This cake uses half a can of cherry pie filling. So that the rest of the can doesn't occupy space in your refrigerator for months, you might want to make two coffee cakes and freeze one. Or freeze the leftover pie filling for later use.

2 cups all-purpose flour
1 teaspoon baking powder
1 teaspoon baking soda
½ teaspoon salt
8 tablespoons (1 stick) unsalted butter, at room temperature
1 cup granulated sugar

2 large eggs
1 teaspoon vanilla extract
½ teaspoon almond extract
1 cup sour cream
1 cup cherry pie filling
½ cup (1¾ ounces) sliced natural almonds

Heat oven to 350°F. Butter a 9-inch springform pan.

Put flour, baking powder, baking soda, and salt into a small bowl; stir to mix well.

In a large bowl, beat butter with an electric mixer. When creamy, add sugar, about ¼ cup at a time, beating after each addition.

When mixture is light and fluffy, add eggs, one at a time, beating after each addition. Beat in extracts. Scrape sides of bowl.

With mixer on low, add flour mixture, about ½ cup at a time, alternating with sour cream, about ⅓ cup at a time, beating just until batter is smooth.

Spoon half the batter (about 2 cups) into prepared pan; add half cherry pie filling and swirl it once through batter with a rubber spatula. Spoon remaining batter evenly over top and then remaining cherry pie filling (but don't swirl it). Sprinkle with almonds; press almonds lightly into surface.

Bake 60 to 65 minutes, or until cake is brown on top and shrinks slightly from sides of pan and a wooden toothpick inserted in center comes out clean.

Cool in pan on wire rack for 15 minutes. Remove pan sides. Serve cake warm. *Makes 12 generous servings.*

SHOPPING GUIDE

2 cups all-purpose flour
1 cup granulated sugar
1 teaspoon baking powder
1 teaspoon baking soda
1 teaspoon vanilla extract
½ teaspoon almond extract
1 21-ounce can cherry pie filling
½ cup (1¾ ounces) sliced natural almonds
2 tablespoons pure olive or vegetable oil

Fresh fruits for fruit platter
1 pound red or white thin-skinned potatoes ("new" potatoes)
1 onion (1 cup sliced)
1 small red bell pepper
1 small green bell pepper (or you can use 2 green)

1 pound sweet Italian sausage

1 8-ounce container sour cream
8 tablespoons (1 stick) unsalted butter
22 large eggs
⅓ cup (1½ ounces) freshly-grated Parmesan cheese

(Coffee? Tea? Add what you need. If you wish, add butter for the table and white or pumpernickel bread to serve, toasted, with the eggs.)

For Dad, with Love, Too

M E N U

FOR 4

FRESHLY-SQUEEZED
ORANGE JUICE

*SPAGHETTI FRITTATA

SALSA OR CHILI SAUCE

*PARMESAN TOAST

*RECIPE FOLLOWS

Why is it that traditionally mother is served breakfast in bed on her day, while father helps cook his own? Perhaps it is because so many fathers already enjoy making weekend breakfasts with their kids. In fact, I've written the recipe for Parmesan Toast for children to use, with close adult supervision, of course.

This menu requires a small conspiracy: a spaghetti dinner a few days beforehand so that there is cooked spaghetti in the refrigerator. (Of course, if there aren't any leftovers, you can always cook spaghetti the night before just for this dish.) Not only is the frittata easy to make, but children take great delight in having spaghetti for breakfast.

While everyone is enjoying the fruits of their labor, you can amaze and confuse the children. Tell them that a frittata is an omelet in Italian and that it is usually served flat (like this one), unlike a French omelet, which is folded over or rolled up before serving. Then ask them what a Spanish omelet is in America. After they've told you that it has ham, tomatoes, and green peppers in it and is served folded over, tell them that in Spain an omelet is usually served flat and that in Spain an omelet is called a tortilla.

Spaghetti Frittata

Serve the frittata with salsa or chili sauce.

4 teaspoons pure olive or vegetable
  oil
1½ cups cooked spaghetti
6 large eggs
2 tablespoons freshly-grated
  Parmesan cheese

1 tablespoon milk
¼ teaspoon salt
⅛ teaspoon freshly-ground pepper

Choose a nonstick skillet that measures 7 to 8 inches across the bottom and has a lid.

Put olive oil in skillet and heat over moderately-high heat. Add spaghetti and toss with two wooden spoons until it is coated with oil. Then spread spaghetti over bottom of pan.

Reduce heat to moderate and fry spaghetti about 5 minutes. Turn it over and fry 5 minutes longer on second side. Spaghetti will become lightly browned and crisp.

While spaghetti browns, break eggs into a medium-sized bowl. Add cheese, milk, salt, and pepper. Beat eggs with a wire whisk or a fork until they are well broken up and you can no longer tell yolk from white. (The mixture will be pale yellow and there will be a little froth on the top.)

Pour eggs over hot spaghetti. Reduce heat to moderately-low. Cover and cook 8 to 9 minutes, but uncover the pan every minute or two. Notice how the egg starts to set around the edge. Take a pancake turner (a wooden or plastic one that won't scratch the nonstick skillet) and lift up the cooked egg in two or three places around the edge to let uncooked (still runny) egg flow underneath cooked part.

Soon all the egg will be set. The frittata is done. Remove pan from heat right away so egg stops cooking. Have a large serving plate nearby and slide frittata out of the pan onto the plate. (If you don't have a large flat plate, a board will do just fine.)

Cut frittata in wedges like a pie and put a wedge on each person's plate. Mangia! *Makes 4 servings.*

GAME PLAN

UP TO 2 DAYS BEFORE:
◆ Cook spaghetti.

THE NIGHT BEFORE YOU MAY:
◆ Slice French bread; store in plastic bag.

ABOUT 40 MINUTES BEFORE SERVING:
◆ Take butter out of refrigerator to soften.
◆ Squeeze oranges for juice.
◆ Set table.
◆ Butter French bread; put on cookie sheet; sprinkle with Parmesan.
◆ Heat broiler.
◆ Make frittata; cover and keep warm for a few minutes while you broil Parmesan Toast.
◆ Slide frittata onto a serving plate or board.
◆ Put Parmesan Toast on a plate or in a basket.

OLIVE OIL

Since olive oil was reclassified as "healthy" (hurray!), I have been experimenting with it in a wide variety of recipes, even for baking. I've found that it can add a full, rich flavor, yet not be discernible as olive oil.

Look for olive oils labeled "pure" or "light" (light in flavor, not in calories). Save virgin and extra-virgin oils for salads and meats.

SHOPPING GUIDE

1½ cups cooked spaghetti (4 ounces before cooking)

Salsa or chili sauce

4 teaspoons pure olive or vegetable oil

12 juice oranges or 1 to 2 quarts refrigerated orange juice

1 long loaf crusty French or Italian bread (about 8 ounces)

1 tablespoon milk

2 tablespoons butter

6 large eggs

4 tablespoons (1 ounce) freshly-grated Parmesan cheese

(Milk to drink? Coffee? Tea? Add what you need.)

Parmesan Toast

Parmesan is a cheese that originated in Italy. It is allowed to age for several months, making it very hard and dry. You can buy Parmesan from Italy or you can buy delicious Parmesan that is made in Wisconsin. Most people buy packaged, grated Parmesan, but try buying store-grated Parmesan instead. For best flavor, buy a small wedge of Wisconsin Parmesan at the dairy counter and grate it yourself.

1 long loaf crusty French or Italian bread (about 8 ounces)
2 tablespoons butter, at room temperature

2 tablespoons freshly-grated Parmesan cheese

Ask an adult to cut 8 or more slices of bread, each about 1-inch thick. (A knife with a serrated, or saw-toothed, edge is best for cutting bread.)

Heat broiler or ask an adult to do it for you.

Butter slices of bread on one side. Put slices flat on a cookie sheet, buttered side up, as close together as you can. Sprinkle tops lightly with cheese. Spread slices out a little.

Slide cookie sheet carefully under broiler and broil toast for 5 to 6 minutes. Watch toast carefully and be ready with oven mitts. As soon as toast is golden brown, remove cookie sheet very carefully from oven and put it down where it won't burn the surface.

Use a pancake turner to lift toast off cookie sheet onto a large plate. The cookie sheet will stay hot for a while so be sure to warn everyone not to touch it.

Serve Parmesan Toast with frittata. *Makes 4 servings.*

Weekend Breakfast on the Porch

When I have house guests, I find it best to be very laid-back about breakfast time. A selection of smoked fish is not only one of my favorite breakfasts, it adapts perfectly to early risers, late sleepers, and neighbors who drop by. Think of it as a very elegant and luxurious picnic. Put out the food and let your friends eat at their own pace, coming back to try a different smoked fish, or another spoonful of Crunchy Cucumber Salad. The Farmer Cheese with Blueberries is soothing and mildly sweet; it is delicious eaten with a cinnamon-raisin bagel to finish the meal.

You'll find a great deal of information about smoked fish because, even though it is costly, it makes a delightful breakfast for many occasions and it is incredibly easy to serve. It's worth knowing some of the many types of smoked fish available so you can try several and discover which ones you enjoy most.

MENU

FOR 8

*MELON, CHERRY, AND GRAPE PLATTER

*SMOKED FISH PLATTER

DARK BREADS BAGELS

*SUPERB HORSERADISH SAUCE

*CRUNCHY CUCUMBER SALAD

*FARMER CHEESE WITH BLUEBERRIES

*RECIPE FOLLOWS

GAME PLAN

The day before you may:

- Make Farmer Cheese with Blueberries.
- Slice and salt cucumbers for Crunchy Cucumber Salad; drain; refrigerate.
- Make Superb Horseradish Sauce.

About 1 hour before serving:

- Wash fruit; arrange on platter.
- Finish cucumber salad.
- Chop onion; cut lemon wedges; pick dill sprigs.
- Arrange fish on platter(s); let come to room temperature. (Remove fishy smell from fingers by rubbing with a cut lemon half.)
- Slice bagels in half; arrange breads and bagels in baskets.

SHOPPING GUIDE

½ cup confectioners' sugar
1 teaspoon vanilla extract
¼ teaspoon nutmeg, freshly-grated or from a jar
3 tablespoons light olive or vegetable oil
2 tablespoons red wine vinegar or rice vinegar
⅛ teaspoon Worcestershire sauce
¾ teaspoon Dijon mustard

continued

Melon, Cherry, and Grape Platter

Buy plenty of cherries because they always disappear fast—sometimes even from the refrigerator before the guests arrive. If you have a grapevine in the garden, clip a few leaves to lay under the melon or grapes.

1 or 2 melons, depending on size and whatever is best in the market
2 to 3 pounds fresh sweet cherries
2 pounds red or green seedless grapes

Edible flowers, if available (see page 189)

Cut the melon into wedges and cut the rind off each wedge.

Shortly before serving, rinse cherries and grapes. Snip grapes into small bunches. Arrange fruits in groups on a platter. Decorate with edible flowers. *Makes 8 generous servings.*

Smoked Fish Platter

2 to 3 ounces sliced boneless smoked fish per person (1 to 1½ pounds for 8)

Lemon wedges
Finely chopped sweet onion
Fresh dill sprigs

Arrange fish slices, slightly overlapping, on a large platter, keeping the types of fish separate. Put lemon wedges and onion in mounds on the platter and garnish fish with dill sprigs.

Superb Horseradish Sauce

Consider doubling this recipe, since the sauce keeps for at least a week and also tastes wonderful with baked potatoes, grilled fish, and raw vegetables.

1 8-ounce container sour cream
1 tablespoon snipped fresh chives or 2 tablespoons thinly-sliced scallion greens

4 teaspoons prepared white horseradish
⅛ teaspoon Worcestershire sauce
½ teaspoon salt
Few grinds of pepper

Put all ingredients in a small bowl and stir gently to mix. *Makes 1 cup.*

Crunchy Cucumber Salad

When they're in season, Kirby cucumbers make a particularly satisfying salad. Scrub, then slice them; there is no need to remove the seeds.

3½ to 4 pounds Kirby or 6 medium-
 sized regular cucumbers
2 teaspoons salt
3 tablespoons light olive or
 vegetable oil
3 tablespoons snipped fresh dill

2 tablespoons red wine vinegar
 or rice vinegar
¾ teaspoon Dijon mustard
¼ teaspoon freshly-ground
 pepper

Peel cucumbers and halve lengthwise. If using regular cucumbers, scoop out the seeds with a teaspoon and discard.

Thinly slice cucumbers with a knife or food processor. Put slices into a bowl. Add salt and toss to mix. Cover and refrigerate overnight (or at least 3 hours).

Tip contents of bowl into a colander. Rinse with cold water and drain well. Put cucumber slices into a serving bowl. Add remaining ingredients and mix well. Taste; add more salt or vinegar if you wish. *Makes 8 servings.*

Farmer Cheese with Blueberries

This mixture is soothing and mildly sweet. Enjoy as a spread or as breakfast "dessert." Farmer cheese is similar to pot cheese or a dry-curd cottage cheese, but creamier.

3 7½-ounce packages farmer cheese,
 at room temperature
1 3-ounce package cream cheese, at
 room temperature
½ cup confectioners' sugar

1 teaspoon vanilla extract
¼ teaspoon nutmeg, freshly-grated or
 from a jar
1 pint small fresh blueberries

Put farmer cheese, cream cheese, sugar, vanilla, and nutmeg into a medium-sized bowl. Beat well with a wooden spoon (farmer cheese will remain in curds). Stir in blueberries.

Scrape mixture into a serving bowl. Cover and chill. *Makes 8 servings.*

SHOPPING GUIDE *cont'd*

1 pint small fresh blueberries
2 to 3 pounds fresh sweet cherries
2 pounds red or green seedless grapes
1 or 2 melons, depending on size and whatever is best in the market
Edible flowers for decoration, if available (see page 189)
3½ to 4 pounds Kirby or 6 medium-sized regular cucumbers
1 sweet yellow or red onion
2 or 3 lemons
Fresh chives (enough for 1 tablespoon snipped) or scallion greens (2 tablespoons sliced)
1 bunch dill (enough for 3 tablespoons snipped)

2 to 3 ounces sliced boneless smoked fish per person (1 to 1½ pounds for 8)
1 8-ounce container sour cream
3 7½-ounce packages farmer cheese
1 3-ounce package cream cheese
4 teaspoons prepared white horseradish

Dark breads; bagels (plain, salt, poppy seed, or onion to eat with the fish; cinnamon-raisin to enjoy with the Farmer Cheese with Blueberries; other flavors as you wish).

(Coffee? Tea? Add what you need; also, butter for the table.)

SMOKED FISH

The selection of smoked fish available will vary according to where you live. Smoked fish can be so delicious and so easy to serve that it is worth seeking dependable local sources. The store with the greatest variety of fish is not necessarily the best. Better a smaller selection with a fast turnover.

Once you've found a good source, look for someone there who knows how to slice smoked fish properly. Salmon, for example, should be sliced very thin, with the blade of the knife almost parallel to the cutting board, so that each slice is as large as possible.

There are two distinctly different smoking techniques: *cold* and *hot*. *Cold-smoking* produces the lox or smoked salmon most of us are familiar with; it is deep orange red and translucent. Depending on the species, *hot-smoked* fish is much whiter or browner, and, in fact, looks something like normal cooked salmon or tuna—which is to be expected, since it is fully cooked before or during the smoking.

Smoked fish is available whole, by the piece, or sliced. *Whole* fish should have smooth skin and good color. Tacky skin or salt crystals are signs of aging, but if the fish smells good, you can remove the skin and still eat the fish. *Sliced* cold-smoked fish should have a moist, slightly iridescent appearance. If it feels tacky or smells bad, don't eat it.

Smoked fish has become so popular that virtually anything that swims is being smoked, not always with delectable results. Ask to taste a small amount of an unfamiliar smoked fish before buying in quantity; the salesperson should always be willing to give you a tiny sample.

Here are buying tips for the smoked fish that taste good for breakfast:

TUNA. *Cold-smoked tuna* is a deep reddish-mauve color. Buy it sliced about ¼-inch thick. *Hot-smoked tuna* is very mild (less smokey and salty than most cold-smoked) with firm, compact white flesh. It is usually sold by the piece (it can't be sliced thin). Put it on the serving platter and let guests cut off a chunk.

WHITEFISH. This fish is wonderfully rich, with mild flavor and moist texture. Large fish are sold by the pound, including bones and skin. Young whitefish, called chubs, are sold whole. You can fillet whitefish in the kitchen (instructions follow), or put the small whole fish on the serving platter and let everyone take a piece. *To fillet a chub:* Pull off the golden skin and put the fish flat on one side on a board. Insert a blunt knife along the natural separation that runs from head to tail; slowly push the meat off one side of the backbone and then the other. Turn fish over and repeat.

Before you put the chunks of fish on the serving platter, feel them with your fingers and carefully remove any bones. Chubs and larger whitefish have lots of very fine bones.

MARLIN. There *is* something better to do with marlin than stuff them and hang them on walls as trophies: smoke and eat them! Marlin is usually hot-smoked. It has a drier texture and deeper flavor than tuna, and it is usually sold sliced ½-inch thick. When eating marlin, cut away any very dark streaks, which have a very fishy flavor.

SABLEFISH. Sablefish is Pacific (not Atlantic) black cod that's been smoked. A coarse-grained fish, it is usually sold sliced slightly thicker than smoked salmon. Sablefish is extremely delicious to eat. You may also find whole sides of fish, called sable plates.

STURGEON. A firmer fish that is almost always hot-smoked, sturgeon is mild and very delicious. It is sold thinly sliced, vertically, rather than diagonally. Take money!

SALMON. If you go to a store that carries an extensive selection of smoked fish, you will probably find smoked salmon from several countries. You may also see lox and gravlax. You may wonder at the wide range of prices, and debate which is best, which to choose.

Salmon from cold Atlantic water are richer in oil than salmon from the warm Pacific. This gives the smoked fish more flavor and a more melt-in-the-mouth texture. So let your first choice be smoked salmon from Norway, Scotland, Ireland, the Faroe Islands, or Nova Scotia; which is made from cold-water (Atlantic) fish.

Lox and gravlax are salt-cured salmon, although sometimes lox is lightly smoked too. Gravlax (a Scandinavian favorite) is delicious as a summer lunch or as an appetizer. Lox, the favorite in New York delis, is delicious with bagels and cream cheese for breakfast, lunch, a snack, or any time.

For a party, consider buying a whole side of sliced smoked salmon, sealed in heavy plastic. It can weigh from 1 to 5 pounds and is generally an excellent and reliable buy. At the other end of the scale, small sealed packages (about 3 ounces) are available in the refrigerator section of most supermarkets.

Kippered salmon, sometimes called baked salmon, is hot-smoked. Unlike smoked salmon, which should be sliced very thin, kippered salmon is sold by the chunk. It is mild, juicy, and flavorful.

TROUT. Trout is widely available and has a delicious, mild flavor. Allow a small whole fish per person. Put on salad or dinner plates and garnish with greens. Or fillet the fish in the kitchen (follow directions for chub, above) and arrange the fillets as neatly as possible on individual plates.

WHITING. Smoked whiting, mild and delicious, is sold as small whole fish. Serve whole or remove the bones as described for chub.

Not all the smoked fish you see are meant to be eaten as is. Kippers and bloaters (two kinds of cured herring) should be grilled with a little butter. Smoked haddock, sometimes sold as "finnan haddie" (originally from Findon, in Scotland), should be lightly poached. When in doubt, try to find a knowledgeable salesperson.

Breakfast with a Southwestern Flavor

Chilies and cheese give scrambled eggs a warm, rich flavor that is good any time of the year. But I like to serve this breakfast in the summer when casual entertaining is very much in order. If you wish you can omit the avocado and even the salsa; the eggs and tortillas are delicious just by themselves.

Here's how the main course goes together: each person spreads a tortilla with some of the avocado, spoons on scrambled eggs, and tops with salsa. The filled tortilla can then be eaten with a knife and fork or rolled up and eaten with fingers, making this breakfast suitable for enjoying while leaning against a porch railing. (But be sure to have a plate in one hand!)

Most of this breakfast can be prepared a day ahead: the salsa made, the coffee cake baked, the pineapple cut up and mixed with the sugar and cinnamon. You may be surprised to find canned peaches recommended for the Bellinis. The reason is that fresh peaches are rarely ripe or flavorful; if you use canned peaches you don't have to worry.

M E N U

FOR 6

*BELLINIS OR NEW BELLINIS

*CINNAMON PINEAPPLE

*SCRAMBLED EGGS WITH
CHILIES AND CHEESE

*SALSA CILANTRO

*MASHED AVOCADO

*WARM TORTILLAS

*APRICOT STREUSEL
COFFEE CAKE

*RECIPE FOLLOWS

GAME PLAN

The day before:

◆ Bake Apricot Streusel Coffee Cake. Or measure and organize all the ingredients; grease pan; make topping.
◆ Chill wine and purée canned peaches for Bellinis; pour into a pitcher.
◆ Make Salsa Cilantro.
◆ Grate cheese.
◆ Chop green pepper.
◆ Prepare Cinnamon Pineapple.

About 1½ hours before serving:

◆ Pack glasses with crushed ice and put in freezer.
◆ Heat oven to 375°F. Make coffee cake batter; put cake in to bake.
◆ Wrap tortillas in foil.
◆ Cook green pepper and onion in skillet for eggs.
◆ Beat eggs.
◆ Mash avocado.
◆ Make and serve Bellinis.
◆ Heat tortillas.
◆ Reheat coffee cake if made ahead (15 minutes, covered, at 350°F.).
◆ Scramble eggs.

Bellinis

Canned peaches have a more intense and reliable flavor than fresh peaches. If you can get really ripe peaches, peel and pit them (see page 187) and purée them with ⅓ cup peach or pear nectar.

1 16-ounce can juice-packed sliced peaches, chilled
1 750-ml. bottle dry Champagne or sparkling wine, chilled

2 tablespoons Drambuie liqueur
About 5 cups crushed ice

Purée peaches with their liquid in a blender or food processor. Pour into a large pitcher.

Up to 2 hours ahead, pack up to ten 6-ounce Champagne or wine glasses with ½ cup crushed ice each and put in freezer.

Just before serving, pour Champagne and liqueur over peach purée. Stir very gently, just until mixed. Pour ½ cup over crushed ice in each glass. *Makes 10 4-ounce drinks.*

New Bellinis: Follow above recipe but use sparkling white grape juice instead of wine, and 2 tablespoons frozen apple juice concentrate instead of Drambuie.

Cinnamon Pineapple

Many supermarkets now have a machine that will peel, core, and slice a pineapple for you, neatly eliminating that prickly chore.

1 ripe medium-sized pineapple (3½ to 4 pounds)

2 teaspoons granulated sugar
¼ teaspoon ground cinnamon

Peel pineapple (see page 187), quarter lengthwise, and cut out core. Cut each quarter in half lengthwise and slice crosswise into ¼-inch-thick chunks.

Put pineapple into a mixing or serving bowl (or even a heavy plastic bag for overnight refrigeration). Sprinkle with sugar and cinnamon and toss to mix. Cover and refrigerate at least 1 hour before serving. *Makes 8 servings.*

Scrambled Eggs with Chilies and Cheese

You can use 1 to 3 tablespoons minced seeded fresh green chilies instead of the canned. Add them with the onion and bell pepper.

3 tablespoons butter	¼ teaspoon freshly-ground pepper
½ cup finely-chopped green bell pepper	2 or 3 drops hot-pepper sauce
	3 tablespoons drained canned chopped green chilies
¼ cup thinly-sliced scallions	
10 large eggs	2 ounces sharp cheddar cheese, shredded (½ cup)
¼ teaspoon salt	

In a skillet 9 to 10 inches across the bottom (nonstick works best), melt butter over moderate heat. Add green pepper and scallions. Cook 4 to 6 minutes, stirring often, until pepper is crisp-tender and onions are soft, but not brown.

Meanwhile, break eggs into a large bowl. Add salt, pepper, and hot-pepper sauce. Beat with fork or wire whisk until eggs are well broken up.

Shortly before serving, pour egg mixture into skillet over moderately-low heat and start to scramble (see page 193). When creamy, add green chilies and cheese and continue to scramble until eggs are almost as firm as you like them.

Remove from heat. Serve from skillet or spoon onto a warm dish. *Makes 6 servings.*

Salsa Cilantro

2 tablespoons pure olive oil	¼ cup chopped fresh cilantro or flat-leaf parsley
1 tablespoon cider vinegar	
1 pound ripe tomatoes, cored and diced (about 2 cups)	¼ teaspoon salt
¾ cup chopped sweet onion or ½ cup thinly-sliced scallions	

Whisk oil and vinegar in a medium-sized bowl. Add remaining ingredients and toss to mix. This recipe makes more than you'll need, but the salsa keeps well and is delicious with many foods. *Makes about 3 cups.*

SHOPPING GUIDE

2 cups plus 2 tablespoons all-purpose flour

⅔ cup plus 2 teaspoons granulated sugar

¼ cup brown sugar

2 teaspoons baking powder

½ teaspoon ground coriander seed

¼ teaspoon ground cardamom seed

¼ teaspoon ground cinnamon

¼ cup (1 ounce) pecans, chopped

1 cup (4½ ounces) dried apricots

1 4-ounce can chopped green chilies

1 16-ounce can juice-packed sliced peaches

2 or 3 drops hot-pepper sauce

2 tablespoons pure olive oil

1 tablespoon cider vinegar

1 ripe medium-sized pineapple (3½ to 4 pounds)

1 green bell pepper (½ cup finely chopped)

2 or 3 scallions (¼ cup thinly sliced)

1 pound ripe tomatoes (about 2 cups diced)

1 medium-sized sweet red or yellow onion (¾ cup chopped) or 1 bunch scallions (½ cup thinly sliced)

1 or 2 large ripe avocados (about 1¼ pounds)

Small bunch fresh cilantro (also known as coriander or Chinese parsley) or flat-leaf parsley (enough for ¼ cup chopped)

continued

SHOPPING GUIDE *cont'd*

6 or more corn tortillas

¾ cup milk

11 tablespoons (about 1½ sticks) unsalted butter

12 large eggs

2 ounces sharp cheddar cheese (½ cup shredded)

1 bottle (750 ml.) dry Champagne, sparkling wine, or sparkling white grape juice

2 tablespoons Drambuie liqueur or 2 tablespoons frozen apple juice concentrate

5 cups crushed ice

(Coffee? Tea? Add what you need; also, butter for the table.)

Mashed Avocado

Buy 1 or 2 avocados, depending on how much you think guests will eat. A ½-pound avocado yields about ½ cup mashed; a 1-pound avocado about 1½ cups. Buy a ripe avocado or allow time for it to ripen at home, at room temperature. An avocado is ripe when it yields to gentle pressure. California avocados have more oil and a richer flavor than Florida ones, but calorie watchers may appreciate the lower oil content of the Florida variety.

TO PREPARE: Cut avocados in half and discard pits. Using a small spoon, scoop avocado flesh onto a plate; mash smooth with a fork. Put into a serving bowl. Cover with plastic wrap, placing wrap right on the surface. Serve chilled or at room temperature.

Warm Tortillas

If you want to heat additional tortillas, make a separate package. Tortillas heat better stacked no more than six high.

6 corn tortillas

Stack tortillas and wrap in aluminum foil. *Either:* Heat 10 to 15 minutes in 250°F oven or toaster-oven. *Or:* Put foil-wrapped tortillas on wire rack over a skillet or saucepan of simmering water. Turn package every 2 or 3 minutes so tortillas heat through evenly. Six tortillas heat in about 8 minutes.

Microwave: Wrap stack of tortillas in a cloth napkin. Place on a microwave-safe rack or inverted plate. Heat in (650- to 700-watt) microwave oven 4 minutes on 100% power. Let stand 5 minutes.

Apricot Streusel Coffee Cake

1 cup (4½ ounces) dried apricots, diced

¾ cup milk

8 tablespoons (1 stick) unsalted butter

TOPPING:

¼ cup pecans, chopped

¼ cup packed brown sugar

2 tablespoons all-purpose flour

½ teaspoon ground coriander seed

BATTER:

2 cups all-purpose flour

⅔ cup granulated sugar

2 teaspoons baking powder

¼ teaspoon ground cardamom seed

¼ teaspoon salt

2 large eggs, at room temperature

Heat apricots and milk in a small saucepan for 2 to 3 minutes over low heat. (Milk may curdle; don't worry.) Remove from heat and add 5 tablespoons of butter (keep remaining butter cold; it goes into the Topping). Let stand 10 minutes while apricots soften and butter melts.

Meanwhile, heat oven to 375°F. Butter a 9-inch round baking pan. Mix all Topping ingredients in a small bowl. Cut remaining butter in small pieces; add to nut mixture and mash with a fork until crumbly.

Mix flour, sugar, baking powder, cardamom, and salt in a large bowl. Pour in apricot mixture. Add eggs. Stir and beat with a wooden spoon just until batter is smooth. Scrape batter into prepared pan. Sprinkle Topping over surface.

Place cake pan on a cookie sheet and bake 40 to 45 minutes, until light golden brown and a wooden toothpick inserted in center comes out clean.

Cool cake in pan. Serve warm or cold. *Makes 12 servings.*

Fourth of July Steak Breakfast

M E N U

FOR 8

*FRESH BLUEBERRIES AND STRAWBERRIES IN ORANGE JUICE

*NORTH DAKOTA BREAKFAST STEAKS

*IRVING RUBIN'S PILLOW POTATOES

*BASIL TOMATOES

*HONEY-GLAZED RAISIN AND SUNFLOWER-SEED TWIST

OR
*DETROIT FRIED CHEESE DANISH

*RECIPE FOLLOWS

One of my fondest breakfast memories is of grilled steak on a North Dakota sunflower ranch after a magnificent hot-air balloon ride over acres of deep-gold sunflowers. Wherever you live, a hearty steak breakfast is perfect before joining the town parade to celebrate America's birthday. So fire up the grill; cooking the main course outside will help keep the house cool.

The potatoes that accompany the breakfast steaks are also cooked on the grill. They are first sliced and wrapped in foil packets for even cooking and easy handling. As the potatoes cook they create steam, causing the little foil packets to puff up and look like little silver pillows. As you will find out when you open one, the foil wrapping also holds in all the flavor and aroma of the potatoes and seasonings.

When my friend Miriam Rubin (daughter of Irving) first described Detroit Fried Cheese Danish to me, I'll admit I was incredulous. *Fried* danish? It turns out that when Miriam was at Wayne State University, these were a specialty of Cappy's near the Art Institute. One taste convinced me my misgivings were unfounded. Be sure to start with top-quality danish. And wait half an hour or so after everyone has finished the main course before frying and serving them, otherwise it's just too much food at once.

Fresh Blueberries and Strawberries in Orange Juice

This is for people who can't decide whether they prefer drinking juice or eating fresh fruit, because it combines the two pleasures. Make each serving in an 8- to 10-ounce glass (stemmed or not), and place each glass, with a teaspoon alongside, on a small plate lined with a small napkin to prevent skidding. Sip the juice; eat the fruit with the teaspoon. In high summer, when fresh fruit is abundant, I sometimes double the amount of berries.

8 teaspoons granulated sugar
1½ quarts orange juice, preferably
        freshly-squeezed

1 pint fresh blueberries
2 pints fresh strawberries, sliced
        (leave whole if very small)

Put 1 teaspoon sugar and ¾ cup orange juice in each glass; stir to dissolve sugar. Add fruit shortly before serving. *Makes 8 servings.*

North Dakota Breakfast Steaks

2 tablespoons pure olive or vegetable oil
1 tablespoon freshly-ground pepper
2 teaspoons salt

8 boneless beef sirloin steaks, about 6
        ounces each

TO GRILL: Mix oil, pepper, and salt in a cup; brush steaks on both sides with oil mixture. Grill over moderately-hot coals about 2 minutes per side for rare, 2½ to 3 minutes per side for medium.

TO PAN-FRY: Sprinkle both sides of steaks with salt and pepper. In a heavy skillet 10 to 12 inches across the bottom, heat 1 tablespoon of oil over high heat. When oil starts to smoke, add four steaks and cook about 2 minutes on each side, turning once. Remove to plates. Cook remaining meat the same way.

Makes 8 servings.

GAME PLAN

UP TO 1 WEEK AHEAD YOU MAY:
◆ Bake and freeze Honey-Glazed Raisin and Sunflower-Seed Twist.

THE DAY BEFORE:
◆ Transfer the sunflower-seed twist from freezer to refrigerator.
◆ Scrub potatoes.

ABOUT 1 TO 1½ HOURS BEFORE SERVING (WORK OUT TIMING ACCORDING TO METHOD YOU USE TO COOK POTATOES AND MEAT):
◆ Slice potatoes and onion. Wrap in foil packages as directed and start cooking them.
◆ Slice tomatoes; arrange on platter; sprinkle with dressing.
◆ Mix oil, pepper, and salt for steaks.

LAST MINUTE:
◆ Grill or pan-fry steaks.
◆ When, or after, steaks are served, put foil-wrapped honey bread in oven to heat (10 minutes at 250°F.) or on side of grill.

SHOPPING GUIDE

3½ cups all-purpose flour

1 envelope active dry yeast

½ cup honey

½ cup plus 2 teaspoons granulated sugar

3 tablespoons instant nonfat dry milk (optional)

4 tablespoons pure olive oil

¼ cup (1½ ounces) hulled but not toasted sunflower seeds

¼ cup (1½ ounces) golden raisins

Ground nutmeg (optional)

2 pounds red or white thin-skinned potatoes ("new" potatoes)

1 medium-sized onion

3 pounds (about 6 medium-sized) ripe tomatoes

1 pint fresh blueberries

2 pints fresh strawberries

1 bunch fresh basil (enough for ¼ cup chopped)

8 boneless beef sirloin steaks, about 6 ounces each

2 large eggs

16 tablespoons (2 sticks) unsalted butter

1½ quarts freshly-squeezed or refrigerated orange juice

(Coffee? Tea? Add what you need. If you opt for the Detroit Fried Cheese Danish, add eight small (4 to 5 ounce) cheese danish— cheese with raisins is even better.)

Irving Rubin's Pillow Potatoes

Mr. Rubin makes these individual foil-wrapped packets of steaming-hot potatoes, winter or summer, city or country. He says this recipe evolved from the high-fat cottage fries he used to make.

2 pounds red or white thin-skinned potatoes

1 medium-sized onion, sliced

4 tablespoons (½ stick) unsalted butter, cut in small pieces

½ teaspoon salt

¼ teaspoon freshly-ground pepper

Heat grill; or heat oven to 425°F. Tear off eight 12-inch lengths of foil. Spread out on countertop and spray with nonstick cooking spray.

Scrub, but don't peel potatoes; slice them thin. Divide into eight portions. Arrange each portion, slices overlapping, in two rows side by side in center of a sheet of foil. Arrange some onion slices on top and sprinkle with butter, salt, and pepper. Fold up each piece of foil to form a packet and tightly crimp edges together.

To GRILL: Put foil packets over direct heat, at least 4 inches from coals; cover grill. Turn packets after 15 minutes. Cook 5 to 10 minutes longer; packets will puff up like pillows when potatoes are done. If breakfast isn't quite ready, potatoes can be kept warm for about 30 minutes at edge of grill. Or reheat briefly on grill just before serving.

In OVEN: Place packets directly on oven rack. Cook 35 to 40 minutes, until packets are slightly puffed and potatoes are tender (pierce one packet with a knife to test).

Makes 8 servings.

Basil Tomatoes

If you prefer, you can grill tomato halves, but in the summertime I prefer this light, juicy almost-salad.

6 medium-sized ripe tomatoes (about 3 pounds)

¼ cup coarsely-chopped fresh basil

2 tablespoons pure olive oil

½ teaspoon salt

¼ teaspoon freshly-ground pepper

Core tomatoes and cut into thick slices. Arrange slices on a platter. Mix remaining ingredients in a small cup.

Shortly before serving, spoon dressing over tomatoes. Serve right away, or cover and refrigerate up to 30 minutes. *Makes 8 servings.*

Honey-Glazed Raisin and Sunflower-Seed Twist

This is easiest to make in an electric mixer with paddle and dough hook attachments. Otherwise, see hand method at end.

DOUGH:

½ cup very warm water (105° to 115°F.)

¼ cup honey

1 envelope active dry yeast

3 to 3¼ cups all-purpose flour

6 tablespoons (¾ stick) unsalted butter, at room temperature

2 large eggs, at room temperature

3 tablespoons instant nonfat dry milk (optional)

½ teaspoon salt

¼ cup (1½ ounces) hulled but not toasted sunflower seeds

¼ cup (1½ ounces) golden raisins

GLAZE:

6 tablespoons (¾ stick) unsalted butter

6 tablespoons granulated sugar

¼ cup all-purpose flour

¼ cup honey

Dough: Put water, honey, and yeast in large bowl of electric mixer fitted with paddle. Mix at low speed until well blended. Turn off machine and let mixture stand 2 or more minutes; yeast will swell and dissolve.

Add to bowl 1 cup of the flour, the butter, eggs, dry milk, and salt. Mix, then beat 2 minutes on medium speed. With mixer on low speed, gradually add enough of remaining flour until a soft dough forms and leaves sides of bowl. Mix in seeds and raisins.

Change paddle to dough hook and knead on medium speed 4 to 5 minutes, until dough is smooth and elastic.

Grease a medium-sized bowl. Put dough in bowl and turn dough once to bring greased side up. Cover bowl with plastic wrap and wrap bowl in a towel. Let rise in a warm place 1½ to 2 hours, until doubled in volume.

Grease two 8-inch round cake pans (or two 8- or 9-inch pie plates, or one 10-inch round cake pan). Clench one fist and punch down the risen dough. Turn out onto surface and cut in half. With palms of hands roll each piece of dough into a 1-inch-thick rope. Starting at the outside, coil a roll of dough into each prepared pan, leaving a space between each coil. Loosely cover and let dough rise again, about 35 minutes, until almost doubled in volume.

Heat oven to 350°F. (Time heating so oven is hot when dough is ready.) Meanwhile, make glaze.

Glaze. Melt butter in a small saucepan. Remove from heat and stir in remaining ingredients until smooth.

Spoon glaze over risen dough. Bake 25 to 35 minutes, until golden

continued

brown and a wooden toothpick inserted in center comes out clean. Let cool in pans at least 30 minutes before serving. Cut in wedges and serve from pans. *Makes 2 twists, 6 servings each.*

To serve later, let twists cool completely, then wrap in foil (in pans). Leave at room temperature if serving next day. Freeze for longer storage.

HAND METHOD: Mix water, yeast, and sugar in a large mixing bowl; let stand 2 minutes. Add dry milk, eggs, butter, salt, and 1 cup of flour; mix smooth, then beat for 2 minutes with a wooden spoon. Stir in enough of remaining flour to make a soft dough. Turn out onto a well-floured surface (use some of the measured flour); sprinkle with raisins and seeds and knead 6 to 8 minutes, until dough is smooth and elastic, adding only as much flour as needed to prevent dough from sticking. Put dough to rise in a clean bowl and continue as directed above.

Detroit Fried Cheese Danish

6 tablespoons (¾ stick) unsalted butter   Ground nutmeg (optional)
8 small (4- to 5-ounce) cheese danish,
    preferably with raisins

Heat 2 tablespoons of butter in a large heavy nonstick skillet over moderate heat. When bubbling, add three of the danish, top sides down, and fry 2 to 3 minutes, just until they begin to brown. Turn danish over carefully and cook 2 to 3 minutes longer, until undersides are lightly browned. Remove from skillet and keep warm.

Wipe out skillet with a piece of paper towel and fry remaining danish in same way. Sprinkle with a little nutmeg before serving. Serve with a knife and fork. *Makes 8 servings.*

Light Breakfast for a Hot Day

Enjoy this easy-to-prepare menu after an early-morning tennis match or before heading for the beach.

The Swiss Almond Muesli is based on Bircher-Muesli, the precursor of all contemporary granolas. A breakfast of fruit, milk, honey, and soaked but not cooked oats, it was first devised by a Swiss diet expert, Dr. Bircher-Benner. (For a crunchy, toasted, more *au courant* granola, see page 168.) With the muesli serve fresh peaches and a selection of berries. Depending on which part of the country you live in, you may be able to get blackberries, blueberries, tay berries, or olallie-berries instead of raspberries. If you have a garden and the right climate, you already know that the best berries are those that are fresh-picked.

M E N U

FOR 4 TO 6

*SWISS ALMOND MUESLI

*FRESH PEACHES AND
RASPBERRIES

YOGURT   FRESH CREAM

*PLUM UPSIDE-DOWN
COFFEE CAKE

*RECIPE FOLLOWS

GAME PLAN

THE DAY BEFORE:
◆ Make muesli.

THE DAY BEFORE YOU MAY
ALSO:
◆ Mix dry ingredients for coffee cake (leave at room temperature). Wrap bottom of 9-inch springform pan in foil; grease pan with butter; refrigerate.

ABOUT 1½ HOURS BEFORE
SERVING:
◆ Remove cake pan from refrigerator. Heat oven to 350°F
◆ Add sugar and plums to buttered springform pan.
◆ Prepare coffee cake batter; bake.
◆ Prepare berries.

NOT MORE THAN 30 MINUTES
BEFORE SERVING:
◆ Peel and slice peaches.

Swiss Almond Muesli

The oats in this muesli are not toasted, and the mixture is only slightly sweet. In case you are wondering about eating "raw" oats, know that before oats are rolled, they are steamed, which in effect cooks them.

2 cups old-fashioned oats
¾ cup (3 ounces) diced dried apples
½ cup toasted wheat germ
½ cup (3 ounces) raisins
½ cup (2 ounces) slivered blanched
   almonds

¼ cup (1½ ounces) hulled but not
   toasted sunflower seeds
2 tablespoons packed light brown
   sugar

Mix all ingredients in a large bowl or airtight container. Store in cool dry place or in refrigerator. Best eaten within a couple of weeks. *Makes 4 cups.*

Fresh Peaches and Raspberries

Guests may like to spoon the fruit over the muesli, but don't do it ahead of time. Serve with sugar.

4 to 6 ripe peaches   1 pint fresh raspberries or other berries

Peel peaches (see page 187) and slice into shallow serving bowl or bowls. Rinse berries; sprinkle them over the peaches. *Makes 4 to 6 servings.*

Plum Upside-Down Coffee Cake

TOPPING:

2 tablespoons unsalted butter, at room temperature

2 or 3 tablespoons packed light brown sugar

1 pound round black plums, pitted and sliced (3 cups)

BATTER:

1½ cups all-purpose flour

2 teaspoons baking powder

1½ teaspoons ground cinnamon

½ teaspoon nutmeg, freshly-grated or from a jar

¼ teaspoon baking soda

¼ teaspoon salt

½ cup packed light brown sugar

6 tablespoons (¾ stick) unsalted butter, melted and cooled

2 large eggs

½ cup sour cream

Heat oven to 350°F.

Topping. Place a 9-inch springform pan on a sheet of aluminum foil and wrap foil about halfway up sides (foil will catch drips from fruit), place pan on a cookie sheet. Heavily butter pan bottom and lightly grease sides with 2 tablespoons of butter. Sprinkle with sugar (use 3 tablespoons if plums are tart). Spread out plums on top of sugar.

Batter. Mix flour, baking powder, spices, baking soda, and salt in a large bowl.

Put sugar, butter, and eggs in a medium-sized bowl; whisk until smooth. Whisk in sour cream. Scrape into flour mixture and stir with a wooden spoon just until well mixed.

Carefully pour batter over plums and spread gently. Bake 30 to 40 minutes, until cake is lightly browned and firm to the touch and a wooden toothpick inserted halfway between edge and center comes out clean.

Remove pan from oven. Let stand 10 minutes, then invert onto serving plate and loosen and remove pan sides. Serve warm. *Makes 10 servings.*

SHOPPING GUIDE

2 cups old-fashioned oats

1½ cups all-purpose flour

½ cup toasted wheat germ

About 1 cup light brown sugar

2 teaspoons baking powder

½ teaspoon baking soda

1½ teaspoons ground cinnamon

½ teaspoon nutmeg, freshly-grated or from a jar

½ cup (3 ounces) raisins

2 ounces dried apples (¾ cup diced)

½ cup (2 ounces) slivered blanched almonds

¼ cup (1½ ounces) hulled but not toasted sunflower seeds

4 to 6 ripe peaches (white peaches are most delicious)

1 pint fresh raspberries or other berries

1 pound round black plums (such as Black Beauty, Black Amber, or Friar)

Yogurt, cream, and milk to serve with fruit and Swiss Almond Muesli

½ cup sour cream

8 tablespoons (1 stick) unsalted butter

2 large eggs

(Coffee? Tea? Add what you need; also, sugar to serve with fruit and muesli.)

Happy Birthday!

M E N U

FOR 8 CHILDREN

*FROZEN RED AND GREEN
GRAPES

*DUTCH BABY

*STRAWBERRY SAUCE

*BREAKFAST BIRTHDAY
CAKE

*RECIPE FOLLOWS

B reakfast can be an ideal time to celebrate a child's birthday, particularly if it falls in the summer when school is out. Children are delighted by the unusual hour for a party and by having somewhere to go first thing in the morning.

The Dutch Baby is a close relative of popovers and Yorkshire pudding. Think of it as a giant pancake that puffs up magically when baked. Here I suggest a fruit sauce for the Dutch Baby, but salsa or chili sauce is good, too, depending on the tastes of your young guests.

No birthday party is complete without a birthday cake. The Breakfast Birthday Cake is the fastest ever to make and bound to be a hit. You simply pack the honoree's favorite flavor of frozen yogurt, ice milk, or ice cream into a cake pan and freeze it. After turning out the "cake" you can decorate it as elaborately as you wish. Birthday candles and a suitable inscription are a must, but you could also stand graham cracker teddy bears around the sides and decorate the top and sides with candies.

Frozen Red and Green Grapes

1½ pounds red seedless grapes   *1½ pounds green seedless grapes*

Wash grapes well under cool running water. Pull grapes off stems. Put grapes into individual ramekins or paper cups or into a baking pan. Freeze grapes several hours or overnight. Serve frozen. *Makes 8 servings.*

Dutch Baby

Before you begin, check that your oven is wide enough for two 9-inch metal pie pans to bake side by side or diagonally opposite each other, with space for hot air to circulate between the pie pans and oven walls. Use regular metal pie pans; disposable ones tend to bend dangerously. Adult supervision and participation are definitely in order here, but it's good to teach children respect for heat and cooking tools at an early age, while also introducing them to the pleasures of cooking

7 large eggs	*2 teaspoons vanilla extract*
1¼ cups all-purpose flour	*½ teaspoon salt*
1¼ cups milk	*2 tablespoons light olive or vegetable*
3 tablespoons (about ½ stick)	*oil (olive tastes better here)*
unsalted butter, cut in small	*2 tablespoons confectioners' sugar*
pieces	

Place one shelf in the middle of the oven and heat oven to 450°F.

Put all ingredients, except oil and confectioners' sugar, in an electric blender in order given. (Food processor method below.) Process until a smooth batter forms. Stop machine, scrape sides, and blend 30 seconds longer.

Pour 1 tablespoon oil into each pie pan. Heat in oven 5 minutes. Pour batter into pie pans. Bake 20 minutes; do not open oven door during that time. After 20 minutes it's okay to peek; pancakes should have puffed up beautifully around the edges. Turn oven down to 350°F. and bake 20 minutes longer, until sides are very crisp. (If you take pancakes out too soon, sides will collapse.)

Remove pans from oven. Sprinkle pancakes with confectioners' sugar. Cut each pancake into four wedges with a blunt knife and serve from pans. *Makes 8 servings.*

FOOD PROCESSOR METHOD. Put flour, salt, and butter into work bowl. Process about 30 seconds, until butter is in tiny pieces. Add remaining ingredients except oil and confectioners' sugar. Process to a smooth batter, stopping machine once to scrape sides. Continue as in blender method.

GAME PLAN

THE DAY BEFORE:
- Rinse grapes; pluck from stems; freeze.
- If using frozen strawberries for sauce, transfer them from freezer to refrigerator to thaw.
- Make Breakfast Birthday Cake.

ABOUT 1½ HOURS BEFORE SERVING:
- Heat oven to 450°F.
- Make Dutch Baby batter.
- Heat oil in pie pans; pour batter in pans; bake.
- Decorate birthday cake.
- Make Strawberry Sauce; put in serving bowl.
- When Dutch Baby is baked, sift confectioners' sugar over the top and serve.

SHOPPING GUIDE

1¼ cups all-purpose flour
2 tablespoons confectioners'
    sugar
2 teaspoons vanilla extract
2 tablespoons light olive or
    vegetable oil (olive oil tastes
    better here)
Sprinkles; tube of cake-writing
    gel; birthday candles and
    holders

1½ pounds red seedless grapes
1½ pounds green seedless
    grapes
2 pints fresh strawberries and 2
    tablespoons granulated sugar
            (or)
1 or 2 16-ounce containers fro-
    zen strawberries in light
    syrup

1¼ cups milk
3 tablespoons (about ½ stick)
    unsalted butter
7 large eggs
½ gallon frozen yogurt, ice
    milk, or ice cream

(Milk? Chocolate milk? Coffee
    and tea for adults? Add what
    you need.)

Strawberry Sauce

If good fresh berries are not available, just thaw one or two containers of frozen strawberries in light syrup. (Light here means with less sugar, not with artificial sweetener.)

2 pints fresh strawberries   *About 2 tablespoons granulated sugar*

Rinse berries; pull off green hulls. Put berries on a kitchen plate. Hold one berry at a time and mash to a pulp with a fork (wear an apron to catch any splashes). Alternatively, use a potato masher, but do not use a blender or food processor as you do not want strawberry purée.

Put mashed berries into a bowl; stir in sugar. Let stand about 10 minutes (but no longer than 30) while sugar dissolves. Taste for sweetness before serving. *Makes about 2½ cups.*

Breakfast Birthday Cake

½ gallon frozen yogurt, ice milk, or ice   Sprinkles; tube of cake-writing gel;
*   cream   birthday candles in holders*

Spray an 8- or 9-inch round layer cake pan with a little vegetable cooking spray, or grease lightly. Line pan with a long strip of plastic wrap, letting excess hang over edge.

If necessary, put frozen yogurt, ice milk, or ice cream in refrigerator or leave at room temperature a few minutes to soften slightly. Pack firmly into plastic-lined cake pan (greasing pan prevents plastic wrap from skidding). When pan is full, level the surface. Cover tightly with plastic wrap or foil; freeze until hard, several hours or overnight. Put a serving plate in the freezer near the "cake."

Turn out cake onto the very cold plate and peel off the plastic wrap. Decorate top with sprinkles. Write greetings on top of cake with the cake-writing gel.

Cover cake and freeze. Just before serving, unwrap cake and insert candles. Cut into wedges and serve with a metal spatula. *Makes 8 or more servings.*

A Breakfast Smorgasbord

In Scandinavia, and Israel, too, cheese is popular for breakfast. It is a little-work idea, and I enjoy serving it to friends. You may arrange all the food on a sideboard or kitchen counter (covered perhaps with a blue-and-white checkered cloth) and invite friends to help themselves before they sit down.

This is a breakfast to linger over as you sample the many possible combinations of cheeses, breads, and vegetables.

The Irish Oat Bread is delicious with cheese and marmalade or other preserves, and it is easy to make because it is leavened with baking soda, not yeast, and therefore requires no rising time. If you are not familiar with baking soda breads, you should know that when made entirely with white flour, or a mixture of white and whole-wheat flours, they generally rise high and have a crumblier texture and a softer crust than yeast bread. But because of the high proportion of oats, this particular bread has a dark crumb that is very moist and compact. The soft dough is simply spread on a cookie sheet and rises very little. The baked bread is about one and a half inches high and has a wonderful country look. Serve it on a round wooden breadboard. Slice the bread or break off chunks. Soda breads are the kind that used to be baked over peat fires long ago in Scottish and Irish cottages.

M E N U

FOR 8 TO 10

BERRIES
AND *THICK YOGURT

*PLATTER OF SLICED
CHEESES

*COTTAGE CHEESE WITH
CHOPPED FRESH
VEGETABLES

*IRISH OAT BREAD

CRISPBREADS

DARK BREADS

FRESH RADISHES

MARMALADE

BLACK CURRANT
PRESERVES

*RECIPE FOLLOWS

GAME PLAN

THE DAY BEFORE YOU MAY:

◆ Mix cottage cheese, sour cream, salt, and pepper for Cottage Cheese with Chopped Fresh Vegetables; refrigerate.

◆ Wash and trim radishes; slice 8 for cottage cheese; wrap tightly.

◆ Slice cucumber; wrap tightly.

◆ Drain yogurt.

◆ Bake Irish Oat Bread. Or grind oats in food processor; add other dry ingredients; leave at room temperature.

ABOUT 1 TO 1½ HOURS
BEFORE SERVING:

◆ Heat oven to 400°F. Complete bread dough; put in to bake.

◆ Complete Cottage Cheese with Chopped Fresh Vegetables.

◆ Arrange sliced cheeses in groups on platters. You might want to prepare at least two platters; cover and refrigerate one to bring out when first one begins to look ragged.

◆ Arrange breads and crispbreads in baskets.

◆ Rinse berries. Put berries and yogurt into separate serving bowls from which guests may help themselves.

LAST MINUTE:

◆ Arrange all food on table.

Thick Yogurt

1 to 1½ quarts plain yogurt

To make yogurt thicker you remove some of the water. Doing this is strictly optional; you can serve the yogurt as it comes from the carton.

There are several ways to thicken yogurt. One is to use a gadget for making yogurt cheese. I know of two such gadgets: one, a grommeted cheese bag that you fill with yogurt and hang up to drain; the other, a funnel of fine plastic mesh. If you don't have one of these, the next most efficient way is to pour the yogurt into a cone-shaped coffee filter, set it in its holder in the coffee pot (to catch drips), and let the yogurt drip for 20 to 30 minutes before scraping it into a serving dish.

Yogurt can also be drained in a strainer lined with a double thickness of white paper towels or two regular coffee filters and suspended over a bowl. Let yogurt drain for at least 30 to 40 minutes. Yogurt can be drained a day or two ahead.

Surprisingly little water will come out in the short draining time, but it is enough to make the yogurt seem richer. (Of course, if you let the yogurt drain for several hours you will end up with yogurt cheese; this is good for breakfast, too, as a spread, but not what you want to serve with the berries.)

Very thick yogurt that contains egg yolk (check ingredient list on container) or Greek or Mediterranean yogurt (available in some markets) is so thick it needs no draining.

Platter of Sliced Cheeses

The best breakfast cheeses are firm ones, free of distracting flavors such as herbs, spices, garlic, or mushrooms. Although I love them at any other time of day, I don't find blue cheeses or rich triple-crème cheeses appealing in the morning.

For your breakfast table, select three to five kinds of cheese. When possible, ask to have them sliced. If that can't be done, provide a cheese slicer (sometimes called a cheese plane) so guests can do the slicing. Most firm or semi-firm cheeses taste best sliced thin.

Here are some good cheeses to try: Jarlsberg, Gouda, Nokkelost Supreme, Havarti, Muenster, Mimolette, Cantal, Tilsit, Sainte Nectaire, Samsoe, and Beaufort.

Cheeses should be fresh and in good condition. Cheeses that smell moldy or of ammonia are past their prime.

You might also include Norwegian Gjetost. Many consider it to be an acquired taste; I love it. Usually sold tightly wrapped in foil and packed in a red box, Gjetost is brown and mild-tasting. It makes a great breakfast, lunch, or snack cheese. Gjetost is made from whey, rather than whole milk, and keeps for weeks. Be sure to slice it with a cheese plane.

Cottage Cheese with Chopped Fresh Vegetables

There are two ways to serve this refreshing dish. Mixed, as described, or spread cottage cheese in a shallow serving bowl, sprinkle with vegetables, and top with sour cream. Serve with a large spoon. I also enjoy this as a cooling evening meal on a sweltering summer night. Juicy tomatoes are a must for best results.

1 pound (2 medium-sized) ripe tomatoes, diced (2½ cups)

3 medium-sized Kirby cucumbers, halved and sliced thin; or 1 medium-sized regular cucumber, peeled, halved, seeded, and sliced (2 cups)

8 radishes, thinly sliced (about 1 cup)

½ cup thinly-sliced scallions

1 16-ounce container creamed small-curd cottage cheese

½ cup sour cream

¼ teaspoon salt

⅛ teaspoon freshly-ground pepper

Put vegetables into a large serving bowl and mix gently.

Add cottage cheese, sour cream, salt, and pepper and mix gently until blended. Serve at once or refrigerate up to 1 hour. *Makes 10 servings.*

SHOPPING GUIDE

2 cups all-purpose flour

2¾ cups quick oats

1 teaspoon baking soda

1½ teaspoons caraway seeds (optional)

One or two kinds of preserves such as a dark orange marmalade, and black currant or damson plum preserves

Dark breads, crispbreads (Many crispbreads are imported from Norway. Made with whole-grain rye or wheat flours, they are practically fat-free.)

1 or more kinds of berries such as raspberries, strawberries, blueberries, huckleberries, blackberries, olallieberries; allow ½ to 1 cup per person

3 large Kirby cucumbers or 1 medium-sized regular cucumber

2 or 3 bunches radishes

1 pound (2 medium-sized) ripe tomatoes (2½ cups diced)

1 bunch scallions (½ cup sliced)

2 cups (1 pint) buttermilk or 1½ cups plain yogurt

1 to 1½ quarts plain yogurt

½ cup sour cream

4 tablespoons (½ stick) unsalted butter

1 16-ounce container creamed small-curd cottage cheese

Sliced firm cheeses, 5 to 6 ounces per person (3 to 3¾ pounds total)

(Coffee? Tea? Add what you need; also, butter for the table.)

BUTTERMILK

Buttermilk adds flavor and richness to many pancakes, waffles, and coffee cakes. When mixed with baking powder or baking soda (and other ingredients, such as flour), it also acts as a leavening agent, creating bubbles that are trapped when the batter is heated. This makes pancakes or coffee cakes light.

If a recipe calls for buttermilk and you have none on hand, you can use plain yogurt instead. Or put 1 tablespoonful lemon juice or white vinegar into a glass cup measure and fill it to the 1-cup mark with fresh whole or skim milk. Let stand 5 minutes before using.

Keep a tin of dried buttermilk powder on hand to use in baked goods; look for it near canned and powdered milk in most supermarkets.

It is not a good idea to arbitrarily change milk to buttermilk in a recipe (or vice versa).

Irish Oat Bread

2½ cups quick oats
2 cups all-purpose flour
1 teaspoon salt
1 teaspoon baking soda
4 tablespoons (½ stick) unsalted
    butter, cut into small pieces

2 cups buttermilk; or 1½ cups plain
    yogurt mixed with ½ cup
    water
1½ teaspoons caraway seeds
    (optional)
3 tablespoons oats, for top

Check that one shelf is in middle of oven and heat oven to 400°F.

Put the 2½ cups oats, flour, salt, and baking soda into a food processor. (Hand method below.) Process 25 to 30 seconds to mix and to partially chop up oats.

Add butter; process 15 to 20 seconds, until mixture looks like fine crumbs. Pour buttermilk over top; sprinkle with caraway seeds. Process a few seconds, until a soft, sticky dough forms.

Scrape dough onto an ungreased cookie sheet and spread to a 9-inch circle. (Leave edges uneven.) Sprinkle with 3 tablespoons oats; press them down lightly with heel of hand.

Bake 25 to 30 minutes, until brown on the bottom and lightly browned on top. Bread will feel springy when touched in center and sound hollow when tapped.

Slide bread onto a wire rack and let cool at least 30 minutes before serving. Leave uncovered if it is to be served within 3 hours, so that crust stays chewy. Store in plastic bag, at room temperature (up to 2 days), or in freezer. *Makes 8 to 10 servings.*

HAND METHOD: Add ¼ cup water to buttermilk or to yogurt mixture. Coarsely grind oats, about half at a time, in an electric blender and put them into a large bowl. Add flour, salt, and baking powder; mix well. Add butter and cut in with a pastry blender or two knives or rub in with fingers, until mixture looks damp and crumbly. Add caraway seeds; toss to mix. Pour in buttermilk; stir well with a wooden spoon, until a soft dough forms. Proceed as directed above.

Lazy August Breakfast

When you feel like company on a summer Sunday morning—while it is still cool enough to enjoy eating—this breakfast is a luscious yet simple way to lure your friends. The French toast can be baked in the oven or cooked on the rangetop, and the combination of the rich toast with the tart-sweet plums is sheer heaven. The sausage is optional, as is the cream, but a small amount of cream poured over the plums is a special treat. Round black plums, with their deep, rich flavor, are the best choice here. (Black plums also seem less tart than red plums.) If you can't get challah (egg bread) for the French toast, try for a brioche loaf, or a firm-textured, homemade-style white bread that you can slice yourself, or have the bakery slice for you.

M E N U

FOR 6

*NUTMEG FRENCH TOAST

*SIMMERED PLUMS

FRESH CREAM

SPICY BREAKFAST SAUSAGE

*RECIPE FOLLOWS

GAME PLAN

THE DAY BEFORE YOU MAY:
◆ Simmer plums; refrigerate.

ABOUT 1 HOUR BEFORE
SERVING:
◆ Take butter out of refrigerator to soften; butter jelly-roll pan while butter is still hard.
◆ Heat oven to 425°F.
◆ Cook sausage.
◆ Prepare Nutmeg French Toast and put in to bake.
◆ Gently reheat plums.
◆ Pour cream into pitcher.
◆ Serve French toast with plums and cream.

Nutmeg French Toast

I've given directions for baking this special French toast, but if you don't want to turn on the oven, cook it on the rangetop in one or two skillets. Serve with the Simmered Plums and a pitcher of fresh cream.

4 tablespoons (½ stick) unsalted butter, at room temperature
4 large eggs
1 cup milk
1 cup heavy cream
3 tablespoons confectioners' sugar
1 teaspoon vanilla extract
¼ teaspoon nutmeg, freshly-grated or from a jar
1 1-pound loaf challah bread, sliced ½-inch thick (18 good slices, discard the small ends)
Confectioners' sugar, for the top

Heat oven to 425°F. Grease two 15 × 10 inch jelly-roll pans with 1 tablespoon of butter each.

Break eggs into a large bowl. Add milk, cream, 3 tablespoons sugar, vanilla, and nutmeg; beat with a fork or wire whisk until well blended.

Dip each piece of challah into egg mixture, turning to coat both sides, and arrange in a single layer on buttered pans. Smear remaining butter on top of bread.

Bake about 15 minutes, without turning, until French toast is browned. Arrange on platter or plates and sift a little confectioners' sugar through a strainer over the top. *Makes 6 servings.*

RANGETOP METHOD: Melt 2 tablespoons of butter in one large or two smaller skillets (preferably nonstick) over moderately-high heat. Add enough of the dipped bread slices to cover bottom with a little space between the slices. Cook 2 to 3 minutes, until lightly browned on the bottom. Turn slices and cook 2 to 3 minutes longer until lightly browned. Repeat with remaining butter and dipped bread.

Simmered Plums

Serve these plums with the French toast.

¼ cup damson plum preserves
3 tablespoons granulated sugar
1 tablespoon freshly-squeezed lemon
    juice

1½ pounds round black plums, halved,
    pitted, and cut into chunks (4
    cups)

Mix preserves, sugar, and lemon juice in a medium-sized heavy sauce-pan. Add plums and bring to a boil over high heat. Reduce heat to low; cover and simmer 8 to 10 minutes, until plums are soft but not mushy.

Remove from heat and let cool about 10 minutes before serving. *Makes 6 servings.*

SHOPPING GUIDE

3 tablespoons granulated sugar
¼ cup confectioners' sugar
¼ teaspoon nutmeg, freshly-grated or from a jar
1 teaspoon vanilla extract
¼ cup damson plum preserves

1½ pounds round black plums (such as Black Beauty, Black Amber, or Friar)
1 lemon

1 to 1½ pounds spicy breakfast sausage

1 1-pound loaf challah bread sliced ½-inch thick (18 slices)

1 cup milk
2 cups (1 pint) heavy cream
4 tablespoons (½ stick) unsalted butter
4 large eggs

(Coffee? Tea? Add what you need.)

F A L L

Back-to-School Breakfast Party

Just before school starts, children welcome the opportunity to reconnect with friends they may not have seen all summer. It's a good time, too, to invite any new kids in the neighborhood, and give them a chance to feel they "belong" before that scary first day in school.

French-bread French toast, filled with jam or jelly, makes a great breakfast for kids. (With the morning rush to catch the school bus about to begin again, it's good to know that leftovers freeze beautifully. One slice heats in about thirty seconds in a microwave oven—but be careful; the jam gets very hot.) The size of the bread is important here; buy loaves that are about eighteen inches long and one and a half to two inches high.

For a beverage that kids will find special, but not too out of the ordinary, you might like to serve CJ-OJ, cranberry juice cocktail and orange juice, mixed fifty-fifty.

M E N U

FOR 8 TO 10

*PICK-UP FRUIT WITH CREAMY BANANA DIP

*KANGAROO POCKETS

FRIZZLED HAM

*RECIPE FOLLOWS

GAME PLAN

THE DAY BEFORE YOU MAY:
◆ Cut up melon and pineapple for Pick-Up Fruit.

ABOUT 1 HOUR BEFORE SERVING:
◆ Heat oven to 400°F.
◆ Slice and fill bread for Kangaroo Pockets; dip in egg mixture and bake.

ABOUT 30 MINUTES BEFORE SERVING:
◆ Make Creamy Banana Dip.
◆ Cut up apples or pears; arrange on platters.
◆ Fry ham (see page 32).

Pick-Up Fruit with Creamy Banana Dip

This recipe is merely a guide because it is best to select fruit according to the current whims and fancies of the young people you've invited to breakfast. Forget making the dip if you don't have really ripe bananas; instead use two 8-ounce containers of fruit-flavored yogurt such as banana or lemon. If you want to be more elaborate, you can impale a selection of fruit on wooden skewers. Otherwise, fingers or wooden toothpicks are suitable tools.

1 *ripe cantaloupe or honeydew melon*
1 *ripe pineapple (3½ to 4 pounds) or 1 to 2 14-ounce cans pineapple chunks packed in unsweetened juice, drained*
3 *Golden Delicious apples or ripe pears*
1 *16-ounce container plain yogurt*
4 *teaspoons granulated sugar or 2 teaspoons honey*
1 *large ripe banana*

Seed and peel melon (see page 186), peel pineapple (see page 187), and cut both into bite-size chunks. Peel apples, if desired (pears are best peeled); quarter, core, and cut into wedges.

Make dip about 30 minutes before serving (no longer, or banana will discolor). Mix yogurt and sugar or honey in a medium-sized bowl. Peel banana and mash as smooth as possible on a plate with a fork. Stir into yogurt. Shortly before serving, taste dip and add a little more sugar or honey if needed. *Makes about 2½ cups dip for 8 to 10 servings.*

Kangaroo Pockets

4 tablespoons (½ stick) unsalted
    butter, melted
2 loaves French or Italian bread,
    plain, not seeded (about 10
    ounces each)
½ cup seedless red raspberry jam

2 large eggs
2 cups milk
2 tablespoons confectioners' sugar
2 teaspoons vanilla extract
    Confectioners' sugar for decoration

Heat oven to 400°F. Brush two 15 × 10 inch jelly-roll pans (preferably nonstick) with some of the butter.

Cut each loaf in the following way to make a total of 16 slices of bread with pockets in them: Remove a 1-inch-wide diagonal slice from one end of loaf (offer to birds or reserve for bread crumbs). Holding knife on a slant, cut a deep slash ¾ inch in from cut end; move knife another ¾ inch and cut all the way through the crust, forming a 1½-inch slice of bread with a "pocket" in it. Cut remainder of loaf into 7 more pocketed slices.

Spread about 1½ teaspoons jam in each pocket and press gently so that preserves are hidden.

Beat eggs in a bowl with a fork or wire whisk. Add milk, the 2 tablespoons confectioners' sugar, and the vanilla. Beat to mix well.

Put 2 or 3 filled slices of bread in egg mixture at a time and soak not more than 5 seconds on each side before placing on buttered pans. Brush remaining butter on top of soaked bread. Bake about 12 minutes. Reverse pans on shelves (top pan to bottom and vice versa) and bake 12 to 15 minutes longer, until bread is nicely browned on top. (No need to turn slices; bottoms will brown enough.)

Transfer bread to serving plates or platter and sift confectioners' sugar over the top (doesn't matter if sugar falls on the plates; in fact it makes them look prettier). *Makes 8 to 10 servings.*

SHOPPING GUIDE

4 or more teaspoons granulated
    sugar or 2 or more teaspoons
    honey
About 3 tablespoons confec-
    tioners' sugar
2 teaspoons vanilla extract
½ cup seedless red raspberry
    jam

3 Golden Delicious apples or
    ripe pears
1 cantaloupe or honeydew
    melon
1 ripe pineapple (3½ to 4
    pounds) or 1 or 2 14-ounce
    cans pineapple chunks
    packed in unsweetened juice
1 large ripe banana

2 loaves French or Italian bread,
    plain, not seeded, about 18
    inches long and 1½ to 2
    inches high (about 10 ounces
    each)

1 or 2 slices cooked ham per
    person

2 cups milk
1 16-ounce container plain
    yogurt or 2 8-ounce contain-
    ers banana or lemon yogurt
4 tablespoons (½ stick) unsalted
    butter
2 large eggs

(Cranberry juice cocktail and
    orange juice? Milk? Other
    beverages for young guests?
    Add what you need.)

Portable Breakfast for a Fall Outing

M E N U

FOR 6

*HIGHWAY CHAMPAGNE

GRAPES

*BACON AND EGG
SANDWICHES

*OATMEAL-RAISIN
BREAKFAST COOKIES

CAFFÈ LATTE

*RECIPE FOLLOWS

When you want to get an early start on a trip to see the changing leaves or to hike through the woods, pack these hearty sandwiches and eat breakfast along the way. If you're like me, you'll stop at a farm stand and buy enough apples and cider to feed fifty people for a year. So pack a knife, a jar of peanut butter, and a bar of Swiss milk or bittersweet chocolate to munch along with the crisp fresh apples and the rest of the breakfast cookies on the journey home.

For the Caffè Latte, make espresso coffee if you have an espresso maker. If you don't, make double-strength coffee using Italian- or espresso-roast coffee in a drip coffee maker. Pack the hot coffee in one heated thermos flask and pack very hot, but not boiled, milk in another. Have enough hot milk to mix at least fifty-fifty with the coffee; some people prefer an even higher proportion of milk. Don't forget to pack sugar and sweetener for those who wish it.

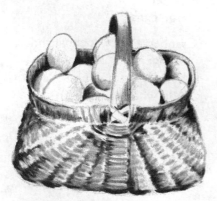

Highway Champagne

Have the beverages well chilled. Pack real glasses or clear plastic alternatives.

Nonalcoholic white wine or a high-quality white grape juice

Seltzer or club soda

Half-fill each glass with nonalcoholic white wine or grape juice. Top up with seltzer.

Bacon and Egg Sandwiches

This takes care of your cholesterol for a week!

6 *crusty rolls, 7 to 8 inches long, weighing 2 to 3 ounces each*
4 *tablespoons (½ stick) unsalted butter, melted*
½ *pound sliced bacon*
16 *large eggs*

2 *tablespoons milk*
½ *teaspoon salt*
½ *teaspoon freshly-ground pepper*
4 *ounces sharp cheddar cheese, shredded (1 cup)*
½ *cup sliced scallions*

Cut about one-third off top of each roll; pull out most of soft insides. (Offer to birds or reserve for bread crumbs.)

Brush insides of rolls and tops with melted butter. Broil rolls and tops (you'll probably need to do this in two batches), until browned, 2 to 3 minutes.

Fry bacon in a large nonstick skillet over moderate heat, until crisp. Drain on paper towels and crumble coarsely.

Drain off all but 1 tablespoon fat from skillet, let skillet cool.

Break eggs into a large bowl. Add milk, salt, and pepper. Beat with a fork or wire whisk until well broken up. Put skillet back over moderately-low heat; heat briefly. Pour in eggs and start to scramble them (see page 193). When creamy, add cheese, scallions, and crumbled bacon; scramble until eggs are almost as firm as you like them.

Spoon scrambled eggs into toasted rolls and put tops back on. Serve right away or wrap in plastic and chill. Do not keep at room temperature for more than 2 hours. *Makes 6 servings.*

GAME PLAN

UP TO 2 WEEKS AHEAD YOU MAY:
◆ Bake and freeze cookies.

THE DAY BEFORE YOU MAY:
◆ Hollow out bread rolls; wrap airtight; leave at room temperature.
◆ Cook bacon in skillet or in microwave oven; drain (save 1 tablespoon fat); crumble; store airtight.
◆ Shred cheese.

ABOUT 1 HOUR BEFORE DEPARTURE:
◆ Remove cookies from freezer.
◆ Rinse grapes; cut into smaller bunches and pack.
◆ Slice scallions.
◆ Brush rolls with melted butter and broil.
◆ Scramble eggs; fill rolls; pack.

SHOPPING GUIDE

¾ cup all-purpose flour
¾ cup old-fashioned oats
½ cup light brown sugar
½ teaspoon baking powder
¼ teaspoon baking soda
¾ teaspoon ground cinnamon
½ cup (3 ounces) dark raisins or
    Zante currants
Dark-roast coffee
Nonalcoholic white wine or
    high-quality white grape
    juice
Seltzer or club soda

1½ to 2 pounds seedless grapes
1 bunch scallions (½ cup sliced)

6 crusty rolls, 7 to 8 inches
    long, weighing 2 to 3 ounces
    each

½ pound sliced bacon

2 tablespoons milk (plus milk
    for Caffè Latte)
10 tablespoons (1¼ sticks)
    unsalted butter
17 large eggs
4 ounces sharp cheddar cheese
    (1 cup shredded)

(Regular coffee? Tea? Add what
    you need.)

Oatmeal-Raisin Breakfast Cookies

6 tablespoons (¾ stick) unsalted
    butter
¾ cup all-purpose flour
¾ cup old-fashioned oats
¾ teaspoon ground cinnamon
½ teaspoon baking powder
¼ teaspoon baking soda
    Few grains of salt
½ cup packed light brown sugar
1 large egg
½ cup (3 ounces) dark raisins or
    Zante currants

Heat oven to 375°F. Melt butter and pour into a small bowl to cool. Grease a cookie sheet.

Put flour, oats, cinnamon, baking powder, baking soda, and salt into a large bowl; stir to mix well.

Add sugar and egg to butter; whisk smooth with fork or wire whisk. Stir in raisins. Pour over flour mixture. Stir to mix well.

Drop heaping tablespoons of batter onto cookie sheet, leaving 2 inches between each. Bake 10 to 12 minutes, until cookies are lightly browned. Let cool a minute or so, then transfer to wire racks to cool completely. *Makes 12 cookies.*

Breakfast from the Oven

M E N U

FOR 6

*HONEY-CRUNCH BAKED
APPLES

*BAKED EGGS WITH HAM
AND GRUYÈRE

*FRESH PEAR AND VANILLA
MUFFINS

*RECIPE FOLLOWS

When the first twinges of fall send you diving into the sweater drawer and you have to turn on the oven for warmth, this is a perfect breakfast to serve. The warm, wonderful smells of apples, muffins, and cheese baking make you glad to feel that first chill.

Even though all the dishes in this menu are baked, you need only one oven. The Fresh Pear and Vanilla Muffins can be baked a day ahead. Even if you decide to bake them the morning of the breakfast, they can be done first because they need to cool for at least thirty minutes for the flavor to develop. While the muffins bake, cut up the apples for the Honey-Crunch Baked Apples. Shortly before you serve the hot apples, put the eggs in the oven. Baked Eggs with Ham and Gruyère looks great, tastes wonderful, and is very easy to make. It can be baked in one large dish, but is even nicer when prepared in individual baking dishes.

GAME PLAN

THE DAY BEFORE YOU MAY:
- Bake Fresh Pear and Vanilla Muffins. When cool, store in plastic bag at room temperature. (Or mix dry ingredients in a large bowl; leave at room temperature. Organize pan and remaining ingredients.)
- Organize ingredients and equipment for Honey-Crunch Baked Apples.

ABOUT 1½ HOURS BEFORE SERVING:
- Heat oven to 375°F. Mix muffin batter; put in to bake.
- Slice apples and prepare topping for Honey-Crunch Baked Apples; bake, remove from oven.
- Turn oven to 325°F.
- Assemble and bake Baked Eggs with Ham and Gruyère.

Honey-Crunch Baked Apples

1½ pounds Golden Delicious apples
2 tablespoons (¼ stick) unsalted butter
1 cup old-fashioned oats
½ cup (2 ounces) walnuts, coarsely chopped
2 tablespoons honey

Heat oven to 375°F. Quarter and core, but don't peel, the apples. Slice apples into wedges about ½-inch thick and put into a baking dish about 11 × 7 inches.

Melt butter in a medium-sized saucepan over low heat. Remove from heat; add remaining ingredients and stir until crumbly. Sprinkle over apples. Bake 35 to 40 minutes, until topping is crisp and browned and apples are tender. Serve warm. *Makes 6 servings.*

Baked Eggs with Ham and Gruyère

Bake this in individual baking dishes about 4½-inches square on the bottom, or oval ones 6- to 7-inches long, or in one large dish (instructions below).

6 thin slices cooked ham (1 to 2 ounces each)
12 large eggs
Salt, freshly-ground pepper
¼ cup light cream or half-and-half
4½ ounces Gruyère cheese, shredded (about 1¼ cups)

Heat oven to 325°F. Butter six individual baking dishes and put a slice of ham in bottom of each. Break eggs over ham. Sprinkle with salt and pepper. Spoon 2 teaspoons cream or half-and-half over eggs in each dish and sprinkle with 3 tablespoons cheese.

Bake about 15 minutes, until eggs are set around edges and lightly puffed. Remove from oven and let stand 5 minutes while eggs complete cooking. Put each baking dish on a plate lined with a napkin to prevent it from sliding. *Makes 6 servings.*

TO MAKE IN ONE BAKING DISH: Butter a baking dish about 13 × 9 inches. Cut ham in roughly 1-inch pieces and scatter in dish. Break eggs over top. Sprinkle with salt and pepper, drizzle with cream or half-and-half, and sprinkle with cheese. Bake about 20 minutes, until eggs are set around edges but still runny in center when dish is gently shaken. Let stand 5 minutes to complete cooking. Serve with a pancake turner.

Fresh Pear and Vanilla Muffins

Allow muffins to cool at least 30 minutes for flavor to develop.

2 cups all-purpose flour
¼ cup granulated sugar
2½ teaspoons baking powder
½ teaspoon baking soda
¼ teaspoon salt
2 large eggs
1½ teaspoons vanilla extract
¾ cup milk
4 tablespoons (½ stick) unsalted butter, melted
1 large ripe Bartlett pear, peeled, cored, and diced (1½ cups)

Heat oven to 375°F. Grease twelve muffin cups or line with foil baking cups.

Mix flour, sugar, baking powder, baking soda, and salt in a large bowl.

In another bowl, whisk eggs and vanilla with a fork, until eggs are well broken up. Whisk in milk and butter. Stir in pear. Pour over dry ingredients and fold in with a rubber spatula, until dry ingredients are just moistened.

Scoop batter into prepared pans. Bake 20 to 25 minutes, until lightly browned and springy to the touch in center.

Remove from pans and let cool at least 30 minutes before eating. *Makes 12 muffins.*

SHOPPING GUIDE

2 cups all-purpose flour
1 cup old-fashioned oats
¼ cup granulated sugar
2½ teaspoons baking powder
½ teaspoon baking soda
½ cup (2 ounces) walnuts, chopped
2 tablespoons honey
1½ teaspoons vanilla extract
Foil baking cups for muffins (optional)

1½ pounds Golden Delicious apples
1 large ripe Bartlett pear
6 thin slices cooked ham (1 to 2 ounces each)

¾ cup milk
¼ cup light cream or half-and-half
6 tablespoons (¾ stick) unsalted butter
14 large eggs
4½ ounces Gruyère cheese (for about 1¼ cups shredded)

(Coffee? Tea? Add what you need including bread for toast if you wish, and butter for the table.)

Celebrate Rosh Hashanah

M E N U

FOR 6

APPLE WEDGES WITH
HONEY

*GRANDMOTHER RUBIN'S
BLINTZES

*WARM CRANBERRY
COULIS

*MIRIAM RUBIN'S HONEY
CAKE

HOT TEA

GLACÉED APRICOTS

*RECIPE FOLLOWS

osh Hashanah, the Jewish New Year, is a joyful holiday to celebrate. Sweet foods are appropriate, representing optimism and hope for the New Year, as are any of the abundant sweet fall fruits such as pumpkins, pears, persimmons, and grapes. Decorate the table with a casual arrangement of these sweet fall fruits in all their glorious colors. As everyone gathers, put out a bowl of honey surrounded with apple wedges to dip in it and eat while toasting the New Year. The blintzes are very rich, so after everyone has enjoyed them it's a good idea to wait a while before serving the honey cake, with glacéed apricots to nibble, and hot tea. Be sure to make the honey cake at least two days ahead so the flavor develops and the texture becomes typically moist. Buckwheat honey, with its very intense flavor, is traditionally used in this cake, but you may use regular clover honey instead. Look for buckwheat honey in your supermarket, or in a specialty or health-food store.

Grandmother Rubin's Blintzes

It is a special privilege to include this recipe from Miriam Rubin's grandmother, Frances. Miriam says that when she asked her 85-year-old grandmother to make the blintzes so she could write down the recipe, her grandmother whipped through the whole process with incredible speed. A blintz is a crêpe rolled up with a filling inside (Frances Rubin calls the crêpes "leaves," a lovely word for them). Making them is a lot of work, but it is a nice project to share and the result is blintzes to dream about. The major problem, says my husband, is deciding whether they are best eaten absolutely plain, or with sour cream, or with sour cream and the cranberry coulis.

They can be made ahead and freeze very well. Don't be tempted to be overefficient and try to make the filling while you're cooking the "leaves." Unless you're a creature of unique ability, either the leaves or the filling will suffer.

Leaves (recipe follows)	*Warm Cranberry Coulis (recipe*
Blintz Filling (recipe follows)	*follows)*
4 tablespoons (½ stick) unsalted butter	*1 or 2 8-ounce containers sour cream*
(for frying blintzes)	

First make the leaves; then the filling. Next fill and roll up the blintzes. They can then be refrigerated for up to 3 days or frozen for longer. Fry blintzes just before serving.

To fill blintzes: Put a rounded tablespoon of the filling on each leaf, about 1 inch from the edge nearest you. Roll up each leaf, spreading the filling a little bit as you roll, but not all the way to the ends. Put filled leaves in a single layer in a baking dish or on a cookie sheet.

When leaves are all filled, you may cover and refrigerate them for up to 3 days or freeze them. When frozen hard, blintzes may be stacked in an airtight container with sheets of wax paper between layers. Thaw before frying.

To fry blintzes: Heat oven to 200°F. so you have somewhere to keep blintzes warm.

Work with two nonstick skillets, each about 10 inches across the bottom. Put skillets over moderate to moderately-high heat and melt 1 tablespoon butter in each. Add six or seven blintzes and cook 1 to 2 minutes per side, until lightly browned, turning once. Don't cook them too quickly, or leaves will scorch before filling is hot.

Arrange on serving platter and keep warm in the oven while you fry remaining blintzes.

Serve warm with Warm Cranberry Coulis and ice-cold sour cream.
Makes 30 to 32 blintzes.

GAME PLAN

UP TO 1 WEEK AHEAD:
◆ Make Miriam Rubin's Honey Cake. Wrap tightly and store at room temperature (but away from hungry eyes).

THE DAY BEFORE:
◆ Make Grandmother Rubin's Blintzes; cover tightly; refrigerate.
◆ Make Cranberry Coulis; refrigerate.

ABOUT 30 MINUTES BEFORE SERVING:
◆ Quarter and core apples; cut into wedges. Arrange on platter with small bowl of honey for dipping. Let everyone toast the New Year.
◆ Fry blintzes.
◆ Warm the Cranberry Coulis.
◆ Put sour cream in a bowl. Serve with blintzes.

LATER:
◆ Slice honey cake. Serve with hot tea and glacéed apricots.

SHOPPING GUIDE

3¾ cups all-purpose flour
½ cup dark brown sugar
7 tablespoons granulated sugar
2 teaspoons baking powder
½ teaspoon baking soda
1 teaspoon ground cinnamon
1 teaspoon ground ginger
½ teaspoon vanilla extract
1 cup (3½ ounces) sliced natural almonds
1½ cups (7½ to 8 ounces) golden raisins
1 tablespoon instant coffee granules
1¼ cups (1 pound) buckwheat honey
About ⅓ cup clover or other honey for serving with apple wedges
Glacéed apricots (buy 1 or 2 per person)
¾ cup vegetable oil
½ cup seedless red raspberry jam

1 12-ounce bag fresh or frozen cranberries
1 or 2 lemons
3 or more apples for serving with honey

1 or 2 8-ounce containers sour cream to serve with blintzes
12 tablespoons (1½ sticks) unsalted butter
10 large eggs
2 7½-ounce packages farmer cheese (preferably *not* unsalted)

(Tea? Coffee? Add what you need including fruits for the table. Check paper towel supply; you need fifteen sheets for the blintzes.)

LEAVES

1 cup all-purpose flour
4 large eggs
1⅓ cups water
3 tablespoons (about ½ stick) unsalted butter, melted

½ teaspoon sugar
Few grains of salt
Melted unsalted butter for skillet, about 4 tablespoons (½ stick)

Line countertop near range with about fifteen sheets of paper towels. As each leaf is made, you will put it on the paper towels. Leaves can be very close together, even slightly overlapping.

To make batter: Put all ingredients, except butter for skillets, into an electric blender. Cover and blend at high speed until smooth, stopping machine and scraping sides 2 or 3 times.

Choose a nonstick skillet, about 5 inches across the bottom. Place skillet over moderate heat for a minute or two. Brush lightly with melted butter.

Have the batter in a bowl or cup measure, close by the range. Have a measuring tablespoon handy, also a small ladle or custard cup. Measure about 1½ tablespoons batter into the ladle or cup and use this amount for each leaf.

To make a leaf: Pick up skillet in one hand and pour in the 1½ tablespoons batter, tipping and tilting skillet as you pour, so that batter coats the bottom of the skillet as completely as possible. Unlike most crêpes, leaves for blintzes are not turned during cooking. A leaf is cooked when it looks dull and starts pulling away from the sides of the skillet. At that point, tip skillet upside down over paper towels so leaf lands upside down. Put pan on heat and start the next leaf. If you can work with two skillets, making the leaves will go faster.

Keep in mind that even pros usually mess up the first two or three crêpes or leaves (this loss has been factored into amount of batter). Also keep in mind that it does not matter if batter doesn't always completely cover the bottom of the skillet. When you roll up the leaves with the filling inside, any small deficiencies will be hidden.

By the time you've used about half the batter, it will have thickened slightly; stir in about 1 tablespoon water. (You can do this any time, even at beginning, if batter seems too thick. The thinner it is, the better.)

When all leaves (about 30 to 32) have been made, fill, roll, and fry them according to directions above.

BLINTZ FILLING

- 2 7½-ounce packages farmer cheese (preferably not unsalted)
- ¼ cup granulated sugar
- 1 large egg
- ½ teaspoon vanilla extract
- 2 teaspoons all-purpose flour
- 1 tablespoon unsalted butter, melted

Put all ingredients into a bowl and stir to mix well.

WARM CRANBERRY COULIS

- 1 12-ounce bag fresh or frozen cranberries
- ½ cup seedless red raspberry jam
- ¾ cup water
- 2 tablespoons granulated sugar

Pick over cranberries, removing any stems and discarding any squishy ones.

Mix all ingredients in a medium-sized saucepan and bring to a boil over high heat.

Reduce heat to moderately low. Simmer 3 to 4 minutes, stirring frequently, until most of the cranberries have popped and are soft. *Makes 2½ cups.*

Miriam Rubin's Honey Cake

2½ cups all-purpose flour
2 teaspoons baking powder
½ teaspoon baking soda
¼ teaspoon salt
1 teaspoon ground cinnamon
1 teaspoon ground ginger
1½ cups (7½ to 8 ounces) golden
    raisins
1 cup (3 ounces) sliced natural
    almonds

⅓ cup water
1 tablespoon instant coffee granules
5 large eggs
1¼ cups (1 pound) buckwheat honey
½ cup packed dark brown sugar
¾ cup vegetable oil
2 teaspoons freshly-grated lemon peel

Heat oven to 325°F. Heavily grease a 12-cup Bundt pan.

Put flour, baking powder, baking soda, salt, cinnamon, and ginger into a large bowl; stir to mix well. Add raisins and almonds; toss to coat with flour.

Measure water in a glass cup measure; add coffee granules and stir until dissolved.

In another large bowl, beat eggs with honey and sugar, until sugar is dissolved. Beat in oil, lemon peel, and dissolved coffee. Pour into flour mixture. Stir with a wooden spoon until well mixed.

Pour batter into Bundt pan. Bake 50 to 60 minutes, until cake has browned and shrunk slightly from sides of pan. A wooden toothpick inserted in the center of cake (between outer and inner edge) should come out clean, that is, without uncooked batter clinging to it.

Place pan on a wire rack to cool at least 30 minutes. Turn cake out onto rack; let cool completely. Wrap tightly and store at least 2 days at room temperature for flavor to develop. *Makes 20 to 24 servings.*

Come Help—Raise Our New Roof, Plant Bulbs, Rake Leaves

Helping friends and neighbors with major projects is a wonderful American custom in the tradition of barn-raisings and quilting-bees. It's important though (as our ancestors knew) to feed helpers well, starting with a hearty breakfast. Sharing food makes the task seem lighter. Of course, feeding the crew should not be too hard on the cook, as this menu takes into account. Use one or two good-sized griddles to bake the pancakes on. (Once cooked, the pancakes can be kept warm successfully for up to half an hour.) Bake the Orange-Almond Coffee Cake well ahead of time and freeze it. Cut up the plums the night before; in the morning they will require scant attention while baking.

Although the Baked Prune Plums works well with almost any kind of plum, my favorite time to make it is during the all-too-short season for Italian prune plums in late summer/early fall. Prune plums freeze very well; pit them before freezing in plastic bags or containers. Enjoy them poached, baked, or in a coffee cake during the winter months.

M E N U

FOR 10 TO 12

*BAKED PRUNE PLUMS

*DOUBLE CORN AND
CHILI PANCAKES

SALSA

SOUR CREAM

HOT-PEPPER JELLY

MAPLE SYRUP

HAM OR SPICY SAUSAGE

*ORANGE-ALMOND
COFFEE CAKE

*RECIPE FOLLOWS

GAME PLAN

UP TO 1 MONTH AHEAD YOU
MAY:
- Bake, cool, wrap, and freeze Orange-Almond Coffee Cake.

THE DAY BEFORE:
- Transfer coffee cake from freezer to refrigerator.

THE DAY BEFORE YOU MAY
ALSO:
- Halve and pit plums for Baked Prune Plums; store in plastic bags. Select baking dishes.

ABOUT 1½ TO 2 HOURS
BEFORE SERVING:
- Heat oven to 400°F. Assemble prune plums in baking dishes; put in to bake. (When done, remove from oven and turn oven to 200°F.)
- Put accompaniments (salsa, sour cream, syrup, jelly) in serving dishes.
- Cook ham or sausage (see page 196); keep warm.
- Prepare Double Corn and Chili Pancake batter. Make pancakes; keep warm in 200°F. oven.
- When you serve pancakes, put foil-wrapped coffee cake in oven to warm for 15 minutes.

Baked Prune Plums

4 pounds Italian prune plums
⅔ cup granulated sugar
6 tablespoons (¾ stick) unsalted butter, cut in small pieces
1 teaspoon ground cinnamon

Heat oven to 400°F. Butter two nonmetallic baking dishes, each about 13 × 9 × 2 inches.

Cut each plum in half and discard the pit. Arrange plums, cut sides up, in single layer in baking dishes. Sprinkle each dish with half the sugar (it will seem like a thick layer). Dot with butter and sprinkle with cinnamon.

Bake 20 to 25 minutes, until plums are tender. Serve warm, spooning the delicious pink syrup that forms during baking over the plums. *Makes 10 to 12 servings.*

Double Corn and Chili Pancakes

Heat oven to 200°F. just before you start making the pancakes so you'll have somewhere to keep them warm. They'll be fine for up to half an hour.

1½ cups yellow cornmeal
½ cup all-purpose flour
2 tablespoons baking powder
½ teaspoon salt
¼ teaspoon freshly-ground pepper
6 large eggs
2 cups milk
8 tablespoons (1 stick) unsalted butter, melted and cooled slightly
4 cups frozen corn kernels
1 4-ounce can chopped green chilies
½ cup coarsely chopped roasted red peppers

Mix cornmeal, flour, baking powder, salt, and pepper in a large bowl. Whisk eggs in another large bowl; add milk and butter; whisk to blend. Stir in corn, chilies, and red peppers.

Pour wet ingredients into dry and stir until dry ingredients are blended.

Heat one or two pancake griddles or large nonstick skillets over high heat. Brush griddles lightly with oil and reduce heat to moderate. For each pancake, pour scant ¼ cup of batter onto griddle and cook 3 to 4 minutes, until lightly browned on the bottom. Turn and cook 2 to 3 minutes longer, until browned.

Put cooked pancakes into a roasting pan or on a cookie sheet; cover loosely with foil and keep warm in oven while you cook remaining pancakes. If batter gets too thick (which it may do if it stands a while) thin it with a tablespoon of milk. *Makes about 64 pancakes.*

Orange-Almond Coffee Cake

2¼ cups all-purpose flour
1 tablespoon baking powder
1 teaspoon baking soda
½ teaspoon salt
3 large eggs
1 cup granulated sugar
12 tablespoons (1½ sticks) unsalted butter, melted and cooled slightly

1 tablespoon freshly-grated orange peel, from navel orange
¾ cup freshly-squeezed orange juice
1 cup (3½ ounces) sliced natural almonds
2 tablespoons orange marmalade

Heat oven to 350°F. Grease two 8-inch round layer-cake pans.

Mix flour, baking powder, baking soda, and salt in a large bowl.

In a medium-sized bowl, whisk eggs, sugar, and butter until well blended. Stir in orange peel and juice. Scrape wet ingredients into dry ingredients and stir until dry ingredients are just incorporated.

Divide batter between pans. Sprinkle with almonds. Bake 20 to 25 minutes, until cakes are lightly browned and a wooden toothpick inserted near the centers comes out clean. Let cool 5 minutes. Brush surfaces with marmalade. Serve warm or cool from pans. *Makes 16 servings.*

SHOPPING GUIDE

2¾ cups all-purpose flour
1½ cups yellow cornmeal
1⅔ cups granulated sugar
3 tablespoons baking powder
1 teaspoon baking soda
1 teaspoon ground cinnamon
1 cup (3½ ounces) sliced natural almonds
1 4-ounce can chopped green chilies
1 7-ounce jar roasted red peppers
2 tablespoons orange marmalade

4 pounds Italian prune plums
1 navel orange
3 or 4 juice oranges (¾ cup juice)

2 10-ounce packages frozen corn kernels, or 1 24-ounce package (4 cups)

Ham or spicy sausage or a selection of both: allow about ⅓ to ½ ham steak per person and 1 or 2 hot Italian sausages.

2 cups milk
26 tablespoons (3¼ sticks) unsalted butter
9 large eggs

(Coffee? Tea? Add what you need, also butter for the table and your choice of salsa, sour cream, hot pepper jelly, and maple syrup to serve with the pancakes.)

Hearty Breakfast for Columbus Day

M E N U

FOR 6

*LEMON-POACHED APPLES

*SWEET OR SPICY ITALIAN
SAUSAGE

*BAKED POLENTA

*CHUNKY SALSA SALAD

*RECIPE FOLLOWS

I love this breakfast on any cool day. The polenta, Italian cornmeal mush, is best made ahead, a feature that makes this meal easy to prepare for guests. If you can buy wonderful Italian sausage, for heaven's sake do. But if locally available products lack distinction, it is easy to make your own. Be sure to make it a day ahead so the flavor can develop. Because this sausage is lean, cook it carefully over moderate heat so it doesn't get too dry. If you'd like a spicy-hot sausage, add a quarter teaspoon crushed red pepper flakes to the mixture.

I know the Chunky Salsa Salad is crossing ethnic lines but it tastes absolutely wonderful with the spicy sausage and the simple polenta. Just think of it as a fresh Italian tomato sauce, spiked with jalapeño instead of crushed red pepper.

Lemon-Poached Apples

Watch liquid carefully as apples poach; if it boils, they may turn to applesauce. Save any liquid left after the apples are eaten and use it to poach more apples.

4 cups water
1 cup granulated sugar
    Peels of 2 large lemons, removed in
        long strips with a vegetable peeler
½ cup freshly-squeezed lemon juice
1 teaspoon vanilla extract

2 cinnamon sticks
4 whole cloves
3 to 3½ pounds (about 7) Granny
    Smith apples, peeled, quartered,
    and cored

Put all ingredients except apples into a large stainless steel or enameled skillet or saucepan. Bring to a boil over moderately-high heat.

Add apples; reduce heat to moderately-low or low and poach 20 to 30 minutes, until apples are tender, regulating heat so liquid doesn't boil.

Serve warm or chilled. *Makes 6 to 8 servings.*

Sweet or Spicy Italian Sausage

1½ pounds lean ground pork
1½ teaspoons whole fennel seed
1 teaspoon salt
½ teaspoon freshly-ground pepper

¾ teaspoon ground coriander seed
    Pure olive or vegetable oil for
        frying sausage

Put all ingredients except oil into a medium-sized bowl and mix lightly with hands or spoon just until well blended.

Cover and chill overnight. Or shape first: form mixture into a 14-inch-long log on a cutting board. Cut into 16 slices. Shape each piece into a patty about 2 inches across.

To cook, heat 1 to 2 teaspoons oil in one or two heavy skillets over moderate heat. Add patties and fry about 8 minutes per side, turning once, until cooked through and nicely browned. If necessary, drain on paper towels. *Makes 16 patties.*

GAME PLAN

THE DAY BEFORE:
◆ Cook cornmeal for Baked Polenta and put in oiled cake pan.
◆ Season ground pork and shape Sweet or Spicy Italian Sausage patties.

THE DAY BEFORE YOU MAY ALSO:
◆ Poach apples.
◆ Make Chunky Salsa Salad.
◆ Grate Parmesan for Baked Polenta.

ABOUT 1 HOUR BEFORE SERVING:
◆ Remove polenta, apples, and salsa salad from refrigerator.
◆ Heat oven to 400°F.
◆ Cut polenta into 8 wedges; cover with foil; bake 25 to 30 minutes.
◆ If desired, heat Lemon-Poached Apples on rangetop or in oven with polenta
◆ Cook Sweet or Spicy Italian Sausage patties.

SHOPPING GUIDE

1 cup yellow cornmeal
1 cup granulated sugar
4 whole cloves
2 cinnamon sticks
¾ teaspoon ground coriander
  seed
1½ teaspoons whole fennel
  seed
1 teaspoon vanilla extract
¼ cup pure olive or vegetable
  oil

3 to 3½ pounds (about 7)
  Granny Smith apples
3 large lemons
2 limes (or an additional lemon)
1 bunch scallions (¾ cup sliced)
1½ pounds fresh ripe tomatoes
1 or 2 fresh or pickled jalapeño
  peppers (2 to 3 teaspoons,
  minced)
1½ pounds lean ground pork

2 tablespoons (¼ stick) butter
¼ cup (1 ounce) freshly-grated
  Parmesan cheese

(Coffee? Tea? Add what you
  need.)

Baked Polenta

4 cups water
½ teaspoon salt
1 cup yellow cornmeal
¼ teaspoon freshly-ground pepper
  Pure olive oil
¼ cup freshly-grated Parmesan cheese
2 tablespoons butter, cut in small
  pieces

In a large (4 to 5 quart) nonstick saucepan or Dutch oven bring water and salt to a boil over high heat. Stirring constantly, pour in cornmeal in a slow, steady stream. Continue stirring and reduce heat to moderately-low or low, so cornmeal cooks but doesn't spatter over your arms too much (a long-handled spoon helps). With a nonstick pan you only need to stir every few minutes; otherwise stir more or less constantly for the entire 15 to 20 minutes cornmeal takes to cook. Mixture will become very thick. When done, remove from heat. Stir in pepper.

Grease an 8-inch round cake pan with a little olive oil. Pour in polenta and spread smoothly. Cover and chill overnight.

Heat oven to 400°F. Cut polenta in pan into 8 wedges. Cover with foil and bake 25 to 30 minutes, until heated through.

Remove from oven and discard foil. Heat broiler. Sprinkle polenta with cheese and dot with butter. Broil 6 to 8 minutes, until surface is browned. *Makes 8 servings.*

Chunky Salsa Salad

1½ pounds ripe tomatoes, cut into
  large chunks
¾ cup thinly-sliced scallions
2 tablespoons freshly-squeezed lime
  or lemon juice
2 to 3 teaspoons minced seeded fresh or
  pickled jalapeño pepper
2 tablespoons pure olive or
  vegetable oil
½ teaspoon salt
⅛ teaspoon freshly-ground pepper

Put all ingredients into a bowl and mix well. Serve soon or cover and refrigerate. Salad keeps for up to 3 days. *Makes about 3½ cups.*

A New England Breakfast

No matter where you live, when you serve this breakfast you can at least dream about autumn weekends in New England—antiquing trips, country auctions, local crafts fairs, roadside markets piled high with apples and pears, and long walks along country lanes scuffling through piles of leaves, trying to catch the leaves as they fall. (When I was a child, legend had it that for every leaf you caught you'd have a happy day the next year.) This is a very hearty breakfast so do plan one of those long country walks (or a swim, or visit to a gym) later in the day!

There are two recipes for the main course. Homemade Corned Beef Hash is strictly from scratch, including cooking the corned beef brisket. If you're pressed for time, or if this is the first time you've made this New England specialty, I suggest you give thanks for frozen hash-browns and corned beef in a can, and make Corned Beef Hash in a Hurry. Whichever recipe you choose, the secret to crisp, well-browned hash is to press it down firmly in the skillet and turn it in clumps. If you enjoy chili sauce or salsa with corned beef hash, the Special Chili Salsa is better than either.

M E N U

FOR 6

*HONEY-BAKED PEARS AND PRUNES

*HOMEMADE CORNED BEEF HASH

POACHED EGGS

*SPECIAL CHILI SALSA

TOASTED ENGLISH MUFFINS

*SUPERSTICKY CINNAMON ROLLS

*RECIPE FOLLOWS

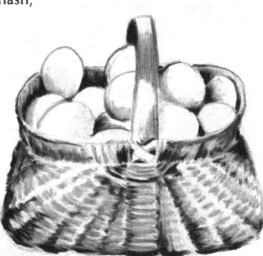

UP TO 1 WEEK AHEAD:

- Cook, trim, and dice corned beef for Homemade Corned Beef Hash. Freeze meat if keeping longer than 3 days.
- Make and freeze Supersticky Cinnamon Rolls.

THE DAY BEFORE:

- Make Homemade Corned Beef Hash mixture; cover and refrigerate.
- Transfer Supersticky Cinnamon Rolls from freezer to refrigerator.

THE DAY BEFORE YOU MAY ALSO:

- Poach eggs (see page 191); refrigerate in bowl of cold water.
- Make Special Chili Salsa.

ABOUT 2 HOURS BEFORE SERVING:

- Heat oven to 350°F. Prepare Honey-Baked Prunes and Pears and put in oven to bake. (When done, remove from oven and turn oven to 200°F.)

ABOUT 30 MINUTES BEFORE SERVING:

- Fry corned beef hash.
- Poach eggs and keep warm in bowl of very warm water; or transfer refrigerated poached eggs to bowl or skillet of hot water to warm.
- Toast muffins.
- Put foil-wrapped cinnamon rolls in oven to heat for 10 minutes.

Honey-Baked Pears and Prunes

3 pounds (about 6 medium-sized) firm ripe pears
1 cup (6 ounces) pitted prunes
¼ cup honey
¼ cup freshly-squeezed lemon juice
½ teaspoon vanilla extract

Heat oven to 350°F. Peel (a vegetable peeler works well), halve, and core pears. Cut pears into 1-inch chunks (you'll have about 7 cups).

Mix prunes and pear chunks in a shallow baking dish about 13 × 9 × 2 inches.

Measure honey in a 1-cup glass measure, add lemon juice and vanilla, and stir to blend. Pour over fruit and toss gently to mix. Bake, uncovered, about 1 to 1¼ hours, stirring three or four times, until pears are very soft and caramel-colored and most of the juices have evaporated. Serve warm. *Makes 6 servings.*

Homemade Corned Beef Hash

Don't make this with canned corned beef or with ready-cooked corned beef from the deli department. Corned beef is beef brisket, cured (corned) in a brine with spices, which gives it its unique flavor. Look for corned beef in the meat counter; it is usually sold sealed in heavy plastic, and you may see a bay leaf or peppercorns floating in the small amount of pickling juice packed with the meat. Look carefully at the meat before you buy; try to find as lean a piece as possible. (Often a thick layer of fat is hidden behind a pretty picture on the label of lean, lean meat.)

You can cook the corned beef ahead, dice it, and freeze it for a few days, but the hash mixture does not freeze satisfactorily.

1½ to 2 pounds russet (baking) potatoes

2 tablespoons pure olive or vegetable oil

1 cup finely chopped onion

1 large red, yellow, or green bell pepper, seeded and cut into ¼-inch pieces (1 cup)

Salt, freshly-ground pepper

About 2½ cups diced cooked corned beef (recipe below)

¼ cup milk

Scrub potatoes and boil in water to cover until tender when pierced with a knife, about 30 minutes. Drain, and when cool enough to handle, remove skin and dice or coarsely chop potatoes.

To make hash mixture, heat 1 tablespoon oil in a small saucepan over moderately-low heat. Stir in onion and pepper and cook 6 to 7 minutes, until onion is translucent and tender.

Put vegetables into a large bowl. Stir in 1 teaspoon salt and ½ teaspoon pepper. Add 2½ cups meat and 4 cups potatoes. (If you have more meat, add it along with about ¾ cup potatoes per ½ cup meat.) Sprinkle with milk. Mix with a large fork or spoon. Taste; add more seasoning if you wish, but keep in mind that flavor will develop on standing. Cover hash and refrigerate until next day.

To brown hash, heat 1 tablespoon oil in one or two large nonstick skillets over moderate to moderately-high heat. Add hash mixture and press down with pancake turner. Cook 5 to 6 minutes, until browned on bottom. Turn hash in three or four large chunks, press down again, and cook 5 to 6 minutes longer. Repeat once more. Hash should be nicely browned and very hot. Keep warm in 200°F. oven until ready to serve. *Make 6 servings.*

CORNED BEEF FOR HASH

1 2 to 2½ pound uncooked corned beef brisket

Flavorings: 1 small carrot; 2-inch piece celery stalk; 5 peppercorns; 1 clove; 1 sprig parsley

Remove corned beef from package and rinse with cold water. Put into a medium-sized pan, add enough water to just cover, and bring to a boil over moderately-high heat. Add flavorings and boil about 2 minutes. Reduce heat, until water is no longer boiling but just giving an occasional bubble. (If meat boils fast during the entire cooking time, it may toughen.)

Cook meat about 3 hours, or until fork-tender (poke in several places). When done, remove pot from heat and let stand 15 minutes or longer. Remove meat from liquid (discard liquid) and let stand until cool enough to handle. (Or cover and refrigerate until next day.)

Remove fat from cooled meat. Cut meat into ¼- to ½-inch dice. You should have about 2½ cups meat.

SHOPPING GUIDE

(If you elect to make Corned Beef Hash in a Hurry, add ingredients and delete those in Homemade Corned Beef Hash.)

2½ cups all-purpose flour

½ cup plus 1 tablespoon dark brown sugar

3 tablespoons granulated sugar

1 envelope active dry yeast

1½ teaspoons ground cinnamon

1½ teaspoons vanilla extract

5 peppercorns

1 clove

1 cup (3½ ounces) broken pecans or very small pecan halves

3 tablespoons (1 ounce) Zante currants or dark raisins

1 cup (6 ounces) pitted prunes

¼ cup honey

½ cup chili sauce

½ cup salsa

2 tablespoons pure olive or vegetable oil

English muffins, ½ or more per person

2 or 3 lemons

3 pounds (about 6 medium-sized) firm ripe pears

1 medium-sized onion (1 cup chopped)

1 large red, yellow, or green bell pepper (1 cup chopped)

1½ to 2 pounds russet (baking) potatoes

For flavoring: 1 small carrot; 2-inch piece celery, parsley sprig

1 2- to 2½-pound uncooked corned beef brisket

continued

SHOPPING GUIDE *cont'd*

6 tablespoons milk

3 tablespoons (about ½ stick) unsalted butter

Eggs to poach or fry, 1 or 2 per person

(Coffee? Tea? Add what you need, also butter for the table.)

CORNED BEEF HASH IN A HURRY

1 12-ounce can corned beef

6 3-ounce frozen hash-brown potato patties, thawed

½ teaspoon freshly-ground pepper
 About 3 tablespoons pure olive or vegetable oil

1 cup finely chopped onion

1 large red, yellow, or green bell pepper, seeded and cut into ¼-inch pieces

Scrape off any exterior fat from corned beef and crumble meat into a bowl. Break up hash-brown patties, add to beef, sprinkle with pepper, and mix well.

Heat 1 tablespoon of oil in a nonstick skillet 8 to 10 inches across the bottom. Add onion and bell pepper and cook 4 to 5 minutes over moderately-high heat, stirring several times, until wilted. Add to corned beef mixture and mix well.

Add remaining 2 tablespoons oil to skillet and place over moderately-high heat. When oil is hot, add hash mixture; press down firmly with pancake turner and cook 7 to 8 minutes, without stirring, until browned on the bottom. Turn hash in three or four clumps (add another tablespoon of oil if pan seems dry). Press hash down again and reduce heat to moderate. Cook about 10 minutes longer, turning hash and pressing it down twice more, until crisp and well browned. *Makes 6 servings.*

Special Chili Salsa

½ cup chili sauce

½ cup salsa

Mix sauces together. *Makes 1 cup.*

Supersticky Cinnamon Rolls

Cinnamon Roll Dough (recipe
    follows)
1 cup (3½ ounces) broken pecans or
    very small pecan halves
½ cup packed dark brown sugar

2 tablespoons milk
3 tablespoons granulated sugar
1½ teaspoons ground cinnamon
2 tablespoons unsalted butter, at
    room temperature

Make up the dough, and while it is rising heat oven to 375°F. Spread pecans on a cookie sheet and bake 8 to 12 minutes, shaking once or twice, until lightly toasted (turn off oven).

Grease a 9-inch springform pan. Place it on a 12-inch length of foil and bring foil up around the sides. (Springform pans are rarely water-tight, and foil will catch drips.)

Put brown sugar and milk in springform pan and stir until sugar dissolves and forms a syrup. Spread syrup evenly in bottom of pan.

Mix pecans, granulated sugar, and cinnamon in a small bowl.

Punch down dough with clenched fist. Put dough onto a lightly floured board and, using a lightly floured rolling pin, roll dough into a rectangle about 12 × 7 inches (have a long side nearest you).

With a rubber spatula, spread butter over dough leaving a ½-inch border all around. Sprinkle with pecan mixture. Starting with long side nearest you, roll up dough like a jelly-roll. Cut roll into 12 slices. Place slices flat in prepared springform pan. Cover and let rise 15 to 25 minutes, until nearly doubled in bulk. Heat oven to 375°F. when dough seems to be almost ready.

Place springform pan on a cookie sheet and bake 20 to 25 minutes, until rolls are browned. Immediately invert pan onto a round serving platter; let stand at least 2 minutes, while syrup runs down sides. Remove pan. Let rolls cool at least 20 minutes before eating. *Makes 12 rolls.*

Cinnamon Roll Dough

If you don't have an electric mixer with a dough hook, use hand method at end, or start with mixer and switch to hand method when the going gets too tough for your mixer.

⅔ cup very warm water (110° to 115°F.)

1 tablespoon packed dark brown sugar

1 envelope active dry yeast

2 to 2¼ cups all-purpose flour

1 tablespoon unsalted butter, at room temperature

1 teaspoon vanilla extract

½ teaspoon salt

3 tablespoons (1 ounce) Zante currants or dark raisins

Put water, sugar, and yeast in bowl of an electric mixer fitted with a paddle (or beaters, if no paddle). Mix on low speed, then let stand 2 minutes; yeast will swell and dissolve.

Add 1 cup of the flour, then butter, vanilla, and salt. Mix on low speed, then beat on medium speed for 2 minutes. Mix in enough of remaining flour to make a soft dough that begins to leave sides of bowl (or, if you are using beaters, as much flour as the machine can handle). Mix in currants.

Switch to a dough hook and knead at medium speed for 2 to 3 minutes, until dough is smooth and elastic. (Or remove dough to floured countertop, work in as much flour as needed, and knead dough by hand for 10 minutes.) Transfer dough to a large greased bowl and turn dough over so greased side is up. Cover bowl with plastic wrap and let rise in a warm place 30 to 45 minutes, or until dough is doubled in volume. Punch down dough. Roll and fill as directed above.

HAND METHOD: Put water, sugar, and yeast into a large bowl; stir briefly until yeast dissolves. Add butter, cut in small pieces; add vanilla, salt, and 1 cup of flour. Stir, then beat with a wooden spoon about 2 minutes. Stir in enough of remaining flour to make a fairly stiff dough that leaves sides of bowl. Mix in currants. Turn out dough onto a floured board (use some of remaining flour) and knead 8 to 10 minutes, until dough is smooth and elastic. Transfer dough to a large greased bowl and continue as directed above.

Breakfast Treats for Pumpkin Pickers

It's fun to have a breakfast party before driving to the nearest farm stand to pick up pumpkins for carving. I particularly enjoy going to a place where you can walk around the pumpkin patch and make your own selection. Of course, living as I do in a tiny city apartment, it is the cutest small pumpkin that goes home with me. I also go through the boxes of apples and pick out lots of little ones. We have found that young children are enchanted when given a bag of very small apples as a "treat."

If I have to make do with pumpkins from a city Greenmarket, then I like to invite children and adults to a costume-making session preceded, of course, by a hearty breakfast. For spooky fun, draw the curtains and serve breakfast by candlelight. The tangerines-turned-into-pumpkins will glow in the light, as will the appropriately blood-red Cranberry-Red Zinger Tea.

M E N U

FOR 6

*TANGERINES MASQUERADING AS PUMPKINS

RAISINS AND PUMPKIN SEEDS

*CHOCOLATE CHIP PANCAKES

VANILLA YOGURT

*CRANBERRY-RED ZINGER TEA

*RECIPE FOLLOWS

GAME PLAN

THE DAY BEFORE YOU MAY:
- Mix dry ingredients for pancakes.
- Mix raisins and pumpkin seeds in one or more serving bowls.

ABOUT 1 HOUR BEFORE SERVING:
- Make Tangerines Masquerading as Pumpkins.
- Put vanilla yogurt in a serving bowl.
- Heat oven to 200°F. to keep pancakes warm.
- Mix pancake batter; make pancakes; keep warm.
- Make Cranberry-Red Zinger Tea.

Tangerines Masquerading as Pumpkins

The first tangerines of the new season usually appear in the supermarket just in time to do this Halloween trick!

6 tangerines
Whole cloves

Broken pieces of cinnamon stick (optional)

In one side of each tangerine insert two cloves for the "pumpkin's" eyes and one for the nose. With the point of a small sharp knife, cut a mouth shape in the tangerine skin and remove the piece of skin.

Make a small hole in the skin in the top of each tangerine. Then stick in a small broken piece of cinnamon stick or another clove for the "pumpkin's" stem.

Put a "pumpkin" on a small plate at each place setting. *Makes 6 "pumpkins."*

Chocolate Chip Pancakes

For an adult party you may want to use 3 to 5 ounces of bittersweet Swiss chocolate, chopped into tiny chunks, instead of the chocolate chips. You may also add 2 tablespoons dark rum to the batter.

2½ cups all-purpose flour
2 tablespoons granulated sugar
2 tablespoons baking powder
½ teaspoon salt
4 large eggs
2 cups milk
8 tablespoons (1 stick) unsalted butter, melted and cooled

1 teaspoon vanilla extract
1 cup (6 ounces) semisweet chocolate minichips
Vegetable oil
About 1 tablespoon confectioners' sugar

Mix flour, granulated sugar, baking powder, and salt in a large bowl.

Beat eggs in a medium-sized bowl with a fork or wire whisk until frothy. Add milk, butter, and vanilla. Whisk to mix. Pour into flour mixture; add chocolate chips. Stir until about half mixed, then beat briefly to get rid of flour lumps.

Heat oven to 200°F. to keep pancakes warm.

Heat a griddle or large nonstick skillet over moderately-high heat. Brush lightly with oil; reduce heat to moderate. For each pancake, spoon a scant ¼ cup batter onto griddle. Cook about 2 minutes, until bubbles form on top and undersides are browned. Turn and cook 1 to 2 minutes longer. Arrange on serving platter. Sprinkle with the confectioners' sugar; serve with vanilla yogurt. *Makes 25 to 30 pancakes.*

Cranberry-Red Zinger Tea

This drink is delicious hot or chilled.

6 cups water
4 Red Zinger tea bags

1 48-ounce bottle cranberry juice
cocktail

Bring water to a boil in a large stainless steel or enameled saucepan or Dutch oven; add tea bags. Cover pan, remove from heat, and let tea infuse 5 minutes.

Remove tea bags. Add cranberry juice. Heat to a simmer or chill. *Makes 12 1-cup servings.*

SHOPPING GUIDE

2½ cups all-purpose flour
2 tablespoons granulated sugar
About 1 tablespoon confectioners' sugar
2 tablespoons baking powder
18 to 24 whole cloves
Few pieces broken cinnamon sticks (optional)
1 teaspoon vanilla extract
1 cup (6 ounces) semisweet chocolate minichips
2 cups (about 12 ounces) sunflower seeds or pumpkin seeds, hulled, but not toasted
1½ cups (7½ to 8 ounces) raisins
1 48-ounce bottle cranberry juice cocktail
4 Red Zinger tea bags
Vegetable oil

6 tangerines

2 cups milk
2 8-ounce containers vanilla yogurt
8 tablespoons (1 stick) unsalted butter
4 large eggs

(Coffee? Tea? Add what you need, also butter for the table.)

Hearty Fare for a Country Weekend

M E N U

FOR 8

*BAKED APPLE FANS

*OATMEAL HOTCAKES

BROWN-SUGAR SYRUP
OR
MAPLE SYRUP

*HOMEMADE SAGE AND
THYME SAUSAGE PATTIES

*PUMPKIN WALNUT
MUFFINS

*RECIPE FOLLOWS

Your houseguests may threaten to become permanent boarders when you serve them this warming breakfast, which is full of good flavors we associate with fall: apples, oatmeal, brown sugar, sage, thyme, and pumpkin. This menu works best if you have two ovens, one in which you can keep the hotcakes warm, while the apple fans bake in the other. Pretty to look at and delicious to eat, the apple fans are simply a refined version of baked apples (and much easier to eat).

Because they contain a relatively high proportion of oatmeal, the hotcakes are moister and less fluffy than regular pancakes and have a wonderful oat flavor. The recipe makes three or four pancakes per person, which is just right if you're making the complete menu. If you're not serving the muffins, you may want to increase the hotcake recipe by half. You'll find the quantities to use at the end of the hotcake recipe.

Baked Apple Fans

Choose an apple that doesn't turn to mush when baked. Look on country farm stands for Golden Delicious apples with brown russeting on the skin; I find these apples have the best flavor.

4 large apples such as Golden
   Delicious, Granny Smith, or
   Greenings

2 tablespoons unsalted butter, melted
1 tablespoon granulated sugar
⅛ teaspoon ground cinnamon

Heat oven to 425°F. Peel, halve, and core apples. Put each half, cut side down, on a board and slice very thinly crosswise, keeping the slices together. Put each sliced half on a nonstick cookie sheet and push down lightly with heel of hand so it fans slightly.

Brush apple fans thoroughly with melted butter. (Apples may be refrigerated for about an hour at this point; if sealed well with butter, they won't brown.) Mix sugar and cinnamon; sprinkle over apples. Bake about 15 minutes, until apples are tender. If desired, broil briefly to brown edges. *Makes 8 apple fans.*

Oatmeal Hotcakes

Quantities are given below for increasing the hotcake recipe by half.

1 quart milk
1½ cups old-fashioned oats
4 tablespoons (½ stick) unsalted
   butter, cut in small pieces
3 cups all-purpose flour

1 tablespoon baking powder
½ teaspoon salt
1 large egg
⅓ cup packed dark brown sugar
   Vegetable oil

In a medium-sized saucepan heat milk until bubbles appear around the edge. Remove from heat and stir in oats and butter. Let stand 20 minutes, while oats soften and cool and butter melts.

Meanwhile, mix flour, baking powder, and salt in a small bowl. Beat egg and sugar in a large bowl until sugar dissolves. Add oat mixture and flour mixture; stir until flour is incorporated (mixture will still look slightly lumpy).

Place griddle or large nonstick skillet over high heat. When hot, brush lightly with oil and reduce heat to moderate. Make pancakes, using ¼ cup batter for each. Cook 1 to 2 minutes, until pancakes are browned on the underside and bubbles break on surface. Turn pan-

GAME PLAN

UP TO 2 DAYS AHEAD:
◆ Mix ingredients for Homemade Sage and Thyme Sausage Patties; cover and refrigerate.
◆ Make Brown-Sugar Syrup (see page 7).

THE DAY BEFORE YOU MAY:
◆ Make Oatmeal Hotcakes batter. (Or mix dry ingredients and leave at room temperature.)
◆ Mix dry ingredients for Pumpkin Walnut Muffins batter; get out pan and remaining ingredients.

ABOUT 1½ HOURS BEFORE SERVING:
◆ Heat oven to 400°F. Prepare muffin batter and bake.
◆ Cut apples for Baked Apple Fans; brush with butter; refrigerate.
◆ Shape sausage patties and cook.
◆ When muffins are baked, turn oven to 425°F. Bake apple fans.
◆ Put Brown-Sugar Syrup on to warm.
◆ Cook Oatmeal Hotcakes; as soon as apple fans are baked, turn oven to 200°F. (leave door open a few minutes to cool oven) so you can keep hotcakes warm.

SHOPPING GUIDE

4½ cups all-purpose flour
1½ cups old-fashioned oats
1 pound light brown sugar or
  maple syrup
⅔ cup dark brown sugar
2 tablespoons granulated sugar
5 teaspoons baking powder
1 teaspoon baking soda
1⅛ teaspoons ground cinnamon
¼ teaspoon ground ginger
½ teaspoon nutmeg, freshly-
  grated or from a jar
1½ teaspoons dried sage leaves
1 teaspoon dried thyme leaves
½ cup (3 ounces) dark raisins or
  Zante currants
¾ cup (3 ounces) walnuts
1 16-ounce can plain pumpkin
1 tablespoon Worcestershire
  sauce
2 tablespoons pure olive or vegetable oil
Foil baking cups for muffins

4 large apples (Golden Delicious, Granny Smith, or
  Greenings)

2 pounds coarsely-ground lean
  pork

1 quart milk
10 tablespoons (1¼ sticks)
  unsalted butter
3 large eggs

(Coffee? Tea? Add what you
  need, also butter for the
  table.)

cakes and cook 1 to 2 minutes longer. Serve at once or cover loosely and keep warm for up to 30 minutes. *Makes 26 to 28 pancakes.*

TO INCREASE: Use these quantities for 1½ times recipe: 1½ quarts (6 cups) milk, 2¼ cups oats, 6 tablespoons (¾ stick) butter, 4½ cups flour, 1 tablespoon plus 1½ teaspoons baking powder, ¾ teaspoon salt, 2 eggs, ½ cup packed brown sugar.

Homemade Sage and Thyme Sausage Patties

Homemade sausage tends to be leaner and therefore drier than store-bought, but today most people welcome the reduction in fat and accept the difference in texture. The patties may be frozen before cooking.

2 pounds coarsely ground lean pork
1 tablespoon Worcestershire sauce
1½ teaspoons salt
1½ teaspoons dried sage leaves, crumbled
1 teaspoon dried thyme leaves, crumbled
¾ teaspoon freshly-ground pepper
2 teaspoons pure olive or vegetable oil

Put all ingredients except oil into a large bowl and mix well with hands or a large wooden spoon. Cover and refrigerate 1 to 2 days for flavor to develop.

Divide sausage in half and form each half into a 10-inch log. Cut into 10 pieces and shape each piece into a 2½-inch patty.

Heat oil in two large nonstick skillets over moderately-high heat. (Or cook sausage in two batches and keep warm in 200°F. oven.) Add patties and fry 6 to 8 minutes on each side, until browned and cooked through. Drain on paper towels. *Makes 20 patties.*

Pumpkin Walnut Muffins

1½ cups all-purpose flour
2 teaspoons baking powder
1 teaspoon baking soda
1 teaspoon ground cinnamon
½ teaspoon nutmeg, freshly-grated or from a jar
¼ teaspoon ground ginger
¼ teaspoon salt
2 large eggs
⅓ cup packed dark brown sugar

1 16-ounce can plain pumpkin
4 tablespoons (½ stick) unsalted butter, melted and slightly cooled
½ cup (3 ounces) raisins or Zante currants
¾ cup (3 ounces) walnuts, chopped
1 tablespoon granulated sugar mixed with a few grains cinnamon or nutmeg

Heat oven to 400°F. Grease twelve nonstick muffin cups or line with foil baking cups.

Mix flour, baking powder, baking soda, spices, and salt in a large bowl.

Whisk eggs and brown sugar in a medium-sized bowl until smooth. Whisk in pumpkin and butter. When incorporated, stir in raisins.

Scrape wet ingredients into dry and stir until well mixed. Fill muffin cups with batter. Place walnuts on top of batter, pressing them in just a little. Sprinkle with spiced sugar mixture.

Bake 25 to 30 minutes, until lightly browned and springy to the touch. Remove from pan and cool on wire rack. *Makes 12 muffins.*

Thanksgiving Day

M E N U

FOR 8

PLATTER OF FALL FRUITS

*MULLED CIDER AND
ORANGE JUICE

*SQUASH WAFFLES

BROWN-SUGAR SYRUP

DOUBLE-SMOKED BACON

*JIM DODGE'S NUTMEG
PEAR PIE

*RECIPE FOLLOWS

I feel strongly that a good breakfast can make a substantial contribution to a harmonious Thanksgiving celebration. The big dinner is often not served until late, late, late, by which time a temper or two may have flared—often provoked by sheer hunger. Try a hearty breakfast to keep everyone feeling well fed and friendly. I also feel that pie is appropriate fare, since our Thanksgiving celebration began in New England, where pie for breakfast is a very old custom. At breakfast time, too, you can enjoy the flavor of pie, rather than trying to force a mouthful or two when the turkey is gone and you're the one who's stuffed. No need to hunt up your pie pan! This lovely pie is assembled and baked on a cookie sheet, preferably one that has at least one side without an edge, so you can slide the pie off onto a serving board or plate. The recipe was originally developed for *Woman's Day* by Jim Dodge, the super-duper pastry chef, teacher, and writer, who now owns The American Baker in San Francisco.

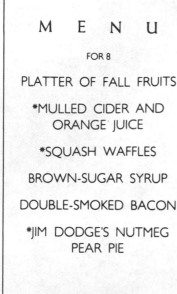

Mulled Cider and Orange Juice

Serve this cider hot or chilled.

1 *navel orange, scrubbed*
3 *whole cloves or ⅛ teaspoon ground cloves*
    About 2¾ cups orange juice (refrigerated or made from frozen concentrate)

½ *gallon apple cider or juice*
¼ *cup (1½ ounces) raisins or Zante currants*
1 *cinnamon stick (3 to 4 inches) or ½ teaspoon ground cinnamon*

Remove the peel from the orange with a knife or vegetable peeler, leaving most of the white pith behind. (Try for a pretty spiral of peel.) Stick whole cloves into the orange peel.

Squeeze orange; measure juice and add purchased juice to total 3 cups.

Put all ingredients into a large stainless steel or enameled saucepan. Cover and bring to a boil over high heat. Remove from heat and let stand at least 30 minutes to allow flavors to blend. Serve hot. Or refrigerate overnight and serve hot or chilled the next day. *Makes 11 cups.*

GAME PLAN

THE DAY BEFORE YOU MAY:
- Make Jim Dodge's Nutmeg Pear Pie.
- Make Mulled Cider and Orange Juice; refrigerate.
- Make Brown-Sugar Syrup (see page 7).
- Mix dry ingredients for Squash Waffles; leave at room temperature.

ABOUT 1 HOUR BEFORE SERVING:
- Cook bacon (see page 195).
- Rinse fruit; arrange on platter.

ABOUT 30 MINUTES BEFORE SERVING:
- Complete waffle batter; start making waffles; keep warm in 200°F. oven.
- Heat Mulled Cider and Orange Juice; serve as guests arrive.
- Heat Brown-Sugar Syrup.
- Reheat bacon briefly.

LATER:
- Serve pie.

SHOPPING GUIDE

5½ cups all-purpose flour
2 tablespoons quick-cooking
    tapioca
1 pound plus ⅓ cup light
    brown sugar
⅓ cup granulated sugar
5 teaspoons baking powder
½ teaspoon baking soda
3 whole cloves, or ⅛ teaspoon
    ground cloves
½ teaspoon ground cinnamon
3- to 4-inch cinnamon stick; or
    an additional ½ teaspoon
    ground cinnamon
½ teaspoon ground ginger
1 teaspoon nutmeg, freshly-
    grated or from a jar
1 teaspoon vanilla extract
¼ cup (1½ ounces) dark raisins
    or Zante currants

½ gallon (2 quarts) apple cider
    or apple juice
2¾ cups refrigerated orange
    juice or 1 6-ounce can frozen
    orange juice concentrate
Selection of apples, pears, and
    grapes for the fruit platter
1 navel orange
6 medium-sized ripe pears

1 12-ounce package frozen
    puréed winter squash

Double-smoked bacon (or other
    bacon), 2 or 3 slices per per-
    son

2½ cups milk
½ cup plus 1 tablespoon heavy
    cream
24 tablespoons (3 sticks)
    unsalted butter
3 large eggs

continued

Squash Waffles

3 cups all-purpose flour
5 teaspoons baking powder
½ teaspoon baking soda
½ teaspoon ground cinnamon
½ teaspoon ground ginger
½ teaspoon nutmeg, freshly grated or
    from a jar
⅛ teaspoon salt
⅛ teaspoon freshly-ground pepper

3 large eggs
⅓ cup packed light brown sugar
2½ cups milk
1 12-ounce package frozen puréed
    winter squash, thawed (1⅓
    cups)
12 tablespoons (1½ sticks) unsalted
    butter, melted and cooled

In a large bowl mix flour, baking powder, baking soda, cinnamon, ginger, nutmeg, salt, and pepper.

Break eggs into a medium-sized bowl; add brown sugar. Beat with a fork or wire whisk until any lumps of sugar have dissolved. Whisk in milk, squash, and butter. Pour over dry ingredients and mix with a spoon, until all ingredients are moistened.

Heat waffle iron and heat oven to 200°F. to keep waffles warm. Make waffles, using a scant 1 cup batter for a four-square waffle. To keep cooked waffles warm and crisp, place them directly on a rack in the oven (not on a cookie sheet). *Makes 8 waffles.*

Jim Dodge's Nutmeg Pear Pie

For a richly flavorful pie, choose pears at the peak of ripeness.

PIE CRUST:

2¼ cups all-purpose flour
 1 tablespoon granulated sugar
 ¼ teaspoon salt

12 tablespoons (1½ sticks) cold
     unsalted butter, cut in ½-inch
     pieces
 ½ cup heavy cream

FILLING:

 ¼ cup granulated sugar
 2 tablespoons quick-cooking tapioca
 1 teaspoon vanilla extract
 ½ teaspoon nutmeg, freshly-grated or
     from a jar

 6 medium-sized ripe pears, peeled,
     quartered, cored, and cut in ¾-
     inch chunks (about 6 cups)
 1 tablespoon heavy cream
 2 teaspoons granulated sugar

To make pie crust: Mix flour, sugar, and salt in a medium-sized bowl. Add butter. Rub in with your fingers (or cut in with pastry blender or 2 knives), until butter pieces are the size of small peas. Add cream and mix with rubber spatula until dough comes together and is pliable. Divide dough in half. Shape into flattened rounds. Wrap in plastic or wax paper and refrigerate.

To make filling: Mix sugar, tapioca, vanilla, and nutmeg in a large bowl. Add pears and toss until evenly coated. Heat oven to 425°F.

To assemble pie: Have a cookie sheet ready. On a lightly floured surface roll out one portion of dough to a 10-inch-diameter circle. Trim ragged edges. (Save scraps.) Transfer to ungreased cookie sheet. Spread filling over dough to within 1 inch of edge, mounding it in center. Brush edge with water. Roll out remaining dough in same way and place over filling. Press edges to seal, then fold up and crimp with fork. Brush top crust with cream.

To decorate pie: Roll out some of the scraps, cut into leaf shapes, and mark veins with knife. Form more of the scraps into small pears and insert a clove for the stem. Arrange leaves and pears on pie; brush with cream. Cut four ½-inch steam vents in top crust. Sprinkle sugar over top.

Bake 15 minutes, then reduce oven temperature to 375°F. Bake 40 minutes longer, or until top is golden brown and steam comes out of vents in crust. If pastry decorations brown too quickly, cover them loosely with foil. Cool on cookie sheet on wire rack. Carefully lift to serving plate using two wide spatulas, or slide pie onto a flat board. Serve at room temperature. *Makes 8 servings.*

SHOPPING GUIDE *cont'd*
(Coffee? Tea? Add what you
 need, also butter for the
 table.)

WINTER

Sally Maria Stinson

Come Trim the Tree

This festive menu will enhance the season's merry mood. There's creamy-rich hot cereal, lots of fruit (you may want to choose two out of the three fruit dishes), and a fruited quick bread shaped like a tree. Since guests often arrive bearing gifts of holiday cookies, leave space for a trayful on the buffet.

Advice from one who learned the hard way: if you'll be decorating a live Christmas tree in a pot, be sure to get it in place the night before, so you aren't vacuuming spilled soil as guests drive up to the house! Set out the decorations on a table near the tree, and don't forget ribbons or wires to hang them with. Looping tiny lights on the tree can be done ahead, too, and cranberries and popcorn can be readied for stringing.

This get-together is a nice indulgence for adults, especially for good friends who may be far from your fold on Christmas Day itself.

M E N U

FOR 10 TO 12

*CHESTNUT AND ORANGE BOWL

*PINK GRAPEFRUIT SECTIONS WTH HONEY

*CRANBERRY-POACHED PEARS

*FINNISH BARLEY PORRIDGE

FRIED HAM STEAKS

*BAKED MUSHROOMS

*ROSEMARY HOME-FRIES

CHRISTMAS COOKIES

*QUICK CHRISTMAS TREE BREAD

*RECIPE FOLLOWS

GAME PLAN

Check to be sure you have enough skillets: one large or two smaller ones for the potatoes; one large one (or a griddle) for the ham steaks.

UP TO 2 WEEKS AHEAD:

◆ Make and shape Christmas Tree Bread; freeze unbaked.

THE DAY BEFORE:

◆ Wipe mushrooms clean with paper towels (do not wash mushrooms a day ahead); trim stem ends. Quarter mushrooms; put in a bowl; cover with plastic wrap; refrigerate.

◆ Make Cranberry-poached Pears and Pink Grapefruit Sections with Honey.

THE DAY BEFORE YOU MAY ALSO:

◆ Bake Quick Christmas Tree Bread (if frozen, do not thaw); when cooled, wrap tightly and leave at room temperature.

◆ Cook and cut up potatoes for Rosemary Home-fries (although flavor is best when they are boiled the day they are to be fried).

ABOUT 1½ TO 2 HOURS BEFORE SERVING:

◆ Heat oven to 425°F. and bake Quick Christmas Tree Bread.

◆ Boil and cut up potatoes for Rosemary Home-fries.

◆ Turn oven down to 400°F.

continued

Chestnut and Orange Bowl

This is one of my all-time favorites—the sweet chestnuts contrasting with the tart oranges. It is a dessert that has migrated to breakfast because whenever I serve it for dinner, I hope there will be some left for the next morning!

10 small navel oranges *1 10-ounce jar chestnut pieces (or whole chestnuts) in heavy syrup*

Peel the oranges (see page 186). Slice thinly crosswise and put into a serving bowl. Pour chestnuts and syrup over oranges. Cover and chill at least 12 hours, turning oranges gently once or twice. *Makes 10 servings.*

Pink Grapefruit Sections with Honey

For a pretty effect, scatter pomegranate seeds over the grapefruit just before serving (see page 188).

½ cup honey *9 pounds pink or ruby red grapefruit*

Measure honey in a 2-cup measure.

Peel grapefruit (see page 186).

Working over a bowl, cut out each grapefruit section until you're left with a handful of membrane. Squeeze membrane over honey to extract remaining juice.

When all grapefruit are peeled and sectioned, mix juice and honey. Add to grapefruit sections and mix gently. Refrigerate until serving time. *Makes 10 to 12 servings.*

Cranberry-poached Pears

Choose firm, ripe pears—Comice, Anjou, Bosc, or Bartlett all work well. Cranberry juice imparts a lovely flavor and a deep mauve pink color. There is bound to be poaching liquid left after all the pears are gone; save it for poaching more pears (or apples), or add ice and seltzer for a refreshing drink.

117

W   I   N   T   E   R

2 12-ounce cans frozen concentrated	1½ cups water
cranberry juice cocktail	3 pounds (about 6) firm, ripe pears

Bring cranberry juice and water to a boil in a deep stainless steel or enameled saucepan or Dutch oven.

Peel, halve, and core pears; cut each half into 3 wedges.

Add pears to liquid. Reduce heat to low so that liquid does not boil or even simmer, but so that an occasional ripple breaks the surface. Cook 15 to 25 minutes, until pears are just tender; gently move pears around with a rubber spatula once or twice during cooking. Cool in pan or transfer pears and liquid to serving bowl. Cover and refrigerate overnight. *Makes 12 servings.*

Finnish Barley Porridge

This porridge is usually made with pearl barley, which takes close to an hour to cook. I use barley flakes, which not only cook more quickly but have more of the whole grain. Buy barley flakes where health food is sold. Even though it is slightly sweet, barley or rice porridge is often served in Scandinavia as part of the main course at a holiday meal. Hide a whole blanched almond in the porridge; it is said that the person who finds it will have a very lucky New Year. The currants are a personal addition.

9 cups water	½ cup heavy or light cream or half-
1 1-pound package barley flakes	and-half
1 teaspoon salt	½ teaspoon vanilla extract
4 cups (1 quart) milk	½ cup (2¼ ounces) Zante currants
¾ cup granulated sugar	1 blanched almond (optional)

Bring water, barley flakes, and salt to a boil in a heavy 6- to 8-quart saucepan over high heat. Reduce heat to low, cover, and simmer 20 to 25 minutes, stirring two or three times, until practically all water has been absorbed.

Add milk and bring to a boil over moderately-high heat. Reduce heat to low, cover, and simmer 10 minutes longer, until thickened and creamy. Remove from heat. Stir in sugar, cream, and vanilla. Add currants. To keep porridge hot, place saucepan in a larger pan of simmering water for up to 30 minutes. Add a little more milk or water if porridge thickens on standing, but do not stir it too much. Add almond just before serving. *Makes about 12 cups, 15 to 20 servings.*

GAME PLAN *cont'd*
- Start cooking Finnish Barley Porridge (keep warm as directed).
- Prepare mushrooms and bake (add cornstarch after 20 to 25 minutes).
- Fry Rosemary Home-fries.

LAST MINUTE:
- Fry ham steaks (see p. 197); keep warm in 200°F. oven up to 20 minutes.

CURRANT CONFUSION

Zante currants are a dried tiny grape. Look for them next to raisins (also a dried grape) in the supermarket.

Fresh red and black currants (there are white ones, too) are now turning up more frequently in farmers' markets and specialty produce stores. Put a string of red or black currants in your mouth, pull off the cranberry-size fruits with your teeth, and pop the tart-sweet berries against the roof of your mouth. Red currants and black currants grow on bushes; they are not related to Zante currants, which are the fruit of a vine. If you don't see fresh currants, try red currant jelly or black currant preserves.

SHOPPING GUIDE

Ingredients are included for one Quick Christmas Tree Bread. Check the recipe and add additional ingredients if you elect to make two breads.

2½ cups all-purpose flour
1 1-pound package barley flakes (resemble old-fashioned oats; check hot-cereal section of health-food store)
2 teaspoons cornstarch
About 1 cup granulated sugar
1 tablespoon baking powder
1½ teaspoons pumpkin pie spice or ground cinnamon; or ¾ teaspoon ground cinnamon and ¾ teaspoon ground cloves or ground allspice
½ teaspoon vanilla extract
¾ cup (3¾ ounces) Zante currants
¾ cup (4 ounces) diced dried-fruit mix (or make your own, mixing raisins, currants, snipped dried apricots, apples, and prunes)
1 blanched almond (optional)
1 10-ounce jar chestnut pieces (or whole chestnuts) in heavy syrup
½ cup honey
6 tablespoons pure olive oil
¼ cup vegetable oil

9 pounds (about 9) pink or ruby red grapefruit
10 small navel oranges
3 pounds (about 6) firm, ripe pears
1 lemon

continued

Baked Mushrooms

Although you can find several exotic kinds of mushroom in supermarkets, common white mushrooms are best for this delicious, easy-to-serve dish.

1½ pounds (about 8 cups) fresh mushrooms, quartered
1 cup sliced scallions
2 tablespoons freshly-squeezed lemon juice
2 tablespoons unsalted butter, cut in small pieces
2 tablespoons pure olive oil
½ teaspoon salt
¼ teaspoon freshly-ground pepper
2 teaspoons cornstarch
1 tablespoon cold water

Heat oven to 400°F. Put mushrooms in a baking pan or dish approximately 13 × 9 inches. Add scallions, lemon juice, butter, olive oil, salt, and pepper; mix well.

Bake 20 to 25 minutes, stirring 3 or 4 times, until mushrooms are tender and have released their juices.

Mix cornstarch and water in a cup; stir into mushrooms. Bake 10 minutes longer, stirring 3 or 4 times, until mushroom juices are slightly thickened. *Makes 10 to 12 servings.*

Rosemary Home-fries

Simply the best breakfast potatoes.

3 pounds all-purpose potatoes, scrubbed
¼ cup vegetable oil
¼ cup pure olive oil
2 cups sliced onions
1 teaspoon salt
½ teaspoon freshly-ground pepper
1½ teaspoons chopped fresh rosemary leaves; or ¾ teaspoon dried rosemary, crumbled

Put potatoes in a large pot; add water to cover. Cover pot and bring to a boil over high heat. Reduce heat to moderately-low and simmer 20 to 25 minutes, until potatoes are fork-tender. Drain, cool, and cut into 1-inch chunks (no need to peel).

Choose one deep heavy skillet 10 to 11 inches across the bottom, or two smaller skillets. Add oils and heat over high heat. Add potatoes, onions, salt, and pepper. Stir well.

Reduce heat to moderate and cook 20 to 25 minutes, turning potatoes frequently, until browned and crisp. Add rosemary and cook 5 minutes longer. *Makes 10 to 12 servings.*

Quick Christmas Tree Bread

You might want to make two of these.

⅔ cup milk
½ cup granulated sugar
1 large egg, yolk and white
 separated
¾ cup (4 ounces) diced dried-fruit
 mix (or make your own,
 mixing raisins, currants,
 snipped dried apricots, apples,
 prunes—whatever's on hand)
2½ cups all-purpose flour
1 tablespoon baking powder

1½ teaspoons pumpkin pie spice or
 ground cinnamon; or ¾
 teaspoon ground cinnamon, and
 ¾ teaspoon ground cloves or
 ground allspice
½ teaspoon salt
8 tablespoons (1 stick) cold, unsalted
 butter, cut in small pieces
 Granulated sugar or Homemade
 Vanilla Pearl Sugar (see page
 29)

Check to see that one rack is in bottom third of oven and heat oven to 425°F.

Measure milk in a 2-cup measure; add sugar and egg yolk; stir to mix well. Stir in dried fruit. Let stand until ready to use.

Put flour, baking powder, spice, and salt into a large bowl; stir to mix well. Add butter and cut in with pastry blender or rub in with fingers, until mixture looks like fine granules.

Stir milk mixture and pour over flour mixture. Stir with a fork until a soft dough forms. Turn out dough onto a lightly floured surface and give 10 kneads. (If very sticky, let stand 3 or 4 minutes or add a little more flour.) Cut off about one-fourth of the dough. Put remaining dough on an ungreased cookie sheet at least 16 inches long. Using both rolling pin and fingers, pat and roll dough into a flat triangle about 12 inches long and 9 inches wide across the bottom. With scissors, make about ten diagonal cuts down each long side of the triangle, cutting to within about 1 inch of the center.

Shape a small piece of reserved dough into a trunk at bottom of tree and remaining dough into a "pot." Dough may now be covered with plastic wrap and refrigerated for a couple of hours or frozen for up to 2 weeks.

Bake tree 10 minutes. Beat egg white with a fork until broken up. Brush over hot bread; sprinkle with sugar. Bake 5 to 8 minutes longer, until light brown. With two spatulas, carefully transfer tree to a wire rack. If possible, cool at least 2 hours before serving. Let guests break off small pieces. *Makes 10 to 12 small servings.*

SHOPPING GUIDE *cont'd*

1 pomegranate (optional)
3 pounds all-purpose potatoes
1½ pounds fresh mushrooms
2 medium-sized onions (2 cups
 sliced)
1 to 2 bunches scallions (1 cup
 sliced)
Fresh rosemary (enough for 1½
 teaspoons chopped) or ¾
 teaspoon dried rosemary

2 12-ounce cans frozen concentrated cranberry juice cocktail

4 or 5 ham steaks, about 12
 ounces each, cut about ⅝
 inch thick

Almost 5 cups (1 quart plus ½
 pint) milk
½ cup heavy or light cream or
 half-and-half
10 tablespoons (1¼ stick)
 unsalted butter
1 large egg

(Coffee? Tea? Add what you
 need.)

Christmas Morning Feast

M E N U

FOR 10

*PROVIDENCE HOT APPLES

*SCRAMBLED EGGS WITH
CHEDDAR AND PARSLEY

*SWEDISH POTATO
SAUSAGE

*EASY GINGERBREAD
PEOPLE WITH
CINNAMON-HONEY
BUTTER

*DUTCH ALMOND
CHRISTMAS PASTRIES

*RECIPE FOLLOWS

After the excited rustling of tissue paper and squeezing of Christmas stockings, guessing what the bumps and bulges could turn out to be, both children and adults are starving. Most of this breakfast can be prepared ahead, making Christmas morning pleasant for the cook, too.

Both the Easy Gingerbread People and the Dutch Almond Christmas Pastries can be made ahead and frozen, unbaked. Both call for baking powder doughs: the gingerbread people, because it saves time over the usual yeast dough; the Dutch pastries, because the traditional puff pastry is very high in calories. In their native Holland, where they are called *banket*, the Dutch pastries are often shaped into an initial. I find a ring much easier to do but, in any case, the baked pastries are less than an inch high.

The Swedish Potato Sausage has meat as well as potatoes in it. If you live in an area with many people of Scandinavian heritage (in Minneapolis, for example), you may be able to buy very good potato sausage at a Scandinavian delicatessen. Otherwise, you'll find it quite easy to make at home.

Providence Hot Apples

This Providence is in Rhode Island, and the recipe is divine. Whenever I stay in a hotel I get a bad case of cabin fever. Early in the morning, I head for fresh air and a local coffee shop for breakfast. That's how, when in Providence for the Newspaper Food Editors and Writers meeting one year, I found a coffee shop called Duck Soup. The enticing breakfast menu included corned-beef hash, Texas-sized French toast, and these eye-opening hot apples.

⅔ cup granulated sugar
1½ teaspoons ground cinnamon

4 pounds (about 8) Granny Smith
or other tart apples

Mix sugar and cinnamon in a large bowl. Peel, quarter, and core the apples; cut them into ½-inch chunks. Add to cinnamon-sugar; toss to coat. If you wish, cover bowl and refrigerate overnight.

Heat oven to 400°F. Butter one or two 13 × 9-inch baking dishes. Add apples (including all the cinnamon sugar) and spread them out. Bake 20 minutes, stirring 3 or 4 times, until apples are tender but not mushy. Serve very hot. *Makes 10 servings.*

NOTE: You'll probably want to do all the apple-peeling ahead of time, but if you do it just before baking, you can put the cut-up apples in the greased baking dish(es), sprinkle them with the sugar and cinnamon, and toss to coat. Note also that the apples will shrink during cooking from about 12 cups raw to 8 cups cooked.

PEELING AND CORING APPLES

A swivel-bladed vegetable peeler is the best tool for peeling apples. To core apples (except when they are to be baked whole), either cut the apple in half and scoop out the core with a melon baller (my friend Miriam Rubin's trick), or quarter the apples and make a V-shaped cut where the core is. An apple corer is used only when you plan to bake apples whole.

GAME PLAN

This menu is easier if you have two ovens, as there are a number of dishes to be baked at the last minute or kept warm.

UP TO 1 MONTH AHEAD:
◆ Make Almond Filling for Dutch Almond Christmas Pastries.

UP TO 2 WEEKS AHEAD:
◆ Make dough for Easy Gingerbread People; shape on foil-lined cookie sheet; freeze hard; wrap tightly.
◆ Make Dutch Almond Christmas Pastries; freeze unbaked; wrap tightly.

THE DAY BEFORE:
◆ Make Swedish Potato Sausage; form into patties (if stuffing into sausage casings, make mixture two days ahead).
◆ Shred cheese.
◆ Chop parsley; refrigerate in two separate batches.
◆ Make Cinnamon-Honey Butter.

THE DAY BEFORE YOU MAY ALSO:
◆ Bake gingerbread people; cool completely; wrap in plastic bags; leave at room temperature.
◆ Peel and cut up apples for Providence Hot Apples; toss with cinnamon and sugar.

continued

GAME PLAN *cont'd*

ABOUT 1½ HOURS BEFORE SERVING:
- Heat oven to 425°F. If not already done, bake gingerbread people (if frozen, do not thaw).
- Bake Dutch Almond Christmas Pastries (if frozen, do not thaw).
- Remove Cinnamon-Honey Butter from refrigerator.
- Turn oven down to 400°F. Bake Providence Hot Apples.

ABOUT 30 MINUTES BEFORE SERVING:
- Cook Swedish Potato Sausage; keep warm in 200°F. oven.
- Break 12 eggs into each of two large bowls; whisk; add milk, salt, and pepper.

LAST MINUTE:
- Scramble eggs.

Scrambled Eggs with Cheddar and Parsley

Eggs scramble better in small batches so to cook enough for ten people, make this recipe twice. Before you scramble the eggs, check basic directions on page 193. Remember: since the eggs will continue to cook once removed from the heat, take them off just before they're as firm as you wish. The fresh parsley gives scrambled eggs a lift.

12 *large eggs*
2 *tablespoons milk*
¾ *teaspoon salt*
¼ *teaspoon freshly-ground pepper*
2 *tablespoons (¼ stick) unsalted butter*

6 *ounces cheddar cheese, shredded (1½ cups)*
2 *tablespoons chopped fresh parsley*

Break eggs into a large bowl. Add milk, salt, and pepper. Beat with a wire whisk until well broken up.

Over moderate heat, melt butter in a nonstick skillet that is 9 to 10 inches across the bottom.

Pour in eggs and scramble (see page 193), adding cheese and parsley as eggs start to thicken. Spoon onto warm serving plate. *Makes 5 or 6 servings.*

Swedish Potato Sausage

I like to shape this mixture into patties, but it may be put into sausage casings (instructions below).

1½ *pounds all-purpose potatoes, peeled and coarsely grated (3 to 4 cups)*
1 *pound lean ground beef*
½ *pound lean ground pork*
¾ *cup minced fresh onion*
1¼ *teaspoons salt*

¾ *teaspoon freshly-ground pepper*
½ *teaspoon nutmeg, freshly-grated or from a jar*
¼ *teaspoon ground allspice*
2 *tablespoons vegetable oil*
2 *tablespoons (¼ stick) unsalted butter*

Put potatoes, ground meats, onion, salt, pepper, nutmeg, and allspice into a large bowl. Stir to mix well.

Tear off a strip of wax paper, about 12 inches long, and put on countertop. Line a cookie sheet with plastic wrap.

Measure ¼-cupfuls of the sausage mixture and place on wax paper. Form into patties and put on plastic wrap in a single layer. Cover with more plastic wrap and refrigerate overnight for flavor to develop.

To cook: In a nonstick skillet that is about 10 inches across the bottom, heat 1 tablespoon each oil and butter over moderate heat. Add half the patties and cook 5 to 6 minutes on each side, turning once, until browned and cooked through. Do not overcook. Remove to serving plate and keep warm. Cook remaining patties in same way. *Makes about 20 patties.*

To put in sausage casings: Buy about 10 feet of sausage casings; rinse insides with cold running water. Using a sausage stuffer or large decorating bag, stuff freshly-mixed meat mixture into casings. Tie at each end and twist into about 10 sausages. Mix 2 quarts water with 4 tablespoons salt in a bowl or deep container. Add sausages (brine should cover them) and refrigerate up to 24 hours. Bring 3 quarts water to a boil over high heat. Add drained sausages and 3 teaspoons salt. Boil 3 minutes. Reduce heat to moderately-low and poach sausages for 30 minutes. Drain. Sausages may now be browned or immediately refrigerated until the next day.

Easy Gingerbread People with Cinnamon-Honey Butter

These are easy to shape and bake, but after baking be careful to pick them up with a pancake turner or two hands because they will break. The breads can be shaped and frozen, then baked shortly before serving. You may want to make this recipe twice to serve 10 people; if so, increase ingredients on shopping list.

⅓ cup milk
⅓ cup light molasses
2 cups all-purpose flour
2 teaspoons baking powder
¼ teaspoon baking soda
1 teaspoon ground cinnamon
1 teaspoon ground ginger
¼ teaspoon ground cloves

7 tablespoons (about 1 stick) cold unsalted butter, cut in small pieces
About 1 dozen raisins or currants for buttons and eyes
Cinnamon-Honey Butter (see recipe below)

Heat oven to 425°F. Measure milk in a glass cup measure; add molasses to the ⅔-cup mark and stir to blend.

Mix flour, baking powder, baking soda, and spices in a large bowl. Add butter and cut in with a pastry blender or rub in with fingers, until mixture looks like fine granules. Stir milk mixture and add to flour mixture. Stir with a fork to form a smooth, rather soft dough.

continued

SHOPPING GUIDE

4½ to 5 cups all-purpose flour
1½ cups granulated sugar
5 teaspoons baking powder
¼ teaspoon baking soda
¼ teaspoon ground allspice
3 teaspoons ground cinnamon
¼ teaspoon ground cloves
1 teaspoon ground ginger
½ teaspoon nutmeg, freshly-grated or from a jar
2 teaspoons almond extract
1½ cups (8 ounces) whole unblanched almonds
About 1 dozen raisins or currants (eyes and buttons for gingerbread people)
⅓ cup light molasses
1 tablespoon honey
2 tablespoons vegetable oil

4 pounds (about 8) Granny Smith or other tart apples
1 medium-sized onion (¾ cup minced)
1½ pounds all-purpose potatoes
Fresh parsley (enough for ¼ cup chopped)

1 pound lean ground beef
½ pound lean ground pork
10 feet of sausage casings (optional, and *only* if you have a sausage stuffer or large decorating bag)

1¼ cups milk
27 tablespoons (about 3½ sticks) unsalted butter
27 large eggs
12 ounces cheddar cheese (3 cups shredded)

(Coffee? Tea? Add what you need.)

To shape: Turn out dough onto a lightly floured surface and give 10 to 12 kneads. Cut dough in half. Knead each half again once or twice, then put smooth side up on an ungreased cookie sheet and shape into an 8 × 3-inch rectangle. Pinch dough about 2 inches from one of the shorter sides, making a head and neck. With scissors or knife, make a 3-inch cut in the middle of opposite end and push or pull dough apart to form legs. Cut a diagonal line in each long side for arms. With your fingers, move arms and legs into jaunty positions; shape head neatly. Pat dough so it is evenly thick. Insert raisins for eyes and buttons.

Bake about 10 minutes, until medium brown. Leave on cookie sheet and cover loosely with a dish towel. Let cool at least 10 minutes before serving or removing to a wire rack. If not serving within an hour or so, as soon as the breads are cooled, wrap them in plastic bags or they will dry out. Let guests break off pieces and eat with Cinnamon-Honey Butter. *Makes 6 to 8 servings, more as part of a buffet.*

CINNAMON-HONEY BUTTER

6 *tablespoons (¾ stick) unsalted butter, at room temperature*	1 *tablespoon honey*
	¼ *plus ⅛ teaspoon ground cinnamon*

In small bowl, beat butter smooth with a wooden spoon. Beat in honey and cinnamon. Serve at room temperature. *Makes about ⅓ cup.*

Dutch Almond Christmas Pastries

These pastries are a Christmas morning treat in Holland, where they are made with puff pastry. I like to use this easy, lower-fat biscuit dough. Thinly-rolled dough is wrapped around a slender cylinder of almond paste, then formed into a ring or an initial. The pastries can be frozen before baking. Make the filling at least 1 day ahead (or up to 1 month) so flavor can develop.

Almond Filling (see recipe below)	⅓ *cup granulated sugar*
2½ *cups all-purpose flour*	⅔ *cup milk*
1 *tablespoon baking powder*	1 *large egg, lightly beaten*
½ *teaspoon salt*	
8 *tablespoons (1 stick) cold unsalted butter, cut in small pieces*	

Scrape Almond Filling onto floured board. Knead lightly with floured hands and cut into four equal pieces.

Heat oven to 425°F. Put flour, baking powder, and salt into a large bowl; stir to mix well. Add butter and cut in with pastry blender or rub in with fingers, until mixture looks like fine granules. Add sugar; toss to distribute.

Add milk and stir with a fork, until a stiff dough forms. Turn dough onto a lightly floured board or countertop. Give 10 to 12 kneads. Cut dough in half.

Shape half the dough into a rectangle, then roll it out to a large rectangle about 20 × 6 inches, with a long side near you. Trim edges straight with knife or scissors; cut dough in half lengthwise. On the countertop between you and the dough, roll one piece of the Almond Filling to a 19-inch cylinder (use palms of hands). Roll it onto lower half of piece of dough nearest you. Brush edges of dough with beaten egg; fold upper half of dough over filling; press edges to seal. Put on ungreased cookie sheet in a ring, or shape into an initial.

Form remaining dough and filling into three more pastries.

Brush with beaten egg. Bake 20 to 24 minutes, until golden brown and shiny. Cool on wire rack. Let guests break off pieces. *Makes 4 pastries, for 8 to 10 servings.*

ALMOND FILLING

*1½ cups (8 ounces) whole unblanched
    almonds
2 large eggs*

*½ cup granulated sugar
2 teaspoons almond extract*

Heat oven or toaster-oven to 350°F. Put nuts in a baking pan and bake 10 to 15 minutes, until light brown. Cool 5 to 10 minutes.

If you have a food processor, use it to process filling ingredients to a grainy paste. Otherwise, grind nuts (in grinder or a few at a time in blender), then mix in a bowl with eggs, sugar, and almond extract.

Store Almond Filling in covered bowl in refrigerator for at least 1 day to develop flavor, and up to 1 month.

Hogmanay—A Scottish New Year

M E N U

FOR 12

CHAMPAGNE

ORANGE JUICE

*GRAPEFRUIT SECTIONS
WITH CAMPARI

*KEDGEREE AND POACHED
EGGS

*MIRIAM RUBIN'S SCOTCH
BREAD PUDDING

SPICY SAUSAGE PATTIES

*BAPS

OATCAKES

TAWNY MARMALADE

*RECIPE FOLLOWS

My mother and my father's parents were born in Scotland, so it's not surprising that Scottish lore and traditions were thoroughly instilled in me and my siblings. Among Scots, Hogmanay, or New Year's, is more important than Christmas, and is celebrated with much whooping, singing, dancing, and haggis, liberally laced with a "wee dram" (a shot of Scotch). Among the many Scottish New Year's traditions is "first-footing," or visiting friends and neighbors on New Year's Day. It is said that if the first person to set foot in your house in a new year is a tall, dark stranger, you'll have good luck all year. So plan a breakfast party and select your guests with foresight.

Welcome guests with Champagne and orange juice, which they can sip solo or mix (about fifty-fifty) to make a Mimosa.

Buy tawny marmalade and Scottish oatcakes in a specialty food department or store. Oatcakes are best crisped for ten minutes on a baking sheet in a 300°F. oven. (Do this the evening ahead, if you like.) Smoked haddock is a marvelous foil for poached eggs, and good soft yeast rolls are essential for mopping up the last creamy bits of egg yolk. Buy the spicy sausage patties or make your own (see page 93).

Grapefruit Sections with Campari

Campari is an Italian aperitif wine with a flavor that adds warm undertones to grapefruit.

⅓ cup Campari
⅓ cup granulated sugar

8 pounds (about 8) large pink
    grapefruit

Mix Campari and sugar in a serving bowl. Peel the grapefruit (see p. 186).

Working over serving bowl, cut out each section of grapefruit and let it drop into bowl. Squeeze membrane over bowl with your hands to extract remaining juice. Mix gently. Cover and chill at least 1 hour, or up to 24 hours, stirring gently once or twice. *Makes 10 to 12 servings.*

Miriam Rubin's Scotch Bread Pudding

This incredibly good bread pudding is wonderful for breakfast. Save any leftovers for a midnight snack. To serve twelve, make two puddings rather than doubling the recipe for one large pudding.

2 cups milk
1 cup heavy cream
2 large eggs
  Yolks of 2 large eggs
⅔ cup granulated sugar
2 tablespoons Scotch whisky

1 teaspoon vanilla extract
3 plain or cinnamon-raisin English
    muffins, split
1 tablespoon (⅛ stick) unsalted
    butter, at room temperature

Heat oven to 325°F. Put milk and cream in a heavy medium-sized saucepan and heat over moderate heat, until bubbles appear around edges.

While milk and cream heat, put eggs, egg yolks, sugar, whisky, and vanilla in a large bowl and whisk with a wire whisk or portable electric mixer, until pale and thick. Keep whisking while you pour in hot milk and cream; pour first half slowly, then add remainder all at once.

Butter a 9- to 9½-inch-square baking dish. Spread muffins with 1 tablespoon butter and arrange them, overlapping, split side up, in two rows in baking dish. Pour custard over muffins.

Put baking dish in a larger baking pan and fill larger pan with ½ inch hot water. (This is easier if you put larger pan in oven first.)

continued

GAME PLAN

You need two ovens to complete the menu.

UP TO ONE WEEK AHEAD:
- Bake Baps and freeze.

THE DAY BEFORE:
- Prepare Grapefruit Sections with Campari; refrigerate.
- Bake oatcakes 10 minutes at 300°F. to crispen. Cool; store airtight.
- Make kedgeree; refrigerate, tightly covered.
- Sieve egg yolk to decorate kedgeree; refrigerate.
- Poach eggs (see page 191); refrigerate in cold water.

ABOUT 2 HOURS BEFORE SERVING:
- Heat oven to 325°F.
- Remove kedgeree from refrigerator and let come to room temperature.
- Assemble pudding and put in oven to bake.
- Remove Baps from freezer; let thaw at room temperature.
- Cook sausages; drain; arrange in oven-proof serving dish.

ABOUT 1 HOUR BEFORE SERVING:
- Heat oven to 325°F. Bake kedgeree.

continued

GAME PLAN *cont'd*

ABOUT 30 MINUTES BEFORE SERVING:

- Remove Scotch bread pudding from oven; let stand 30 minutes at room temperature.
- Arrange Baps on cookie sheet; bake 10 minutes (at 325°F.) to heat.
- Put sausage in oven for last 5 minutes to heat.

ABOUT 10 MINUTES BEFORE SERVING:

- Put Baps in oven (with kedgeree) to warm.
- Slip eggs into very hot water to heat.
- Remove chives and sieved egg yolk from refrigerator.
- Serve Grapefruit Sections with Campari.

LAST MINUTE:

- Drain eggs; arrange on top of kedgeree. Sprinkle with sieved egg yolk and chives.

Bake about 45 minutes, until custard looks jelly-like in center and is firm around edges. Remove pudding and water bath from oven; let stand 10 minutes. Remove pudding from water bath; place on a wire rack to cool for 30 minutes before serving. Serve warm. *Makes 6 to 8 servings.*

Kedgeree and Poached Eggs

This simple and soothing dish of smoked haddock and rice is a longtime English favorite. It is perfect for breakfast because it should be made the day before to give the flavor time to develop. If you can't find good smoked haddock, choose another recipe. You want large, meaty fillets; reject scrawny baby haddocks (usually about 8 inches long) with skin and bones still present. Their flavor is not very good, and you may have as much as fifty percent waste.

Water
2 cups converted white rice
Salt
4 tablespoons (½ stick) unsalted butter
2 to 2½ pounds smoked haddock fillet
½ cup milk

Freshly-ground pepper
2 eggs, hard-cooked and peeled (see page 193)
½ cup half-and-half
12 warm poached eggs (see page 191)
¼ cup snipped chives or thinly-sliced scallions

Bring 5 cups water to a boil in a heavy 4- to 5-quart saucepan over high heat. Add rice and 2 teaspoons salt. Stir until boiling, reduce heat to moderately-low, cover pan, and simmer 20 minutes. Remove from heat; add butter and let stand 5 minutes, until most of the remaining water has been absorbed.

While rice cooks, put fish in a pan or deep skillet, just large enough to hold it. Add milk, and enough water to barely cover fish. Cover skillet and bring to a simmer over moderately-low heat. Reduce heat to low and let poach 5 minutes; liquid should barely quiver. Remove pan from heat and pour off liquid.

When fish is cool enough to handle, break it up with your fingers, discarding any tough skin and feeling carefully for any bones. Break fish into small flakes and put it into a measuring cup; you should have about 4 cups.

Add fish to rice along with about ½ teaspoon salt and a good grinding of pepper. Mix well. Taste; add more salt and pepper as needed, keeping in mind that flavor will develop a little on standing. Kedgeree should have a mild, soothing flavor and not be highly seasoned.

Cut hard-cooked eggs in half, scoop out yolks, and put aside. Chop whites; stir into fish mixture. Spread mixture evenly in two 2-quart baking dishes, or one larger one (about 13 × 9 inches) Cover dishes tightly with foil and refrigerate until the next day.

Tear off a small strip of wax paper. Put egg yolks in a strainer and, using the back of a wooden spoon, press them through the strainer onto the wax paper. Put into a small container, cover tightly, and refrigerate.

Next day, remove kedgeree from refrigerator; let come to room temperature. Heat oven to 325°F. Pour half-and-half over kedgeree; cover and bake 40 to 50 minutes until heated through. Uncover. Arrange poached eggs on top; sprinkle with sieved egg yolks and chives or scallions and serve. *Makes 12 servings.*

Baps

Even the smallest Scottish towns seem to boast at least two bakeries, and I think it's safe to say that every single one of them sells Baps. Baps are pale, soft-crusted light breakfast rolls easily distinguished by their floury exterior. Their mild flavor is perfect with butter and marmalade; their soft texture great for mopping up the last creamy bit of a poached or fried egg. Since you won't want to keep baker's hours, make these ahead and freeze them.

1⅓ cups milk
4 tablespoons (½ stick) unsalted butter
1 envelope active dry yeast
1 teaspoon granulated sugar

3 cups all-purpose flour
⅛ teaspoon salt
Additional flour for dusting and dredging

Heat milk and butter in a small heavy saucepan over moderate heat until very warm (105° to 115°F.). Remove pan from heat.

Put yeast and sugar into a large bowl. Stir in warm milk mixture with a large wooden spoon. Let stand 5 minutes while yeast swells and dissolves.

Add flour and salt. Stir with a wooden spoon to make a fairly stiff dough. Beat with spoon for 2 minutes. (Sit down, hold bowl in lap, and give those biceps a workout. If you have the strength to beat dough for 3 minutes, it will be even smoother and silkier.)

Scrape sides of bowl. Cover with plastic wrap or a damp kitchen towel and put in a warm place, until dough is doubled in volume, about 1 hour.

continued

SHOPPING GUIDE

3 cups all-purpose flour
2 cups converted white rice
1⅔ cups plus 1 teaspoon granulated sugar
1 envelope active dry yeast
2 teaspoons vanilla extract
24 oatcakes (oatcakes come round or triangular; package sizes vary)
1 1-pound jar tawny marmalade

8 pounds (about 8) large pink grapefruit
Freshly-squeezed orange juice
Small bunch chives or scallions (¼ cup sliced)

2 pounds frozen spicy sausage patties

6 plain or cinnamon-raisin English muffins

2 to 2½ pounds smoked haddock fillet

6 cups (1½ quarts) milk
2 cups (1 pint) heavy cream
½ cup half-and-half
10 tablespoons (1¼ sticks) unsalted butter
22 large eggs

Champagne
⅓ cup Campari
¼ cup Scotch whisky

(Coffee? Tea? Add what you need, also butter for the table.)

Beat risen dough with spoon to deflate. Turn dough onto a generously floured work surface or board; flour your fingers and knead dough firmly but lightly for about 3 minutes. (Object is to keep dough as soft as possible, so try not to work in a great deal of additional flour.) Now, cover dough with towel or bowl and let it relax for 5 minutes so it is workable.

Grease a 15 × 10-inch jelly-roll pan. Sprinkle with about 1 tablespoon flour (use a dredger if you have one or sift flour through a small strainer). Shake pan back and forth until lightly coated with flour.

On lightly floured surface roll dough with palms of hands into a 15-inch rope. Cut or snip into 15 pieces. Shape each piece into a ball (see directions below). When balls are all shaped, flatten slightly with palm of hand. Cover loosely with plastic wrap and let rise in warm place, until doubled in size, 30 to 50 minutes (time will depend on how cold dough has become during shaping and how warm your kitchen is). Shortly before dough seems risen enough, heat oven to 375°F. Uncover Baps and sift about 1 tablespoon flour over them (or dust with flour dredger).

Bake 18 to 20 minutes, until Baps are light golden brown and sound hollow when tapped on bottom. Remove from baking pan; prop up on pan sides to cool, or put on cooling rack. When completely cool (allow 2 or more hours as flavor also needs time to develop), rub tops lightly with fingers to give proper floury look, then wrap airtight and leave at room temperature overnight or freeze. *Makes 15 Baps.*

To shape rolls. Here's how to shape each little piece of dough into a roll. With piece of dough on countertop, lift up edge farthest from you with fingertips, bring it forward, and press down into middle of dough. Turn roll slightly and repeat 8 to 10 times, until roll is smooth on underside. (Work fast, you don't want to spend hours doing this; each roll should take just a few seconds.) Turn roll over on board, cup roll in your palms, and give several quick back-and-forth movements to make the roll rounder. Put roll, creased side down, on baking sheet.

After the Ball

When I was eighteen, I spent a year at home, raising chickens and growing flowers in order to pay my cooking school fees. Life wasn't too rough down on the farm, and in the wintertime there were often dances to go to. The Young Farmer's Ball and the Hunt Ball are two I remember well.

One night, driving home from a dance with my escort, we passed my chicken houses. I noticed that the lights had come on. Always curious about life in a chicken house at 3:00 A.M. I climbed up to the window in my ball gown while my escort watched from the safety of his car. To my disappointment the hens were wandering around, eating, scratching about, clucking, and otherwise behaving just as they did at any other time of the day.

Way back then escorts left one at the front door. One of the nice things about growing up and leaving home is that when you have danced all night and return to your very own house hungry, wide-awake, and in need of time to unwind, you can share an early breakfast without waking curious parents. This is a time for food that's sustaining but very quick to prepare. A little advance planning is in order.

M E N U
FOR 2
FRESHLY-SQUEEZED ORANGE JUICE
CHAMPAGNE OR SPARKLING WHITE GRAPE JUICE
*LOX AND BAGELS
OR *SCRAMBLED EGGS AND CAVIAR WITH BRIOCHE OR HOT BUTTERED TOAST
*RECIPE FOLLOWS

GAME PLAN

BEFORE YOU LEAVE:
◆ Put Champagne or sparkling grape juice in refrigerator.

WHEN YOU RETURN:
◆ Squeeze juice; pour chilled wine or juice.
◆ Either make toast, scramble eggs, top with sour cream, caviar, and chives; or put out lox, toasted bagels, and cream cheese and garnish with lemon wedges.

Scrambled Eggs and Caviar

I like red salmon caviar best here, but red or black lumpfish caviar tastes just fine. Or cut a slice of smoked salmon in strips and put that on top of the sour cream. The eggs take only a few seconds to scramble, so before you pour the eggs into the hot skillet, have plates, caviar, and sour cream at hand and pop the bread into the toaster.

4 large eggs
¼ cup milk
  Salt
  Freshly-ground pepper
1 tablespoon chopped fresh parsley,
    chives, green parts of scallions,
    or watercress

1 tablespoon unsalted butter
2 to 4 tablespoons sour cream
2 teaspoons or more caviar

Break eggs into a medium-sized bowl; add milk, salt, pepper, and most of the chopped parsley or other greens (save a little for garnish). Beat with a fork or wire whisk, until eggs are well broken up.

Choose a nonstick skillet that is 6 to 8 inches across the bottom. Heat over moderate heat, adding butter.

Pour in eggs and start to scramble them (see page 193). As soon as eggs are almost firm (in a few seconds), spoon them onto plates. (Eggs will finish cooking in their own heat.) Top each serving with sour cream, caviar, and the reserved chopped greens. *Makes 2 servings.*

Lox and Bagels

For more information on lox and smoked salmon, see page 48. Be sure to put the pepper mill on the table to grind over the salmon.

4 or more ounces lox, Nova Scotia, or
    other smoked salmon of choice
Lemon wedges
4 crusty plain bagels

1 3-ounce package cream cheese or a
    small container of chive cream
    cheese

Arrange the salmon on a serving platter; garnish with lemon wedges.
   Cut bagels in half and toast them. Serve in napkin-lined basket.
   Serve with cream cheese to spread on the bagels. Some people like to make a sandwich with the salmon and bagels; others like to eat the salmon with a fork and munch toasted bagel along with it. *Makes 2 servings.*

SHOPPING GUIDE

6 juice oranges or 1 quart
   refrigerated orange juice

Champagne or sparkling white
   grape juice

For Scrambled Eggs and Caviar:
2 brioches, or 2 or 4 slices
   white or rye bread
Fresh parsley, chives, green part
   of scallions, or a few sprigs
   of watercress (enough for 1
   tablespoon chopped)

1 ounce (2 teaspoons) caviar (it
   will keep at least 2 days, so a
   little extra won't hurt)

¼ cup milk
2 to 4 tablespoons sour cream
1 tablespoon unsalted butter
4 large eggs

For Lox and Bagels:
4 crusty plain bagels (leftovers
   can be frozen)

1 lemon

4 or more ounces lox, Nova
   Scotia, or other smoked
   salmon

1 3-ounce package cream
   cheese or small container
   chive cream cheese

(Decaffeinated coffee? Herb
   tea? Preserves for the last of
   the brioches, toast, or
   bagels? Add what you need,
   including butter for toast.)

Pre-ski Energy Input

M E N U

FOR 6

*ORANGE WEDGES

*PORK CUTLET BREAKFAST
SANDWICHES

*WALNUT CINNAMON-
CHOCOLATE COFFEE CAKE

*RECIPE FOLLOWS

A substantial breakfast is happily a must before heading for the slopes or cross-country trails. With plenty of exercise in store, you can stash a supply of calories and carbohydrates with a reasonably clear conscience.

If you're traveling to a house in the snow and taking supplies with you (who wants to waste ski-time in the supermarket?) you can mix the spices for the Pork Cutlet Breakfast Sandwiches at home. Pack the meat in a cooler and the bread in plastic bags so it does not dry out. Don't forget the chutney, the spices, and the coffee cake from the freezer. Refrigerate the fresh meat as soon as you arrive at the ski house. Leave the coffee cake wrapped; put it in the freezer or leave at room temperature. This is a delicious breakfast with little work or cleanup.

Orange Wedges

6 navel oranges

Just in case your mother didn't give you oranges this way when you were a child, here's how to serve them: Buy good-sized navel oranges. Wash them. Cut each orange into 8 wedges and put on plates, or reshape in small bowls. To eat, pick up a wedge with both hands and bend it back so fruit starts to separate from pith. Put juicy flesh in your mouth and eat it, pulling it off the pith as you do so. *Makes 6 servings.*

Pork Cutlet Breakfast Sandwiches

1½ pounds well-trimmed boneless pork loin, or 12 thin, well-trimmed lean boneless pork cutlets (about 1½ pounds)
½ teaspoon salt
½ teaspoon ground cumin seed
¼ teaspoon freshly-ground pepper
⅛ teaspoon ground cardamom seed (optional)
3 tablespoons pure olive or vegetable oil
About 1 tablespoon Dijon mustard
12 large slices crusty white or rye bread or 6 Kaiser rolls, split
About 4 tablespoons mango chutney

If you purchased the meat whole, cut it into 12 thin slices. Mix salt, cumin, pepper, and cardamom in a small container. Sprinkle spice mixture on both sides of meat.

Heat 2 tablespoons of oil in a large (preferably nonstick) skillet over high heat. Add half the pork and cook 2 minutes on each side, turning once, until browned and cooked through. Do not overcook. Remove to a plate. Add remaining oil to skillet and cook remaining pork in same way (add a touch more oil if pan seems dry).

When pork is cooked, let it stand a minute or two while you spread ½ teaspoon mustard on each of 6 slices of bread (or inside top of each roll).

Spread each remaining slice of bread (or bottoms of rolls) with 2 teaspoons chutney; top with two slices pork and sprinkle with meat juices that have collected on the plate. Close sandwiches with mustard-spread bread and munch away. *Makes 6 servings.*

GAME PLAN

UP TO A WEEK AHEAD YOU MAY:
◆ Bake Walnut Cinnamon-Chocolate Coffee Cake; cool completely; wrap pan tightly in foil and freeze.

THE DAY BEFORE:
◆ Slice meat if it is not already sliced. Wrap tightly and refrigerate.

ABOUT 30 MINUTES BEFORE SERVING:
◆ Heat oven to 325°F.
◆ Mix seasoning for pork cutlets.
◆ Cut up oranges and put on serving plates at each place. (Or invite guests to eat oranges in the kitchen while you make the breakfast sandwiches.)
◆ Warm foil-wrapped coffee cake in oven for about 15 minutes. (If you don't have an oven, the cake is perfectly delicious at room temperature.)
◆ Fry pork cutlets. Make sandwiches; eat while hot.

SHOPPING GUIDE

2¼ cups all-purpose flour
¾ cup light brown sugar
½ cup granulated sugar
1 teaspoon baking powder
1 teaspoon baking soda
1½ teaspoons ground cinnamon
½ teaspoon ground cumin seed
⅛ teaspoon ground cardamom
  seed (optional)
1 teaspoon vanilla extract
1 cup (6 ounces) semisweet
  chocolate chips
1 cup (3½ ounces) walnuts,
  chopped
3 tablespoons pure olive or vegetable oil
About 4 tablespoons mango or
  other chutney
About 1 tablespoon Dijon mustard

12 large slices crusty white or
  rye bread or 6 Kaiser rolls

6 navel oranges

1½ pounds well-trimmed boneless pork loin; or 12 thin,
  well-trimmed lean boneless
  pork cutlets (about 1½
  pounds)

1 cup plain yogurt
12 tablespoons (1½ sticks)
  unsalted butter
1 large egg

(Coffee? Tea? Hot chocolate?
  Add what you need.)

Walnut Cinnamon-Chocolate Coffee Cake

Wonderful!

2¼ cups all-purpose flour
¾ cup packed light brown sugar
½ cup granulated sugar
1½ teaspoons ground cinnamon
½ teaspoon salt
12 tablespoons (1½ sticks) unsalted
  butter, melted and cooled
1 cup (3½ ounces) walnuts,
  chopped

1 cup plain yogurt
1 large egg
1 teaspoon baking powder
1 teaspoon baking soda
1 teaspoon vanilla extract
1 cup (6 ounces) semisweet chocolate
  chips

Heat oven to 350°F Grease a 13 × 9 × 2-inch baking pan.

In a large bowl, mix flour, sugars, 1 teaspoon of cinnamon, and salt. Rub with fingers to break up any lumps of brown sugar. Add butter and stir with a spoon, until damp and crumbly. Take out ¾ cup of mixture and put it into a small bowl. Add remaining ½ teaspoon cinnamon and walnuts and mix with fingers; this will be the topping.

Put yogurt, egg, baking powder, baking soda, and vanilla into another small bowl; beat with a fork until well mixed; stir in chocolate chips. Scrape into flour mixture in large bowl; stir until incorporated. Scrape into prepared pan; sprinkle with topping.

Bake 30 to 35 minutes, until lightly browned and a wooden toothpick inserted in center comes out clean. Place pan on a wire rack to cool. *Makes 15 servings.*

Breakfast with a Southern Flair

Here is a breakfast with an ample helping of that famous Southern hospitality. South or North of the Mason-Dixon line, it tastes great and is easy to do. Use good-quality ham for the steaks, or even Smithfield ham. Some specialty food stores carry vacuum-packed slices of Smithfield ham, or you might cut slivers from a ham you've had for a special occasion. If you do use an intensely flavorful Smithfield or other country ham, serve only small amounts and add scrambled eggs to the menu.

The popularity of hot-pepper jelly has spread far beyond the South, and it is now widely available. In case you can't buy it locally, the recipe tells you how to make your own in the time it takes to heat apple jelly with vinegar and chopped jalapeño pepper. The peppery-apple flavor is excellent with smoky ham.

```
M E N U
FOR 6

*AMBROSIA

*HAM STEAKS WITH HOT-
PEPPER JELLY GLAZE

*PERFECT GRITS

*CREAM BISCUITS

PEACH SPREAD


*RECIPE FOLLOWS
```

GAME PLAN

UP TO 1 MONTH AHEAD YOU MAY:

- Make Cream Biscuits and freeze unbaked.

THE DAY BEFORE:

- Make Ambrosia.

THE DAY BEFORE YOU MAY ALSO:

- Trim and cut up ham steaks; cover and refrigerate.
- Mix dry ingredients for Cream Biscuits in large bowl; cover; leave at room temperature.

ABOUT 1 HOUR BEFORE SERVING:

- Heat oven to 450°F. Make biscuit dough; cut out biscuits; bake (if frozen, do not thaw). When biscuits are baked, turn oven down to 200°F.
- Make Perfect Grits.
- Add pineapple to Ambrosia.
- Fry ham steaks, put on platter; make glaze. Keep ham steaks warm in 200°F. oven while you eat Ambrosia.

LAST MINUTE:

- Pour glaze over ham; take to table with bowl of Perfect Grits.

Ambrosia

Buying pineapple from the supermarket salad bar saves a whole lot of time. I like to mix it with the oranges close to serving time; if mixed the night before it can develop a very acid tang. The orange juice prevents the banana from browning.

2 juice oranges or ⅔ cup refrigerated orange juice
1 ripe banana
6 medium-sized navel oranges
½ pound seedless green grapes
½ cup packaged sweetened shredded coconut
12 ounces fresh pineapple chunks (from the supermarket salad bar) or 1 20-ounce can pineapple chunks in unsweetened pineapple juice

Squeeze juice oranges and put the juice into a blender or food processor along with the peeled banana. Puree until smooth. Pour into a serving bowl.

Peel the navel oranges (see page 186). Cut in half lengthwise and cut out the pith and bitter white navel, if present. Put each half cut side down on a board; cut in four slices lengthwise and four slices crosswise. Add pieces of orange to bowl.

Remove grapes from stems; rinse with cold water and drain. Add to bowl. Sprinkle with coconut. Stir gently with two wooden spoons. Cover and refrigerate overnight.

Cut pineapple into ½-inch chunks; cover and refrigerate separately.

Shortly before serving, add pineapple to bowl and stir gently. *Makes 6 to 8 servings.*

Ham Steaks with Hot-Pepper Jelly Glaze

3 ham steaks, each about 12 ounces, cut about ⅝-inch thick
1 cup apple jelly
3 tablespoons cider vinegar
1½ tablespoons minced, seeded pickled jalapeño pepper
4 teaspoons light olive or vegetable oil
½ cup water

Cut fat off ham steaks and cut each steak into three sections, discarding center bone if there is one.

Put jelly, vinegar, and jalapeño in a small saucepan and bring to a boil over high heat. Strain into a small bowl; discard jalapeño.

Heat oil in a large heavy skillet over moderately-high heat. Add half the pieces of ham and fry 2 to 3 minutes, until browned on the underside. Reduce heat slightly, turn ham, and cook 2 to 3 minutes longer. Remove ham to a warm platter. Repeat with remaining ham.

To make glaze, add water and strained jelly to skillet. Cook 2 to 3 minutes, stirring to incorporate all the flavorful browned bits in bottom of skillet. When glaze is light brown and slightly syrupy, pour it into a small container and cover. Keep glaze warm and pour over ham just before serving. (If you leave glaze in skillet, it may evaporate almost entirely.) *Makes 6 servings, with about ½ cup sauce.*

Perfect Grits

4 cups water
½ teaspoon salt
1 cup quick grits
¼ cup milk

2 tablespoons (¼ stick) unsalted butter
⅛ teaspoon freshly-ground pepper

Bring water to a boil in a 3- to 4-quart heavy saucepan (nonstick is good) over moderately-high heat. Add salt. Slowly sprinkle in grits while stirring constantly. Reduce heat to low and simmer 4 minutes, stirring two or three times.

Remove pan from heat. Stir in milk, butter, and pepper. Cover and let stand 5 minutes. *Makes 8 servings.*

Cream Biscuits

2 cups all-purpose flour
1 tablespoon baking powder
½ teaspoon salt
6 tablespoons (¾ stick) cold unsalted butter, cut in small pieces

1 5-ounce can evaporated milk, or 5 ounces light or heavy cream
⅓ cup milk

Heat oven to 450°F. Put flour, baking powder, and salt into a large bowl; stir to mix well. Add butter and cut in with pastry blender or rub in with fingers, until mixture forms fine granules.

Add evaporated milk and milk; stir with a wooden spoon until a soft dough forms. Turn dough out onto a lightly floured counter or board; give 12 to 15 kneads. Roll dough with a floured rolling pin to a circle

continued

SHOPPING GUIDE

2 cups all-purpose flour
1 cup quick grits
1 tablespoon baking powder
½ cup packaged sweetened shredded coconut
4 teaspoons light olive or vegetable oil
3 tablespoons cider vinegar
1 5-ounce can evaporated milk
1 cup apple jelly
Peach spread (look in jam section of market for a fruit-only spread)
1½ pickled jalapeño peppers (1½ tablespoons minced)

3 pounds (about 6) medium-sized navel oranges
2 juice oranges or ⅔ cup refrigerated orange juice
½ pound seedless green grapes
12 ounces fresh pineapple chunks (from supermarket salad bar), or 1 20-ounce can pineapple chunks in unsweetened pineapple juice
1 ripe banana

3 ham steaks, each about 12 ounces, cut about ⅝-inch thick

¾ cup milk
5 ounces (about ½ pint) light or heavy cream (if not using evaporated milk for biscuits)
8 tablespoons (1 stick) unsalted butter

(Coffee? Tea? Add what you need, also butter for the table.)

about 7 inches in diameter (dough will be about ½-inch thick). Dip a plain or fluted 2-inch biscuit cutter in flour and cut out biscuits as close together as possible. Pat scraps together, reroll, and cut out more biscuits.

Put biscuits on an ungreased cookie sheet—close together for soft sides, slightly apart for crisper sides.

Bake 12 to 14 minutes, until light golden brown. Line a cooling rack with a linen or cotton kitchen towel; put biscuits directly on towel; cover loosely and let cool 10 minutes. Serve warm in a napkin-lined basket or uncover and let cool further. *Makes about 18 biscuits.*

Make-ahead Breakfast

A hearty start to the day in only two easy dishes. The night before, make the applesauce, assemble the bread pudding, and you're ready to go. Choose this menu when you know the morning will be full of distractions. If you can get quinces, do try the Fresh Quince Applesauce. Quinces are appearing more frequently in supermarkets and farmer's markets. Golden-green in color and similar in shape to an apple, they are sometimes covered with a thin layer of fuzzy bloom. Quinces are a very old, romantic fruit. Rock-hard and totally inedible raw, they are delicious when cooked with meat (as in a pot roast) or, as here, with apples.

With or without quince, once you've made this special applesauce you'll be spoiled. Fresh apples are shredded, then cooked briefly, giving you an applesauce that's full of flavor and not watery at all. Experiment with using different kinds of apples; just about any flavorful, aromatic apple works well.

The homey breakfast bread pudding is an old American favorite that's also known as a strata, or a soufflé. It could also be described as a French toast casserole. Whatever the name, it is very easy to make and delicious to eat.

M E N U

FOR 6

*FRESH APPLESAUCE OR FRESH QUINCE APPLESAUCE WITH APPLE-CINNAMON YOGURT

*HAM AND CHEESE BREAKFAST BREAD PUDDING

*RECIPE FOLLOWS

Fresh Applesauce with Apple-Cinnamon Yogurt

FOR APPLESAUCE:

2 pounds tart green apples, unpeeled
¼ cup water
   About 2 tablespoons granulated
   sugar

FOR TOPPING:

2 tablespoons frozen concentrated
   apple juice
1 8-ounce container plain lowfat
   yogurt
Ground cinnamon

- ◆ Make Fresh Applesauce or Fresh Quince Applesauce; refrigerate in baking dish if reheating.
- ◆ Make Apple-Cinnamon Yogurt.
- ◆ Assemble Ham and Cheese Breakfast Bread Pudding.

FOOD PROCESSOR METHOD: Quarter and core unpeeled apples. Using shredding disk, shred apples in food processor. Discard any large chunks of peel.

HAND METHOD: Leave apples whole; shred them on coarse side of a hand grater, shredding down as far as the core.

Put shredded apples and water in a deep, 10- to 12-inch skillet or saucepan and heat over high heat, until water is simmering. Reduce heat to moderate; cover pan and cook 7 to 8 minutes, stirring two or three times, until apples are tender but still have a little "bite" to them. (Apples may discolor slightly, but don't worry.)

- ◆ Remove breakfast bread pudding from refrigerator; uncover.
- ◆ Heat oven to 325°F.; put pudding in to bake.
- ◆ Remove applesauce from refrigerator; if serving warm, bake (covered) 10 to 15 minutes shortly before serving.
- ◆ Let pudding stand 10 minutes before serving.
- ◆ Serve applesauce with ice-cold yogurt.

Stir in 2 tablespoons sugar; taste; add more sugar if desired. Spoon into a serving bowl or individual dishes. Serve warm or chilled. *Makes 6 servings.*

To make topping: Stir apple juice concentrate into yogurt. Spoon over applesauce and sprinkle with cinnamon.

FRESH QUINCE APPLESAUCE

Buy 1½ pounds of apples and 1 to 1½ pounds of quinces. Wash quinces and peel with a vegetable peeler. (Fruit will turn brown; that's okay.) Either shred on shredder, or cut into quarters or sixths, cut out core, and shred the fruit in the food processor. (You need about 3 cups.) Follow Fresh Applesauce recipe (above), except simmer the quince in the water for about 5 minutes before adding apple and an additional 2 tablespoons water.

Ham and Cheese Breakfast Bread Pudding

4 English muffins, split open
1½ tablespoons (about ¼ stick)
    butter, at room temperature
5 large eggs
3 cups milk
¾ teaspoon salt

¼ teaspoon freshly-ground pepper
Few drops hot-pepper sauce
6 ounces cheddar cheese, shredded
    (1½ cups)
1 cup (5 ounces) diced cooked ham

See note at end if you are making the pudding the same day you are serving it. Butter an 8- to 9-inch square baking dish that's at least 2 inches high and holds 2 quarts. Spread muffins with the 1½ tablespoons butter and arrange them, split sides up, in two rows in the baking dish (overlap the muffins in each row).

Whisk eggs in a large bowl; add milk, salt, pepper, and hot-pepper sauce; whisk to mix.

Pour egg mixture over muffins. Sprinkle with cheese and ham. Cover and refrigerate overnight.

The next morning, remove dish from refrigerator and heat oven to 325°F. Uncover dish and bake, in middle part of oven, 40 to 50 minutes, until puffed and no longer liquid in center. Remove from oven and let stand 10 minutes before serving. *Makes 6 servings.*

NOTE: If assembling just before baking, heat milk in a heavy medium-sized saucepan over moderate heat, until bubbles appear around edge. Whisk eggs in a large bowl. Keep whisking while you slowly pour in hot milk. Whisk in salt, pepper, and hot-pepper sauce. Assemble dish as described above and bake. Heating the milk helps the muffins absorb the mixture faster.

SHOPPING GUIDE

About 2 tablespoons granulated sugar
Ground cinnamon
Few drops hot-pepper sauce

2 pounds tart green apples or 1½ pounds apples and 1 to 1½ pounds quinces

2 tablespoons frozen concentrated apple juice

4 English muffins

5 ounces baked or boiled ham (1 cup diced)

3 cups milk
1 8-ounce container plain low-fat yogurt
1½ tablespoons (about ¼ stick) unsalted butter
5 large eggs
6 ounces cheddar cheese (1½ cups shredded)

(Coffee? Tea? Add what you need.)

For a Cold Country Morning

M E N U

FOR 6

*COMPOTE OF FRESH AND DRIED FRUIT

*BEST-EVER OATMEAL

FRESH CREAM

WARM MAPLE SYRUP

BROWN-SUGAR SYRUP

*HERBED CHICKEN LIVERS

CRUSTY FRENCH BREAD

*APPLE ENGLISH MUFFIN PASTRIES

*RECIPE FOLLOWS

When the snow is piled high and there's more on the way, when it's too cold to do anything constructive out of doors, that's the time to invite your favorite neighbors to come with their kids, and spend a relaxed morning with good food and conversation. Welcome everyone with a blazing fire and a big pot of oatmeal on the range; watch the snow blow behind the frosty panes.

After everyone has warmed up with oatmeal, bring on the Herbed Chicken Livers. I'm convinced that the reason people say they don't like chicken livers is that they've only eaten overcooked ones. Overcooked livers are dry, chalky, and bitter, and I don't like them, either! I love these easy-to-make herbed livers. They require only that you concentrate on them during the short cooking time.

The Brown-Sugar Syrup and the fruit can be prepared the night before and reheated in the morning. The chicken livers can be cut up, too. In the morning, a layer of thin apple slices and a few minutes under the broiler turn English muffins into breakfast pastries.

Compote of Fresh and Dried Fruit

1½ cups water
3 tablespoons packed dark brown
    sugar
⅛ teaspoon ground cinnamon
⅛ teaspoon ground ginger

1 8-ounce package mixed dried fruit
1 small orange, scrubbed
1 small lemon, scrubbed
1 Granny Smith or other tart apple
1 ripe pear

Mix water, sugar, cinnamon, and ginger in a heavy medium-sized saucepan. Add dried fruit.

Cut orange and lemon in half crosswise. Squeeze juice from one half of each into pan. Thinly slice other halves, discarding ends. Add to pan.

Peel, quarter, and core apple and pear; cut into ¾-inch chunks; add to pan.

Bring contents of pan to a boil over high heat. Mix fruit very gently with two wooden spoons. Reduce heat to moderately-low, cover, and simmer 30 to 35 minutes, until dried fruits are softened.

Serve warm. Or refrigerate until next day and either serve cold or reheat as directed in Game Plan. Keeps several days in refrigerator. *Makes 6 to 8 servings.*

Best-ever Oatmeal

There are two kinds of oats worth knowing about for breakfast. One is the familiar flat-rolled oat used for cookies and hot cereal. The other is steel-cut oats, which are in little chunks; look for them in health-food stores.

When cooking the old-fashioned or quick oats available in every supermarket, follow package directions. Cooking directions on most packages of steel-cut oats tend to be minimal or inaccurate. One pound of steel-cut oats cooks up into 9 cups of oatmeal, but since it takes a while to cook you might as well cook a whole pound at once. The cooked oatmeal keeps at least three days in the refrigerator (it can be frozen in individual portions) and can be quickly reheated for a weekday breakfast (see note below).

10 cups water   2½ cups steel-cut oats
1½ teaspoons salt

In a heavy 5- to 6-quart saucepan (preferably nonstick), bring water to a boil over high heat. Add salt; stir in oats. When water is boiling

continued

THE DAY BEFORE YOU MAY:
◆ Make Compote of Fresh and Dried Fruit.
◆ Cut up chicken livers. Spread out in shallow dish; cover and refrigerate.
◆ Make Brown-Sugar Syrup (see page 7); leave at room temperature.

ABOUT 1 HOUR BEFORE SERVING:
◆ Put fruit compote over moderately-low heat to warm; move fruit about gently with two wooden spoons every 6 to 8 minutes. (Or heat in 250°F. oven; no need to stir.)
◆ Prepare Apple English Muffin Pastries for broiling. Cover with plastic wrap; leave at room temperature.
◆ Start cooking oatmeal. Warm maple and brown-sugar syrups if you wish.
◆ Heat oven to 200°F. Put in plates to warm for livers; oatmeal bowls, too, if you wish.
◆ Toss livers with flour and seasonings.

LAST MINUTE:
◆ Put cream, warm maple syrup, Brown-Sugar Syrup on table. Also, butter and breads to be served with the chicken livers.
◆ Serve fruit compote. To save jumping up and down from the table you may wish to serve the oatmeal at the same time. If so, serve fruit in bowls set alongside oatmeal.

continued

IN SEARCH OF PERFECT OATMEAL

Not long ago, my three siblings and I went back to Scotland with our father, the first vacation we had spent together since we were teenagers. During our first breakfast together (at Sunlaws House Hotel, in Roxburghshire) Father's incredibly bushy eyebrows suddenly shot up when he noticed his four adult children happily spooning up big bowls of porridge (translation: oatmeal). "But," he said, unable to believe what he was seeing, "you all hated porridge when you were children." We just grinned and kept on eating. Sometimes you have to grow up to appreciate good simple foods such as oatmeal.

Most of the oatmeal we enjoyed on that idyllic Scottish journey tasted better than any I could ever remember. My quest for the secret began. Inquiries revealed that Scottish cooking methods varied little from American ones. I brought home Scottish oatmeal, but no matter how I cooked it, I could not achieve that flavor.

For the last few years I have eaten oatmeal (or other grains) almost every morning. With a little brown sugar, lots of nonfat dry milk, and perhaps a few currants stirred in, it makes a filling, yet modest-calorie start to days that often involve tasting many recipes in the *Woman's Day* test kitchen.

One morning I decided to treat myself to a little cream on my oatmeal. And there it was—the marvelous full, elusive flavor I'd been searching for since my Scottish visit. It's an embarrassing admission for an acknowledged foodie who thinks she's a pretty good recipe detective. But it is made in hopes that even though calories do count, you will pour a little cream on your oatmeal now and then.

GAME PLAN *cont'd*

- Fry chicken livers.
- Broil English muffin pastries; put in oven to keep warm, but leave door open so muffins don't dry out.
- Serve livers very hot. Bring English muffin pastries to the table a few minutes later.

again, reduce heat to low, cover, and simmer 30 minutes, until oats are tender. No need to stir in a nonstick pan; stir every 5 to 8 minutes in a regular pan.

Remove pan from heat and let stand 5 minutes before serving. *Makes 9 cups, 9 servings.*

NOTE. Oatmeal reheats very well in a microwave oven or in a double boiler. If you don't have a double boiler, sit a saucepan of oatmeal in a skillet of simmering water; or put oatmeal in a metal bowl and put over a saucepan of simmering water. Stir oatmeal once or twice to distribute the heat.

Herbed Chicken Livers

The intense flavor of these chicken livers is so satisfying that you don't need to eat too many, especially after a big bowl of oatmeal.

1 to 1½ pounds chicken livers
¼ cup all-purpose flour
1 teaspoon chopped fresh thyme leaves; or ½ teaspoon dried thyme leaves, crumbled

½ teaspoon salt
¼ teaspoon freshly-ground pepper
4 teaspoons pure olive or vegetable oil

Drain chicken livers in a strainer. With a sharp knife, cut each liver into three or four even-sized pieces. Each liver consists of a smaller and a larger lobe. Cut off smaller lobe, then cut larger lobe into two or three pieces more or less equal to the size of the smaller lobe. Pull or cut off any little pieces of yellow fat and also discard any little green pieces. (Green does not mean spoiled! It is part of the bile and tastes bitter.)

Mix flour, thyme, salt, and pepper in a pie plate or other shallow container. Scatter livers over flour and then toss with fingers or a spoon. Flour will quickly get soaked in pink juices and will not coat livers evenly.

Choose a nonstick skillet that is 7 to 10 inches across the bottom. In it, heat 2 teaspoons oil over high heat. (Pan must be very hot.) Add half the livers; after about 30 seconds, turn them over with two wooden spoons. Cook livers for 2 to 2½ minutes, reducing heat slightly after about 1 minute, and tossing them almost constantly with two spoons. Lightly press one or two pieces of liver with a finger; you'll be able to tell when they are still very soft in the center (and therefore too underdone for most tastes) and when they are just done, still slightly pink in the center, but not chalky. Livers will continue to cook in their own heat, so as soon as they are done, transfer them to a warm serving plate. Wipe out skillet with a paper towel and cook remaining livers in the same way. *Makes 6 servings.*

Apple English Muffin Pastries

6 *English muffins, split*
3 *large Golden Delicious apples, unpeeled*
¼ *cup (2 ounces) cream cheese, at room temperature*

2 *tablespoons granulated sugar*
¼ *teaspoon ground allspice*
2 *tablespoons (¼ stick) unsalted butter, cut in small pieces*

Put muffins, split sides up, on a cookie sheet.

Halve and core apples; thinly slice crosswise. (Eat the end pieces.)

Spread each muffin half with about 2 teaspoons cream cheese and cover with one quarter of an apple, fanning out apple slices.

Heat the broiler. Mix sugar and allspice; sprinkle over apples; dot with butter. Broil 6 to 8 minutes, until apple slices are browned and soft. Apples will be very hot, so let pastries cool a few minutes before serving. *Makes 6 servings.*

¼ cup all-purpose flour
1 pound (2½ cups) steel-cut oats (or use old-fashioned oats)
1 pound light brown sugar
3 tablespoons dark brown sugar
2 tablespoons granulated sugar
¼ teaspoon ground allspice
⅛ teaspoon ground cinnamon
⅛ teaspoon ground ginger
1 8-ounce package mixed dried fruit
4 teaspoons pure olive or vegetable oil
Maple syrup to serve with oatmeal

6 English muffins
Crusty French bread to accompany the livers

1 small bunch fresh thyme (enough for 1 teaspoon chopped) or ½ teaspoon dried thyme leaves
3 Golden Delicious apples
1 Granny Smith or other tart apple
1 ripe pear
1 small lemon
1 orange

1 to 1½ pounds fresh chicken livers

Light or heavy cream or milk to serve with oatmeal (½ to 1 pint)
2 tablespoons (¼ stick) unsalted butter
2 ounces cream cheese

(Coffee? Tea? Add what you need, also butter for the table.)

BIG BASHES

Breakfast for a Crowd

Several menus in this book are designed to serve ten or twelve, but occasions may arise for which you'd like to serve breakfast to twice that many. Perhaps someone who is considering running for election would like the opportunity to meet with your group. Or a family reunion is on the horizon, and breakfast is at your house. A farewell breakfast for someone who is leaving to take another job can be much more fun than the usual late afternoon party, as I know from personal experience! The nicest opportunity for an extra-special breakfast party is a wedding. For that reason, I've planned a special menu for twenty-five people, complete with Shopping Guide and Game Plan. It begins on page 154.

Of course, you don't necessarily have to wait for a wedding to make a festive breakfast for a crowd. The wedding breakfast is suitable for any extra-special occasion, and many of the other menus in this book can be extended very successfully. Don't worry about doubling or tripling recipes. Few home kitchens have pots or pans big enough to hold a triple recipe of any coffee cake, let alone scramble forty eggs. It isn't even a good idea to scramble that many eggs at once. It is far better to scramble eggs in batches of not more than twenty at a time, or to make two (or more) separate coffee cakes and bake them one at a time.

If you don't want to do all the cooking yourself, or if the event is to be held in a public place, why not adapt the idea of a covered-dish supper and ask other people to bring the food. Members of a Westport, Connecticut group did this recently when they wanted to bring together civic leaders to learn about a community project. Each member of the host group was assigned to make one batch of a recipe. Muffins and eggs were among the items on the menu; three people were asked to make muffins and five more were asked to make the egg dish. Everyone brought their food in a serving dish or basket and two or three batches were put on the table at once. The breakfast was a huge success; the costs were shared and no one felt overwhelmed by an enormous amount of preparation.

Here are some menus made up of dishes that work well for a crowd and that are easily multiplied or made in two or three batches.

MEMORIAL DAY (page 39)

The main course doubles easily to serve twenty to twenty-five people. The day before, cook the potatoes for the Eggs with Sausage, Peppers, and Potatoes; grate the cheese and cut up the green peppers. Make two batches of the egg recipe. You'll need two skillets, each at least twelve inches across the bottom and two to three inches deep; large Dutch ovens can be used instead.

Make two Cherry-Almond Coffee Cakes and, for a fruit course, combine sliced strawberries and oranges to make a total of about twenty cups of fruit; mix it in one large or two smaller bowls. Peel and slice the oranges (see page 186) the day before, but hull and slice the berries not more than two hours before serving.

WEEKEND BREAKFAST ON THE PORCH (page 45)

The number of people this luxurious breakfast can serve is limited only by the size of your porch and the spending limit on your credit card. The menu requires virtually no cooking and is perfect for any very special occasion.

For twenty-five people, double the amount of fruit and the recipe for the Farmer Cheese with Blueberries; triple the Superb Horseradish Sauce. The recipe for the Crunchy Cucumber Salad makes about four and one-half cups, and twice as much will probably be sufficient.

For the amount of smoked fish to buy, see page 48. If you are feeling a shade ambitious, bake three batches of Plum Upside-Down Coffee Cake (see page 61) to add to the menu.

BREAKFAST WITH A SOUTHWESTERN FLAVOR (page 49)

To increase the food to enough to serve twenty, triple the Cinnamon Pineapple recipe to make twelve cups fruit. Make two double batches (twenty eggs each) of Scrambled Eggs with Chilies and Cheese. Double the Salsa Cilantro recipe to make six cups and buy three avocadoes for the Mashed Avocado. Make three Apricot Streusel Coffee Cakes.

COME HELP—RAISE OUR NEW ROOF . . . (page 89)

This is a delicious country breakfast that's not hard to do for twenty. But before you decide, make sure you have enough oven space and one or two big griddles to bake the pancakes on.

Double the recipe for the Baked Prune Plums; the four dishes can probably fit in one oven. Make two batches of the Orange-Almond Coffee Cake (do this ahead of time and freeze them). You can cook the sausage the day before the party and reheat it. Serve room-temperature slivers of country ham if you choose ham rather than sausage. Make two batches of the Double Corn and Chili Pancake batter and use at least two large griddles to bake them on.

Successful Big Bashes: Advice from a Pro

Preparing the food for your own or someone else's big occasion is one of the nicest things you can do, says young New York caterer and kitchen design consultant Susan Pomerantz. It lends a special and informal air to the occasion.

The secret of pulling off a big deal, such as a wedding breakfast for twenty-five, Susan says, is to plan, plan, plan. Assign friends to help—arrange flowers; do grocery shopping; pick up the bakery order; share the cooking. Be sure to have enough help on party day, too, both to put out the food and keep the kitchen in order (guests love to wander into the scene of action).

Some more do's and don'ts from this experienced party planner:

Give thought to the electrical load. You don't want fuses blowing when coffeemakers, musicians, air-conditioners, ranges, and refrigerators are all merrily rolling along. Coffeemakers are major fuse blowers, and Susan always tries to use two separate lines, even if she has to use a plug in a bedroom.

More advice on coffeemakers. Beautiful they are not. See if you can rent samovars for serving the coffee in; or at least get good-looking pots—perhaps insulated ones—to put on the tables.

Don't go into a tizzy about having enough food. You want to have enough food to look generous, but you don't want to overdo it.

Early on, read recipes carefully and take stock of the cooking equipment you'll need so that on cooking day you don't have to waste time rustling up, or even having to go shopping for, a big enough saucepan or a special cake pan.

Remember the little things such as salt, pepper, sweeteners, lemon wedges, and boiling water for tea. Get them organized well ahead of time so

there isn't a lot of dashing around right in the middle of the party.

Refrigeration can be a hassle, especially in the summertime. Susan sometimes uses dry ice in a cooler. (Handle dry ice with tongs, or with gloves on; remember, dry ice cools what is underneath it, but not what is above it.)

Often when Susan's crew arrives to do a party there's no space in the refrigerator for the food; it's stuffed with bottles of wine. Don't use valuable refrigerator space for beverages. Chill them in shallow (not deep, because bottles can break if piled on top of one another) plastic tubs filled with ice; this way you need only allow thirty minutes to completely chill the contents.

Give thought to what your helpers will wear. Black and white always looks professional. For a special occasion, add bow ties or aprons to match the table linens.

Type out complete, but concise, instructions for your crew. Go over the list with them when they arrive, ideally two hours before the party. Make sure they know exactly what the menu is and what time you want each food served. Also make sure they know the timing for the event and when you want the toast, if there is to be one, so glasses can be refilled. Show helpers where coats will go and where guests can leave gifts.

Lastly, don't announce all the things that have gone wrong. Unless there's a total disaster, keep quiet and fix the problem without getting hysterical. Chances are no one will notice anything amiss. Experienced caterers expect at least one major problem per event—fuses blow, food isn't delivered, the wrong food arrives. So if something goes wrong for you, you're in very good company.

A Wedding Breakfast

Like most children, I was puzzled by the expression wedding "breakfast," when the event seemed to take place at any time other than the usual morning meal time. And in my native England, at least, the food was usually an unsatisfactory hybrid of cocktail-party and tea-party.

Since no grown-up answered my question satisfactorily, a real wedding breakfast has remained a wonderful fantasy, but a fantasy that makes sense. In the heat of summer, the most popular season for weddings, the morning is the prettiest part of the day—and the coolest. A morning ceremony conveniently reduces anxiety time for guests, as well as for members of the wedding. But what to serve?

I called my friend Ann Clark, in Austin, Texas. Ann is a food consultant, cooking teacher, caterer of considerable renown, and an incurable romantic. Had she ever been asked to prepare a wedding breakfast? "No-o" —followed by a thirty-second silence—then, "but what a marvelous idea!" The imaginary party she proceeded to outline included the Festive Fruit Platter and the Rolled Cheese Soufflé with Spinach Filling recipes that appear below. If there's a wedding in your future—your own, or that of friends—and you are looking for a fresh approach, I hope you will consider this real wedding breakfast. Bringing off such an event successfully is indeed a labor of love, but if friends share the work, it is not impossible.

Kir Royale

A Kir is made with dry white wine; when made with Champagne, it becomes Royale. Have nonalcoholic sparkling white grape juice on hand for those who prefer it. Crème de cassis is a liqueur made from black currants; if you can't get it, use Chambord, a lovely black raspberry liqueur, instead.

1 teaspoon to 1 tablespoon crème de   *6 ounces chilled Champagne or*
   cassis   *sparkling white grape juice*

Pour crème de cassis into a wine or Champagne glass. Add Champagne. *Makes 1 serving.*

Mimosa

2 ounces chilled freshly-squeezed orange   *6 ounces chilled Champagne or*
   juice   *sparkling white grape juice*

Pour orange juice into a wine glass. Top up with Champagne. *Makes 1 serving.*

ADVANCE PLANNING

A venture this big requires a lot of planning. Start at least one month ahead.

◆ Make lists and work out your schedule. Accept offers of help. People love to feel they have contributed to the success of the day. Ask others to be responsible for some dishes—for example, the Miniature Ham and Smoked Turkey Biscuits, the Miniature Corn Muffins, the Raspberry Sauce, and even the Festive Fruit Platter if your refrigerator space will be tight.

◆ Check with a party-rental company, especially if your party is in the busy season. See what they have to offer (different colors of linens, for example) and alert them to your needs, although it is too early to know how many guests you will have.

◆ Start making lists of what you will want to rent: chairs and tables; tablecloths and napkins; glasses, plates, and coffee cups; flatware; serving bowls, platters, and tools; ice buckets; shallow plastic tubs to chill beverages in; a wheeled table for the cake; coffee makers (as this is a breakfast party, expect to serve lots of coffee, both regular and decaffeinated; you may want two 55-cup coffee-makers); an extra refrigerator.

continued

ADVANCE PLANNING *cont'd*

- Order wedding cake; arrange for delivery on day of party.
- Order Champage and crème de cassis or Chambord (for Kir Royale). Unused bottles can usually be returned, if labels are undamaged (not soaked in water) and arrangements are made in advance.
- Go through recipes; list cooking equipment needed, including jelly-roll pan and biscuit cutters. Buy or arrange to borrow what you don't already have.
- Decide on platters for the Rolled Cheese Soufflés with Spinach Filling. You need two to four platters, at least 15 inches long and wide enough to hold one or two soufflés. Ovenproof platters you can bake (and serve) the soufflés on are ideal. The party-rental company may have them.
- Arrange for party helpers, either family, or friends, or people hired from a party-help organization. For twenty-five guests, you'll need four people to help out: a bartender; two people to serve the food and clear dirty plates and glasses; and one person to wash up and keep the kitchen in order.
- Buy frozen and nonperishable foods and beverages, including sparkling mineral water and sparkling white grape juice; also plastic wrap and bags, foil, paper goods, and large plastic trash bags.

Miniature Ham and Smoked Turkey Biscuits

The ham biscuits are round; the smoked turkey ones, heart-shaped.

FOR THE HAM BISCUITS:
45 to 50 1½-inch round Miniature Cream Biscuits (recipe below), thawed if frozen
About ¾ cup mango or other chutney
6 ounces thinly-sliced ham, such as Virginia, Black Forest, or Westphalian

FOR THE TURKEY BISCUITS:
45 to 50 1¾-inch heart-shaped Miniature Cream Biscuits (recipe below)
About ½ cup grainy mustard
6 ounces thinly-sliced smoked turkey

Cut all the ham biscuits in half, lining them up on the counter and keeping tops with bottoms. Spread each top and bottom with a dab of chutney. Trim any fat from ham and tear into pieces not much larger than the biscuits. (Pieces do not have to be neat; they should hang out of the biscuits with aplomb.) Put some ham on each bottom; cover with top. Put filled biscuits into an airtight container and refrigerate.

For the turkey biscuits, follow directions for filling the ham biscuits, but spread only one side of each biscuit with mustard.

About 1 hour before serving, arrange biscuits in napkin-lined baskets or on plates. Cover loosely with slightly damp paper towels. Let come to room temperature. *Makes 45 to 50 of each biscuit, a total of 90 to 100.*

MINIATURE CREAM BISCUITS

Bake these ahead and freeze them. For heart-shaped biscuits, use a cutter that's about 1¾ inches from side to side; for round biscuits, use a plain biscuit cutter about 1½ inches in diameter.

4 cups all-purpose flour
2 tablespoons baking powder
1 teaspoon salt
12 tablespoons (1½ sticks) cold, unsalted butter, cut into small pieces

1 cup milk
1 cup heavy cream

Heat oven to 450°F. Put flour, baking powder, and salt into a large bowl; stir to mix well. Add butter and cut in with pastry blender, or rub in with fingers until mixture forms fine granules.

Add milk and cream; stir with a wooden spoon until a soft dough forms. Turn dough out onto a lightly floured surface; give 12 to 15 kneads. Roll dough with a floured rolling pin to a circle 15 to 16 inches in diameter, and about ¼-inch thick.

Dip cutters in flour and cut out hearts and rounds, cutting them as close together as possible. Arrange them close together, but not quite touching, on ungreased cookie sheets. Pat scraps together; reroll and cut out more biscuits.

Bake 8 to 10 minutes until golden brown. Line one or more cooling racks with a linen or cotton kitchen towel; put biscuits directly on towel; cover loosely with another towel. Let cool 30 minutes to 1 hour. *Makes about 98 biscuits.*

Smoked Salmon Endive Leaves

Easy to make, pretty to look at, and refreshing to eat, these are simply Belgian endive leaves with a dab of smoked salmon filling at the base of each. The filling can be made up to 5 days ahead.

1 8-ounce package neufchâtel cheese (light cream cheese), at room temperature
4 ounces smoked salmon
1 tablespoon chopped onion
Freshly-ground pepper

2–3 tablespoons freshly-squeezed lemon juice
6 (1½ pounds) Belgian endives
For garnish: snipped fresh chives, or about 25 thin slices of radish, quartered

Put cream cheese, salmon, and onion in a food processor. Process to a smooth paste. Add a good grating of pepper and 2 tablespoons lemon juice. Scrape down sides; process again. Taste; add more pepper or lemon juice if desired; flavor will develop on standing.

Scrape mixture into one corner of a zip-closure food storage bag; squeeze out as much air as possible; close carefully and refrigerate.

Rinse Belgian endive. Trim ends and separate leaves. Save the tiny center ones for salad. You should have at least 100 usable leaves.

To assemble, bring bag of salmon mixture to room temperature. Snip off point of plastic bag where filling is, making a hole about ¼ inch in diameter. One by one, pick up each leaf and squeeze about ½ teaspoon filling onto each leaf at the base. When you've filled several leaves, arrange them spoke-fashion on a serving plate or tray and sprinkle with chives or stick a tiny piece of radish in the filling. Keep cold until serving time. *Makes at least 100 appetizers.*

GAME PLAN

When there are just two weeks to go before the big day, you should have some idea of how many guests to expect. Keep going over lists and schedules— and start the cooking:

UP TO 2 WEEKS AHEAD:
◆ Bake, wrap airtight, and freeze the Miniature Cream Biscuits and Miniature Corn Muffins.
◆ Make and freeze Raspberry Sauce.
◆ Order miniature croissants and brioches, and heart-shaped vanilla and chocolate cookies from bakery. Arrange for pickup or delivery on party day.
◆ Get back to party-rental company with closer approximation of needs. (Most companies expect final order three days before party.)
◆ Check helpers.
◆ Draw a diagram of where you want to set up tables; plan on separate tables for the Festive Fruit Platter and for the cake. Give thought to traffic patterns and ease of access for the servers.
◆ Draw a diagram of the buffet table, showing where each bowl or platter of food will go and where the plates, flatware, and napkins will go, too.
◆ Start unloading contents of freezer and refrigerator to free space for party fare.

continued

GAME PLAN *cont'd*

UP TO 1 WEEK AHEAD:
- Check all orders in person or by phone including rentals, ice, liquor, baked goods, and wedding cake.
- Double-check helpers.

UP TO 3 DAYS AHEAD:
- Buy remaining ingredients for the Rolled Cheese Soufflés with Spinach Filling; also melons, pineapples, oranges, kiwis, carambolas, lemons, limes, cherry tomatoes.

UP TO 2 DAYS AHEAD:
- Make two recipes of Rolled Cheese Soufflés with Spinach Filling.
- Buy ham and turkey to fill miniature biscuits; ingredients for Smoked Salmon Endive Leaves; fresh herbs for decorating platters; fresh strawberries and raspberries; also milk, cream, and remaining perishables.

THE DAY BEFORE:
- Thaw Miniature Cream Biscuits; fill; refrigerate.
- Prepare fruit for Festive Fruit Platter; cover all fruit tightly and refrigerate.
- Remove stems from tomatoes; discard any squishy ones; leave tomatoes at room temperature. Chop dill; wrap in plastic; refrigerate.
- Slice radishes or snip chives to decorate Smoked Salmon Endive Leaves. Wrap tightly; refrigerate.

continued

Festive Fruit Platter

Serve the fruit platter with Raspberry Sauce (recipe below).

4 ripe honeydew, cantaloupe, or other good-sized melons
2 large pineapples
8 navel oranges
6 kiwi fruit
4 to 6 pints fresh strawberries
2 or 3 pints fresh raspberries
Carambola Stars (optional, see directions below)

The day before the party, halve, seed, and peel the melons (see page 186), cut them in half again lengthwise, then crosswise into ½-inch thick semicircles. Leave the slices together and put the melons in a plastic container (or on a tray). Cover tightly and refrigerate.

Peel pineapples (see page 187); cut in half lengthwise; remove core. Slice pineapple crosswise. Cover tightly and refrigerate.

Peel the oranges (see page 186); do not slice. Refrigerate in a covered container, preferably in one layer so oranges don't get squashed.

Peel kiwi fruit with small knife or vegetable peeler; refrigerate in covered container.

Gently spread strawberries and raspberries out on trays; discard any moldy or squashed fruit but do not wash the berries or hull the strawberries. Cover loosely and refrigerate.

Before arranging fruit on platters, rinse, drain, and hull strawberries; cut up any very large ones. Rinse and drain raspberries.

To arrange fruit: Arrange circles of melon and pineapple slices on one or more platters, fanning slices out slightly. Slice oranges and kiwi fruit; arrange in circles inside the melon slices. Sprinkle strawberries in center and raspberries on top of strawberries. Decorate platter with Carambola Stars. Cover platters with plastic wrap and keep cool until serving time. *Makes 25 servings.*

RASPBERRY SAUCE

You can make this several days ahead and keep it in the refrigerator, or freeze for longer storage. If you freeze it as flat as possible in a zip-closure storage bag, the sauce will thaw in no time at all.

4 10-ounce packages frozen quick-thaw raspberries in syrup

Thaw raspberries. Purée in food processor or blender. Strain to remove seeds. Cover and refrigerate, or freeze. *Makes 4 cups.*

CARAMBOLA STARS

Carambolas, or star fruit, are green and lemony-sharp when unripe, yellow and somewhat bland-tasting when ripe. What they may lack in flavor, they make up for in decorative value. When carambolas are sliced crosswise, each slice is a star.

4 to 6 carambolas

With a small knife or vegetable peeler, remove the brown tip from each "spine." Make a lengthwise incision, about ½-inch deep, between two of the spines. Slice the fruits ⅜- to ¼-inch thick. Use larger stars from the center to decorate the Festive Fruit Platter. Hang one of the smaller stars (from the end thirds of the fruit) on the rim of each wine glass, using the incision you made before you sliced the fruit. *Each carambola makes about 16 stars.*

Sauteed Cherry Tomatoes

In tomato season, mix two or more kinds of little tomatoes if you can get them. Small red cherry tomatoes and yellow pear-shaped ones make a pretty combination.

    You can remove the stems from the tomatoes the day before and leave them at room temperature (refrigerator space is probably at a premium). In the morning, rinse the tomatoes in a colander and let dry at room temperature so they don't spatter when you cook them. Cook tomatoes as close to serving time as possible; loosely covered with foil they will keep warm for 20 to 30 minutes. Use two or more serving dishes rather than piling the tomatoes up high in one, so tomatoes don't crush each other.

About 3 tablespoons pure olive oil	¼ teaspoon freshly-ground pepper
6 pints (2½ pounds) cherry tomatoes	2 tablespoons chopped fresh dill
½ teaspoon salt	

Use two large skillets for speed. Heat about 2 teaspoons oil in each over high heat. Add cherry tomatoes, enough to cover bottom of pans. Sprinkle with some of the salt and pepper. Cook 3 to 4 minutes, shaking pans several times, just until tomatoes are hot and three or four skins have split. Sprinkle with some of the dill; shake pan gently to mix in. Using a slotted spoon, transfer tomatoes to a shallow serving dish; cover loosely to keep warm. Wipe out pans before cooking remaining tomatoes. *Makes 25 servings.*

GAME PLAN *cont'd*

- Transfer Raspberry Sauce from freezer to refrigerator.
- Tape diagrams and instructions where party helpers can see them.

ABOUT 2 HOURS BEFORE
GUESTS ARE DUE:
- Remove Miniature Corn Muffins from freezer to thaw.
- Party helpers arrive; go over duties and timing with them. Bartender sets up; starts chilling beverages in tubs of ice.
- When croissants and brioches arrive, arrange in napkin-lined baskets; cover loosely with plastic wrap. Put on table along with preserves.
- When heart-shaped cookies arrive, put near serving plates. (Helpers can arrange on plates after soufflés are served and there's space in the kitchen.)
- Have party helpers make Smoked Salmon Endive Leaves.

ABOUT 1¼ HOURS BEFORE
SERVING MAIN DISH:
- Heat oven to 350°F. Brush rolled soufflés with butter; sprinkle with cheese; put in to bake.

ABOUT 1 HOUR BEFORE
SERVING:
- Arrange Miniature Ham and Smoked Turkey Biscuits in napkin-lined baskets or on platters. Cover loosely with slightly damp paper towels; leave at room temperature.

continued

GAME PLAN *cont'd*
- Arrange fruit platters; garnish with Carambola Stars; keep cool. (Give smaller Carambola Stars to bartender to hang on rims of glasses.)
- Put Raspberry Sauce in pitchers or sauce boats; cover; leave at room temperature.
- Turn on coffeemakers.
- Cook cherry tomatoes; keep warm.

WHEN GUESTS ARRIVE, OR AFTER THE CEREMONY, IF IT IS AT YOUR HOUSE:
- Serve drinks and appetizers.
- Put Festive Fruit Platter with Raspberry Sauce on table. Invite guests to help themselves.
- Garnish rolled soufflés with fresh herbs.
- Serve Rolled Cheese Soufflés with Spinach Filling, Sauteed Cherry Tomatoes, Miniature Corn Muffins, brioches, croissants, and butter.
- Put plate of cookies on each table. Refill coffee cups. Just before it is time to toast the bride and groom and cut the cake, pour fresh Champagne.

AND DON'T FORGET . . .

Invitations
Music or musicians
Rabbi, minister, or judge
Photographer
Flowers
Coat racks
Umbrella stands
Ice
Table where guests can leave gifts

Rolled Cheese Soufflés with Spinach Filling

This recipe makes two rolled soufflés, each about 15 inches long. For 25 people, make the recipe twice, which will give you a total of four rolled soufflés. First you make a large amount of thick white sauce; half becomes the filling for two soufflés, the other half becomes the two soufflés themselves. Up to 2 days before serving you bake the two soufflés flat in jelly-roll pans, then fill them and roll them. On party day you bake the filled soufflés. Be sure to decide on serving boards or platters well ahead of time so there's no last-minute panic. Just before you take the soufflés to the table, decorate with sprigs of fresh herbs such as sage and thyme.

FOR THE SAUCE:

16 tablespoons (2 sticks) unsalted butter	6 cups milk
1⅓ cups all-purpose flour	Salt
	Freshly-ground pepper

FOR THE SOUFFLÉS:

Nutmeg, freshly-grated or from a jar	4 ounces Swiss gruyère cheese, shredded (1 cup)
12 large eggs	1 cup freshly-grated Parmesan cheese

SPINACH FILLING:

2 10-ounce packages frozen chopped spinach, thawed and squeezed dry	½ cup thinly-sliced scallions
	1 cup heavy cream

FOR FINAL BAKING:

2 tablespoons unsalted butter, melted	2 ounces Swiss gruyère cheese, finely-grated (½ cup)

Initial preparation. Heavily butter the bottom and sides of a 15 × 10-inch jelly-roll pan. Line bottom only with kitchen parchment paper, trimming sheet to fit if necessary. Butter the parchment.

Separate the egg yolks and whites, dropping all the yolks into one small container. Drop 6 of the whites into an electric-mixer bowl and the remaining 6 whites into a small container. Cover containers of whites and yolks; leave at room temperature.

Before you continue, make sure all the remaining sauce and soufflé ingredients are ready, except for the butter and cheese for final baking.

Now make the sauce. Melt the butter in a heavy, 5- to 6-quart pot over moderately-high heat. Reduce heat to moderate and stir in the flour. Cook for 3 minutes, stirring vigorously and constantly, to cook flour. (Mixture will bubble and foam.) Remove pot from heat; pour in all the milk; whisk mixture to blend. Cover pot and let stand 2 minutes.

Put pot over high heat. Uncover and bring to a simmer, whisking every minute at first, then more frequently as sauce begins to thicken. When sauce begins to bubble and boil (it should be smooth at this point), reduce heat to moderately-low and cook 5 minutes, stirring almost constantly with a wooden spoon.

Remove pot from heat. Measure 3½ cups of the sauce and put it into a very large (5 quart) bowl; let cool 5 minutes. Cover sauce remaining in pot with plastic wrap; this sauce will become the spinach filling.

Continue making the soufflés. Check that one shelf is in center of oven and heat oven to 375°F.

To sauce in bowl, add 1¼ teaspoons salt, ½ teaspoon pepper, and ⅛ teaspoon nutmeg. Stir in gruyère and Parmesan cheeses; then add the egg yolks. Beat 3 or 4 minutes with wooden spoon, until sauce is well blended and glossy. Pour 2½ cups of the mixture into a cup measure; cover and set it aside (use this for the second soufflé as soon as you've baked the first one).

Add ⅛ teaspoon salt to the 6 egg whites in the electric mixer bowl. Beat whites at high speed, until stiff peaks hold when beaters are lifted; do not overbeat. Stir a large spoonful into the cheese mixture in the bowl. Fold in the remaining beaten whites with a rubber spatula. Spread the mixture fairly evenly in the prepared jelly-roll pan. Bake for 20 minutes until top starts to feel a little crisp and is nicely browned.

Complete the Spinach Filling while the soufflé bakes. To the sauce reserved for the filling, add the spinach, scallions, heavy cream, 1¼ teaspoons salt, ¼ teaspoon pepper, and ¼ teaspoon nutmeg.

Now fill and roll the soufflé. Clear the countertop. Have ready a clean dish towel and a cookie sheet, both slightly longer and wider than the jelly-roll pan. Make a "lifter" for the rolled soufflé (see instructions below).

When soufflé is baked, remove from oven and place pan on counter with one long side closest to you. Run a knife around the edge of the soufflé, loosening it from the sides of the pan. Place tea towel over soufflé; cover with the cookie sheet turned upside down. Hold cookie sheet and jelly-roll pan together and turn them over. Place on countertop. Lift off jelly-roll pan. Carefully peel off parchment paper, sliding a metal spatula under it to start. Let soufflé cool 5 minutes. Dab half the spinach filling over the surface of the soufflé. Spread gently with a metal spatula to within about 1 inch of edges. Cover remaining filling.

Put foil lifter very close to the soufflé on the long side farthest away from you. Tuck the towel under the soufflé a little and slide lifter about 1 inch under the souffle. Pick up the towel on the side of soufflé nearest you and, using it to guide the soufflé, roll up the soufflé like a jelly

continued

SHOPPING GUIDE

BEVERAGES:

12 to 18 750 ml. bottles Champagne or sparkling nonalcoholic dry white grape juice
1 bottle crème de cassis liqueur
6 to 8 quarts freshly-squeezed orange juice
4 quarts freshly-squeezed grapefruit juice
8 bottles sparkling mineral water
Ground coffee (or coffee beans), regular and decaffeinated, 2 pounds each
Assortment of tea bags
2 quarts milk, half-and-half, or light cream (add extra milk if children will be present)
Sugar, sweetener
Lemon wedges for tea; lime wedges for mineral water

FOOD:

7⅔ cups all-purpose flour
2 cups yellow cornmeal
2 tablespoons granulated sugar
3 tablespoons baking powder
1 teaspoon nutmeg, freshly-grated or from a jar
1 cup pure olive oil
½ cup grainy mustard
¾ cup mango or other chutney
2 or 3 kinds of good-quality preserves
Parchment paper
Heavy duty foil
Foil miniature baking cups for muffins

4 ripe honeydew, cantaloupe, or other good-sized melons
2 large ripe pineapples
8 navel oranges

continued

SHOPPING GUIDE *cont'd*

6 kiwi fruit

4 to 6 pints fresh strawberries

2 or 3 pints fresh raspberries

4 to 6 carambolas (star fruit)

2 lemons

6 pints (2½ pounds) cherry tomatoes, two different colors if available

6 Belgian endives (about 1½ pounds)

1 large onion (1¼ cups chopped)

1 bunch scallions (1 cup sliced)

1 bunch radishes or fresh chives (to decorate the Smoked Salmon Endive Leaves)

Small bunch dill (enough for 2 tablespoons chopped)

Fresh herbs such as sage and thyme (for decorating the rolled soufflés)

4 10-ounce packages frozen quick-thaw raspberries

4 10-ounce packages frozen chopped spinach

2 10-ounce packages frozen corn kernels, or 1 24-ounce package (3 cups)

Wedding cake

2 dozen small brioches

2 dozen small croissants

3 dozen vanilla and chocolate heart-shaped cookies (about 1½ dozen of each flavor)

6 ounces thinly-sliced smoked turkey

6 ounces thinly-sliced ham such as Virginia, Black Forest, or Westphalian

4 ounces thinly-sliced smoked salmon

continued

roll. Maneuver the soufflé onto the foil lifter and remove the towel. (Soufflé usually develops a crevice or two on the top. Crevices should not be so deep that filling is exposed.)

Lift soufflé on its foil lifter onto a tray; cover loosely with towel and refrigerate. When cold, remove towel and cover tray with foil. (Second soufflé can go on same tray, if space allows.)

Make the second soufflé the same way, using the remaining yolk mixture, egg whites, and filling.

About 1 hour before serving, heat oven to 350°F. Lift the soufflés (on foil lifters) back onto jelly-roll pan or a cookie sheet (two can go side by side). Or, slide soufflés carefully onto ovenproof serving dishes. Brush tops with melted butter and sprinkle with the grated gruyère. Bake 35 to 40 minutes, until heated through and slightly crispy on top. Serve on baking dishes. Or slide carefully onto a large serving board or platter, gently pushing the soufflé roll off the lifter with the back of a cookie sheet. Cut each soufflé into 15 slices, lifting slices onto plates with a long metal spatula as you cut. *Makes 2 soufflé rolls, 15 servings each.*

To make lifter: To make a foil platform or "lifter" for the soufflés, cut a piece of cardboard about 15 × 5 inches. Cardboard can be flexible. Tear off a 22-inch strip of 18-inch wide heavy duty foil. Place cardboard lengthwise on foil and wrap foil around it, leaving the ends unfolded. Turn lifter so seam is down. Once the rolled soufflé is on the lifter you will be able to move it by carefully picking up the lifter by the foil ends. You will need one lifter for each soufflé, a total of four.

Miniature Corn Muffins

Bake these in tiny muffin cups—ones that hold about 2 tablespoons—lined with foil baking cups. You can bake the muffins in batches.

- ¾ cup pure olive oil
- 1¼ cups finely chopped onions
- 3 cups frozen corn kernels
- 1 teaspoon salt
- ¼ teaspoon freshly-ground pepper
- 2 cups yellow cornmeal
- 1 cup all-purpose flour
- 2 tablespoons granulated sugar
- 1 tablespoon baking powder
- 4 large eggs
- 1 cup milk

Heat oil in a large skillet or saucepan over moderately-low heat. Stir in onions and cook about 10 minutes, stirring often, until onions are soft and just starting to turn golden. Onions should be very soft, but not browned. Stir in 1½ cups of the corn, salt, and pepper and cook 2 to 3 minutes, stirring once or twice, just until thawed. Remove from heat and let cool 5 minutes.

While onions cook, line muffin cups with foil baking cups. Heat oven to 375°F. Put cornmeal, flour, sugar, and baking powder into a large bowl; stir to mix well.

Break eggs into a blender or food processor; add milk and remaining 1½ cups corn. Process to a coarse purée. Pour into flour mixture; add onion mixture and stir just until dry ingredients are moistened.

Spoon into muffin cups, filling them to the top. Bake 25 to 30 minutes, until lightly browned. Turn out onto a rack to cool. Let muffin pan cool before baking the next batch. *Makes 60 to 66 miniature muffins.*

SHOPPING GUIDE *cont'd*

- 14 cups (3½ quarts) milk
- 3 cups (1½ pints) heavy cream
- 48 tablespoons (6 sticks) unsalted butter plus butter for the tables
- 28 large eggs
- 12 ounces Swiss gruyère cheese
- 2 cups (8 ounces) freshly-grated Parmesan cheese
- 1 8-ounce package neufchâtel cheese

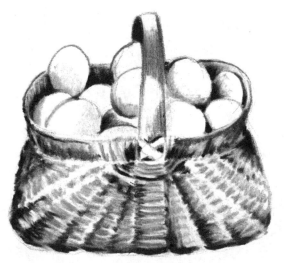

BREAKFAST FOR HEALTH-CONSCIOUS FRIENDS

Great Grains

Often it is the simplest things in life that please people most. Only a few years ago, one would have felt cheap offering oatmeal to company, but the renewed interest in carbohydrates, fiber, and grandmother's food has changed all that. Now health-conscious friends are intrigued and delighted to be offered a grain dish, particularly one they might not have cooked for themselves. Sometimes a simple dish of cooked oatmeal, barley flakes, or buckwheat groats, along with very lovely fruits or juices, is enough to make everyone happy. On another occasion, cooked grains might precede something deliciously wicked, such as bacon and eggs!

Here you'll find directions for cooking grains such as kasha in the simplest possible way. Serve them with milk and light cream, brown sugar, and perhaps raisins or currants. Papa Bear's Breakfast is a festive way to serve oatmeal. With fruit and wheat berries on top, it can stand on its own as a perfect breakfast. Brown Rice Breakfast Pudding is certainly rich and special enough to be the main event.

BUYING AND COOKING GRAINS

When buying whole-grain cereals such as oatmeal, brown rice, barley flakes, or wheat berries, look for a source that has a fast turnover. Whole grains have a shorter shelf life at room temperature than refined ones. In addition to oatmeal and brown rice, which are staples, many supermarkets have extensive "natural" or health-food sections where you may find a wide variety of grains. (To help you when buying them, the weight of the less familiar grains is given in the recipe.)

There are good mail-order sources, too, or perhaps you live near a busy health-food store. Wherever you buy whole grains, once you have opened a package, store it, tightly closed, in the freezer.

Unless the package or a recipe directs otherwise, most grains cook best if added to boiling liquid. This is especially true for oatmeal (but not oat bran), which tends to become gluey if mixed with cold water and brought to a boil.

Even though they require long cooking (up to two hours) whole grains such as wheat berries need little attention or stirring. Use a pan with a tight-fitting lid and adjust the heat so that the water is barely simmering. (If the water boils too quickly it will evaporate, allowing the cereal on the bottom of the pot to scorch.)

Ground grains, such as cornmeal, leave pots sticky. For easiest cleanup, cook cornmeal, oatmeal, and barley grits in nonstick pans—unless the recipe calls for whisking the mixture, since whisking will damage the surface of a nonstick pan. If you can't use a nonstick pan, the next best choice is one with a very thick bottom. Once the cereal is boiling, reduce the heat until the mixture is just giving an occasional "plop." As soon as the cereal is cooked, remove the pan from the heat and let it stand, covered, for three to five minutes. (This helps soften the cereal on the bottom.) Right after you have served the cereal, soak the pot in water. The standing and soaking will speed cleanup.

Many grains cook well in a microwave oven; follow package or manual directions, being sure to use a large enough container to avoid boil overs.

Mush and Milk

Joanne Hayes grew up in Maryland, where her father, who came from Oneida, New York, introduced his family to one of his own favorite childhood breakfasts: hot cornmeal with lots of butter, brown sugar, and milk. Joanne, who is the food editor of *Country Living* magazine, says she and her cousins ate Mush and Milk on snowy winter days before they went sledding. Any leftover mush was chilled in a loaf pan and then sliced, fried, and enjoyed with sausage, bacon, and eggs at another meal.

6 cups water
1 teaspoon salt

1⅓ cups yellow cornmeal
Butter, brown sugar, milk

Bring water to a boil in a heavy or nonstick 3- to 4-quart saucepan over high heat. Add salt. While whisking or stirring water constantly, slowly sprinkle in the cornmeal, keeping water boiling.

When all cornmeal has been added, reduce heat to low, cover, and simmer 15 to 20 minutes until thick and creamy. Pour into bowls. Serve with butter, brown sugar, and milk. *Makes about 6 cups, 6 servings.*

Crunchy Granola

If you like traditional baked granolas, here are two excellent, not-too-sweet ones. They are rich with nuts and seeds, but no raisins, since I feel raisins baked into a granola are something only a dentist can be happy about. You can make this up to one week ahead.

4 cups (10 ounces) old-fashioned oats
1 cup (3 ounces) oat bran
½ cup (about 2½ ounces) untoasted slivered almonds or coarsely chopped hazelnuts (see note)
½ cup (about 3 ounces) hulled but not toasted pumpkin or sunflower seeds

½ cup honey
3 tablespoons light olive or vegetable oil
1 tablespoon vanilla extract
⅓ cup creamy peanut butter, preferably without salt added

Heat oven to 325°F. Get out a large roasting pan or use a 15 × 10-inch jelly-roll pan. (You'll have to use a little restraint when stirring in the jelly-roll pan.) Mix oats, oat bran, nuts, and seeds in the pan. Bake 30 minutes, stirring every 5 to 7 minutes; nuts and oats will acquire a slightly toasted look.

Measure honey in a 2-cup glass measure. Add oil and vanilla. Remove pan of granola from oven. Stir honey mixture until thoroughly blended; drizzle over oat mixture; stir thoroughly with two wooden spoons until coated. Spread evenly; bake 10 minutes more.

Remove pan from oven again. Dab peanut butter over the oat mixture. Mash and stir with the two spoons until peanut butter has melted and coated the oat mixture. Press mixture down in an even layer. Bake 5 minutes longer. Cool completely. Scrape from pan to break up. Store granola in an airtight container (or a plastic bag with a zip-type closure) at room temperature. Keeps well up to 1 week. *Makes 1 pound, 10 ounces granola; 6 cups.*

CALORIES-DON'T-COUNT GRANOLA

Follow directions for Crunchy Granola but reduce the oats to 3 cups and increase the nuts and seeds to 1 cup each. *Makes 6½ cups.*

NOTE: If you can get only *toasted* hazelnuts, add them with the peanut butter.

Breakfast Indian Pudding

Indian pudding is a famous old New England dessert that tastes good for breakfast, too. Although it is usually baked and made with cornmeal (which early New England settlers called Indian meal—hence the name), it's even more delicious made with barley or hominy grits and eaten without baking.

4 cups (1 quart) milk
¾ cup barley grits, or ½ cup hominy
    grits or ½ cup plus 2
    tablespoons yellow cornmeal
¾ teaspoon ground cinnamon

⅛ teaspoon nutmeg, freshly-grated or
    from a jar
½ teaspoon salt
⅓ cup light or dark molasses
2 large eggs

Heat milk in a heavy, nonstick 3-quart pan over moderate heat until bubbles appear around the edge. Mix grits, spices, and salt. Stir into hot milk. When mixture is simmering, reduce heat to low, cover pan, and cook 15 minutes, stirring once or twice.

Measure molasses in a 2-cup measure. Add eggs and whisk with a fork until blended.

Remove grits from heat; let stand 3 or 4 minutes for grits to cool slightly. Quickly stir in the egg mixture. Return pan to heat; stir constantly for about 2 minutes, just until mixture starts to bubble. Remove from heat. Ladle into bowls and serve. *Makes 4½ cups, 4 or 5 servings.*

Brown-rice Breakfast Pudding

For best flavor, make this a day ahead. Serve it warm, or cold—not hot.

1 cup low-fat ricotta cheese	2 tablespoons granulated sugar
½ cup fruit-only apricot spread	½ teaspoon vanilla extract
½ cup milk	3 cups cooked short-grain brown rice
2 large eggs	(see note)
⅓ cup reduced-calorie sour cream	½ cup (3 ounces) golden raisins
(sometimes called sour half-and-	½ teaspoon ground cinnamon mixed
half)	with 1 teaspoon sugar

Heat oven to 325°F. Have ready a 2-quart baking dish, about 10 × 6 inches.

Put ricotta, apricot spread, milk, eggs, sour cream, 2 tablespoons sugar, and vanilla into a medium-sized bowl. Beat to mix thoroughly. Stir in rice and raisins. Pour into baking dish. Sprinkle with cinnamon-sugar.

Bake 50 to 55 minutes until pudding is firm when shaken. Remove from oven. Let cool 20 minutes. Cover and refrigerate several hours or overnight. Serve cold, or uncover and bake about 20 minutes at 300°F., just until warm. *Makes 6 to 8 servings.*

NOTE: To make 3 cups cooked rice, bring 2 cups water to a boil in a medium-sized saucepan over moderately-high heat. Add 2 cups short-grain brown rice and ⅛ teaspoon salt. When boiling, reduce heat to low, cover pan, and simmer 45 to 55 minutes, until rice is tender. May be prepared ahead and refrigerated.

Kasha

Kasha is toasted buckwheat groats and has a warm, earthy flavor. Cooked kasha keeps several days in the refrigerator. It reheats well in a microwave oven, or with a little water in a nonstick saucepan over moderate heat.

5 cups water	½ teaspoon salt
2½ cups (1 pound) kasha	Milk or cream, brown sugar

Bring water to a boil in a heavy 2-quart saucepan. Stir in kasha and salt. When boiling, turn heat to low, cover pan, and simmer 20 minutes until groats are tender and water has been absorbed. Serve with milk or cream and brown sugar. *Makes 8 cups, 8 servings.*

Hot Hulled Barley Cereal

The form of barley most commonly used in cooking (in Scotch broth, for example) is "pearled" barley, from which most of the outer brown husk has been removed, enabling the barley to swell more readily and cook faster. In contrast, hulled barley looks like grains of wheat and is available where health foods are sold. It has more fiber than pearled barley and even when fully cooked, the grains remain chewy and separate. Serve hulled barley with milk and sugar or sprinkle on hot oatmeal. You can also add the cooked grains to soup, or serve them as a side dish with meat.

   7 *cups water*   1 *teaspoon salt*
2½ *cups (1 pound) hulled barley*

Bring water to a boil in a heavy 3-quart saucepan. Add barley and salt. When boiling, turn heat to low, cover, and simmer 1½ hours, checking every 20 minutes or so to make sure water has not all evaporated (add additional ½ cup water if needed). When barley is tender, but still chewy, drain off any remaining water. Barley may be cooked up to 3 days ahead, covered, and refrigerated. Reheat with a little water before serving. *Makes 8 cups cooked barley.*

Wheat Berries

Wheat berries are whole grains of wheat from which only the outer husk has been removed. Look for soft wheat or hard-wheat berries where health foods or "natural" foods are sold. Even after long cooking, the grains remain chewy and separate. They are good with milk, sugar, or honey, and perhaps a few currants or raisins. They taste even better sprinkled over oatmeal as in Papa Bear's Breakfast, page 172.

   5 *cups water*   1 *teaspoon salt*
2½ *cups (1 pound) hard-wheat or*
        2⅓ *cups (1 pound) soft-wheat*
        berries

Bring water to a boil in a heavy, 3-quart saucepan over high heat. Stir in wheat berries and salt. When boiling, reduce heat to low, cover pan, and simmer 2 hours. Berries may be cooked up to 3 days ahead and refrigerated. Reheat before serving in a saucepan over moderate heat. *Makes 7 cups hard-wheat berries, 6 cups soft-wheat berries.*

Buckwheat-Triticale Muffins

Triticale is a hybrid of rye and wheat that is higher in protein than most other grains. These muffins are full of good, whole-grain nutrition, with a light texture and delicate flavor. Warm or cold, they are perfect for breakfast.

½ cup triticale flour
½ cup buckwheat flour
½ cup all-purpose flour
½ cup oat bran
2 tablespoons granulated sugar
1 tablespoon baking powder

¼ teaspoon salt
1 large egg
1 cup milk
4 tablespoons (½ stick) unsalted
    butter, melted

Heat oven to 375°F. Grease twelve muffin cups or line with foil, not paper, baking cups.

Mix flours, oat bran, sugar, baking powder, and salt in a large bowl.

Beat egg with a fork or wire whisk in a small bowl. Whisk in milk and butter. Pour over dry ingredients and fold in with a rubber spatula until dry ingredients are just moistened.

Scoop batter into muffin cups. Bake 20 to 25 minutes, until lightly browned. Remove from pans and cool on wire rack. *Makes 12 muffins.*

BUCKWHEAT-TRITICALE MUFFIN MIX

2 cups triticale flour
2 cups buckwheat flour
2 cups all-purpose flour
2 cups oat bran

½ cup granulated sugar
4 tablespoons baking powder
1¼ teaspoons salt

Thoroughly mix ingredients in a large bowl. Use right away or store airtight in a cool dry place up to 4 months. *Makes enough for 4 dozen muffins.*

To use. Measure 2 cups mix for 12 muffins. Add egg, milk, and butter as in above recipe. Mix and bake as directed.

Papa Bear's Breakfast

Breakfast is one of my favorite times for business meetings, and my favorite site is Sarabeth's Kitchen, on Manhattan's Upper West Side. There are so many good things to choose from that it's hard to decide. Usually I come down to either the pumpkin waffles or one of the stylish presentations of homey oatmeal, wheat berries, bananas, and brown sugar. Here is my own version of Papa Bear's Breakfast, and surely your friends, golden-haired or otherwise, will enjoy it.

Cook the wheat berries one or two days ahead, but make the oatmeal fresh in the morning, using steel-cut or old-fashioned oats. Have everything absolutely ready before you fill the individual serving bowls —the bananas peeled, the berries hulled—then work quickly, so the oatmeal doesn't get cold. This breakfast also works very well as a buffet.

6 servings cooked old-fashioned oats (follow package directions) or Best-ever Oatmeal (see page 145)
1½ cups cooked Wheat Berries (see page 171)

Brown sugar
3 or 4 ripe bananas, thinly sliced
About 12 fresh strawberries, rinsed, hulled, and sliced
Milk, light cream, or half-and-half

Ladle about 1 cup cooked oats into each serving bowl (rimmed soup bowls look nice). Sprinkle ¼ cup cooked Wheat Berries in a small circle in the center and sprinkle about 1 teaspoon brown sugar over them. Arrange bananas in a circle around edge of each dish. Put about 5 slices of strawberry in the center of the wheat berries, and 3 or 5 more slices among the bananas. Serve with milk, light cream, or half-and-half. *Makes 6 servings.*

Recipes for Special Diet Needs

What to do when a breakfast guest announces that he or she is allergic to wheat or milk, or is on a strict low-cholesterol diet and can't eat eggs? Breakfast can be tricky for people with special diet problems. Sometimes the guests (especially those on very strict diets) may simply ask if you mind if they bring their own food. If they do, accept and be thankful. It can save a great deal of worry for both host and guest. Another time you may want to try your hand at making something special. I've found that people on special diets often miss baked goods most, so in this chapter you will find several recipes designed to please, and be safe for, guests with a variety of special diet needs.

When making food for someone who has an allergy—especially a potentially life-threatening one such as an allergy to peanuts—I leave the recipe and the ingredients I used on the counter and quietly invite the guest into the kitchen to make absolutely sure I have not unthinkingly used an unsafe product. (This is especially wise if any packaged foods are used.) For example, a person who is allergic to corn must also avoid corn oil, cornstarch, and most baking powders. A person who is allergic to peanuts is allergic to anything with even a hint of peanut in it. Better to spend a few minutes checking than risk a violent reaction.

The baked goods I have devised are baked in muffin cups, and I've even called some of them muffins. But don't expect them to have the taste and texture of regular muffins. Brown rice flour, for example, imparts a slightly sandy texture. Muffins made entirely with corn, oat, or rice flours simply do not have the structure we expect in those made with wheat flour. In spite of these caveats, I think you and your allergy-prone guests will rate them as very satisfactory.

George Greene's Special Scrambled Eggs

George, who is married to Ellen Greene, my associate at *Woman's Day*, loves scrambled eggs but is on a very strict low-cholesterol diet. He swears that this is closer to the real thing than cholesterol-free egg substitute alone. It's delicious with a spoonful of salsa.

Cholesterol-free egg substitute equivalent   *Whites of 2 large eggs*
  to 1 egg

Beat egg substitute and egg whites with a fork in a small bowl. Spray a small nonstick skillet with vegetable cooking spray. Pour in egg mixture and scramble, stirring mixture very little. *Makes 1 serving.*

No-cholesterol Potato Frittata

Absolutely delicious, whether you are watching your cholesterol intake or not.

1 *pound white thin-skinned potatoes* ("new" potatoes), scrubbed	¼ *teaspoon salt*
2 *tablespoons light or pure olive oil*	¼ *teaspoon freshly-ground pepper*
½ *cup thinly-sliced onion*	*Cholesterol-free egg substitute*
¼ *teaspoon dried thyme leaves,* crumbled	*equivalent to 4 large eggs*

Boil potatoes in water to cover 20 to 25 minutes or until just tender when pierced with knife. Drain in a colander and rinse with cold water. When cool enough to handle, cut into slices about ¼-inch thick (no need to peel).

Heat oil in a 10-inch nonstick skillet over moderately-high heat. Add sliced potatoes and onion; sprinkle with thyme, salt, and pepper. Reduce heat to moderately-low and cook 15 to 20 minutes, turning every 4 or 5 minutes, until potatoes and onions are nicely browned.

Reduce heat to low. Pour in egg substitute. Cover and cook 7 to 9 minutes, uncovering pan every 2 minutes or so and lifting cooked egg around the edges with a spatula, allowing uncooked (still-liquid) egg to flow underneath.

When frittata is firm, remove from heat. Invert onto a serving plate. Cut into wedges and serve. *Makes 4 servings.*

CHOLESTEROL SIMPLIFIED

Cholesterol is found only in foods of animal origin (milk, butter, and cheese; eggs, fish, meat, and poultry). There is no cholesterol in foods of plant origin, including all vegetables, fruits, and grains.

Cholesterol is found in every cell in your body and is essential to life. Your liver manufactures it. So where's the problem? A problem may arise if your body manufactures too much cholesterol, or if you eat too many cholesterol-rich foods, Then the level of cholesterol in your blood rises to a point where it begins to clog your arteries.

Eating too much saturated fat can also contribute to a high cholesterol level. Saturated fats are found in meats, poultry, tropical oils (such as coconut or palm), and hardened or hydrogenated vegetable oils. They are also found in products such as commercial baked goods and non-dairy creamers made with hydrogenated and tropical oils.

CHOLESTEROL-CUTTING TIPS

If you have invited a cholesterol-watching friend to breakfast, you will find it relatively easy to adapt many of the recipes in this book. Some tips:

◆ Use margarine instead of butter as a spread. Look for a margarine that lists *liquid* oil (corn, safflower, canola) as the first ingredient on the package label.

◆ Serve skim milk instead of whole milk or cream; nonfat yogurt instead of sour cream.

◆ In coffee cake recipes, use unsalted stick margarine instead of butter. (Whipped or "light" margarines, which have air or liquid added to them, are often unsuccessful in baking.) Use skim milk instead of whole, and a cholesterol-free egg substitute instead of whole eggs. Purchased coffee cakes usually contain saturated fats as well as cholesterol from eggs. If you bake coffee cakes at home you can control the ingredients.

◆ Cholesterol-free egg substitute can replace whole eggs in most recipes. In recipes that call for both yolks and stiffly beaten egg whites, use egg substitute instead of the yolks (in the amount called for to replace whole eggs) and real, fresh egg whites. (Egg whites contain no cholesterol.) Cholesterol-free egg substitute can even be used for rich sauces such as hollandaise. Believe it or not, it is very hard to tell the difference between the sauce made with real egg and one made with a cholesterol-free substitute.

No-cholesterol Kasha

Kasha is the word for toasted buckwheat groats as well as for this method of preparing them. It's difficult to detect a difference between this version and the traditional kasha made with an egg. It is a delicious breakfast dish served with sautéed mushrooms and grilled tomato halves. Start the meal with fresh fruit and yogurt; the yogurt will balance the vegetable protein in the buckwheat.

1 cup (6½ ounces) kasha (toasted buckwheat groats)
¼ cup cholesterol-free egg substitute
2 cups boiling water
½ teaspoon salt
1 tablespoon light olive oil or margarine

In a heavy, medium-sized, nonstick saucepan mix buckwheat groats with egg substitute. Place over moderate heat and cook, stirring constantly, for 3 to 4 minutes, until grains are separated and dry. Pour in boiling water; add salt and oil. Bring to a boil. Reduce heat to low, cover, and cook 20 minutes until soft. Stir kasha before serving. *Makes 3 cups, 3 or more servings.*

Milk-free, Egg-free Applesauce Muffins

These are moist and delicious. For best flavor, let cool an hour before eating. Good as a breakfast or dinner bread, or for dessert with a big spoonful of applesauce.

1 cup oat bran
½ cup all-purpose flour
2½ teaspoons baking powder
½ teaspoon ground cinnamon
⅛ teaspoon salt
¼ cup light olive or vegetable oil
¼ cup packed light or dark brown sugar
¾ cup unsweetened applesauce
¼ cup frozen apple juice concentrate
½ teaspooon vanilla extract

Heat oven to 375°F. Line nine muffin cups with foil, but not paper, baking cups.

Mix oat bran, flour, baking powder, cinnamon, and salt in a large bowl.

In a medium-sized bowl, beat oil and sugar with a fork or wire whisk until lumps of sugar have dissolved. Add applesauce, apple juice, and vanilla. Whisk to mix. Pour over dry ingredients and fold in with a rubber spatula until dry ingredients are moistened.

Fill each muffin cup with about ⅓ cup batter. Bake 30 to 32 minutes, until browned and springy to the touch. Let cool a few minutes before removing to a wire rack. *Makes 9 muffins.*

Low-sodium, Low-cholesterol Corn Peaks

These breads contain no cholesterol and, because no baking powder or baking soda is used, they are also low-sodium. Air beaten into the egg whites leavens the batter. While they are much denser than regular cornbread or muffins, if you crave corn muffins and are on a low-sodium or low-cholesterol diet, they are very acceptable.

2 cups yellow cornmeal
½ cup all-purpose flour
1½ cups milk
½ cup cholesterol-free egg substitute
2 tablespoons pure olive or vegetable oil

½ teaspoon vanilla extract
Whites of 3 large eggs
2 tablespoons granulated sugar

Heat oven to 425°F. Line twelve muffin cups with foil, but not paper, baking cups.

Put cornmeal, flour, milk, egg substitute, oil, and vanilla into a large bowl. Stir with wooden spoon until well blended.

In a deep, medium-sized bowl, beat egg whites with an electric mixer at high speed until soft peaks form when beaters are lifted. Add sugar and beat until whites are glossy and stiff peaks form.

Using a rubber spatula, stir a spoonful of beaten whites into corn-meal mixture to lighten. Fold in remaining whites. Scoop batter into muffin cups, using about ¼ cup batter for each and filling cups to the tops.

Bake 25 to 30 minutes, until lightly browned. Turn out onto a rack to cool slightly. Serve warm. Breads will be crusty on the outside, quite moist inside. When muffins are cool, wrap in a plastic bag if not serving soon so they won't dry out. *Makes 12 corn peaks.*

Oat Date Nut Muffins

These muffins are wheat- and cholesterol-free and high in fiber. They have a wonderful flavor, but are very crumbly because there is no wheat flour in them. If you don't plan to eat them right away, wrap them in a plastic bag as soon as they are cool to keep them moist.

2¼ cups oat bran

1 tablespoon baking powder

¼ teaspoon salt

½ cup milk

¼ cup packed brown sugar

Whites of 3 large eggs

3 tablespoons vegetable oil

2 tablespoons honey

¼ cup (1½ ounces) chopped dates

¼ cup (1 ounce) walnuts, chopped

Heat oven to 375°F. Line nine muffin cups with foil, but not paper, baking cups.

Mix oat bran, baking powder, and salt in a large bowl.

Put milk, brown sugar, egg whites, vegetable oil, and honey into a medium-sized bowl. Whisk with a fork or wire whisk until sugar dissolves and whites are well broken up. Pour over dry ingredients; sprinkle with dates and walnuts. Fold in with a rubber spatula, until dry ingredients are just moistened.

Scoop the batter into the muffin cups. Bake 20 to 22 minutes until light brown (muffins will rise very little).

Remove from oven and let cool 5 minutes. Remove from pan to a wire rack to cool completely. *Makes 9 muffins.*

Sesame Pecan Brown-rice Muffins

These low-sodium muffins have no gluten, corn, or milk. Eat them for breakfast, or split and fill them with lightly mashed strawberries and a suitable topping for an impromptu dessert. Brown-rice flour (which you can buy at health-food stores) gives the muffins a slightly sandy texture. For best flavor, make a day ahead.

¼ cup hulled sesame seeds

¾ cup brown-rice flour

¾ cup (3 ounces) pecans, coarsely chopped

Whites of 4 large eggs

½ cup granulated sugar

½ teaspoon vanilla extract

Yolks of 4 large eggs

Heat oven to 350°F. Line twelve muffin cups with foil, but not paper, baking cups.

Toast sesame seeds in a small pan over moderate heat, stirring or shaking pan, until seeds begin to pop. Pour seeds into a small bowl. Add brown-rice flour and chopped nuts and mix well.

Put egg whites in a large bowl. Beat with an electric mixer at high speed until soft peaks form when beaters are lifted. Add sugar about one-fourth at a time, beating well after each addition. Whites should be stiff, very white, and glossy.

Turn mixer to low. Add vanilla, then drop in all 4 egg yolks at once. Beat a few seconds until mixture turns pale yellow. Remove bowl from mixer.

Sprinkle pecan mixture over egg mixture and fold in with a rubber spatula, until just evenly distributed. Pour batter into muffin cups, filling them to the top. Bake 20 to 25 minutes, until an even pale brown. Let stand 3 to 5 minutes before removing from pans to a wire rack. When muffins are cool, wrap in a plastic bag. *Makes 12 muffins.*

Lemony Brown-rice Muffins

These muffins are low-sodium, and wheat- and milk-free. They are good warm. Have the oven heated, the pan prepared, and all the ingredients measured before you begin beating the egg whites.

Whites of 4 large eggs	*1 teaspoon freshly-grated lemon peel*
¼ teaspoon salt (omit for low-sodium diets)	*¾ cup brown-rice flour*
2 tablespoons granulated sugar	*2 tablespoons honey mixed with 4 teaspoons freshly-squeezed lemon*
Yolks of 4 large eggs	*juice.*

Heat oven to 350°F. Line ten to twelve muffin cups with foil, but not paper, baking cups.

In a large bowl, beat egg whites and salt with an electric mixer on high speed until soft peaks form when beaters are lifted. Add sugar, 1 tablespoon at a time, beating well after each addition. Whites will be thick and glossy.

Turn mixer to low. Drop in all 4 yolks at once and the lemon peel; beat a few seconds to mix. Sprinkle in rice flour; beat a second or two. Remove bowl from mixer. If rice flour is not completely mixed in, finish with a rubber spatula.

Pour or spoon the batter into the muffin cups, filling them to the top. Bake 18 to 20 minutes, until light golden brown; do not overbake. Remove from pans to a wire rack. While still hot, brush tops of muffins with the lemon-honey syrup, or dip top of each muffin in the syrup until it is all used up. When muffins are cool, wrap in a plastic bag if not serving soon so they won't dry out. *Makes 10 to 12 muffins.*

Apricot Almond Puffs

Low in sodium as well as corn- and milk-free, these have a lovely flavor and are quite moist inside.

1 cup (4½ ounces) dried apricot halves
1 tablespoon freshly-squeezed lemon juice
  Water
1 cup all-purpose flour
½ cup whole-wheat flour
½ cup (2 ounces) toasted slivered almonds

4 tablespoons granulated sugar
2 tablespoons unsalted margarine or vegetable oil (but not corn oil)
  Yolks of 2 large eggs
½ teaspoon almond extract
  Whites of 5 large eggs

In a small saucepan, bring apricots, lemon juice, and 1 cup water to a boil. Cover and simmer about 5 minutes over moderate heat until apricots are tender and have absorbed most of the liquid.

Meanwhile, line twelve muffin cups with foil, but not paper, baking cups. Heat oven to 400°F.

Mix flours, almonds, and 2 tablespoons of the sugar in a large bowl.

Purée apricots with margarine in blender or food processor until apricots are fairly smooth. Add yolks, almond extract, and ¾ cup water; process to blend.

In a deep, medium-sized bowl, beat egg whites with an electric mixer on high speed until soft peaks form when beaters are lifted. Add remaining 2 tablespoons sugar and beat until stiff and glossy.

Pour apricot mixture over flour; stir until smooth with a wooden spoon. Batter will be stiff and a little hard to manage. Stir in about one-fourth of the beaten egg whites to lighten the mixture. Using a rubber spatula, fold in the remainder.

Scoop batter into muffin cups filling them almost to the top. Bake 25 to 30 minutes, until light brown and firm to the touch. Remove to a wire rack; serve warm. *Makes 12 puffs.*

BREAKFAST BASICS

Measuring Ingredients

An ounce or two more or less meat, onion, or carrot in a soup or stew will make little difference to the success of the recipe. With baked goods such as pancakes, muffins, and coffee cakes, however, accurate measuring is essential. Buy good quality tools; buy several sets so you don't have to stop mid-recipe and wash a measure; and keep them handy. If measuring spoons come on a ring, take them off and keep them spoon-end up in a jar on the counter. (Threaten fines, or worse, for anyone who swipes them for other uses.)

Here's how to measure:

DRY INGREDIENTS

Use nested metal cup measures that come in one cup and half, third, and quarter cup sizes. Use exact-size measures; for example, don't try to measure three-quarters cup sugar in a one-cup measure; instead, measure a half cup and a quarter cup.

Flours: For the recipes in this book, do not sift all-purpose flour either before or after measuring. Stir flour in sack or canister and spoon into measuring cup until overflowing. Draw a knife or spatula (anything with a straight edge) across the top of the measuring cup, sweeping off excess. Do not tamp flour down in cup or tap measure on countertop; either way could increase the amount of flour in the cup.

Granulated sugar, rice, lentils, and other, heavier dry ingredients: Use nested measuring cups but, with these heavier ingredients, it is fine to scoop them up from bag or canister, or pour the ingredient into the cup measure before leveling off the surface. (Put a sheet of wax paper on the counter to catch excess flour, sugar, or rice, then pick up the paper and shoot the excess back into the bag or canister.)

Brown sugar: Pack brown sugar into the measuring cup and press down with fingertips until surface of sugar is level with edge of cup.

Baking powder, baking soda, herbs, and spices: Use metal measuring spoons. Dip into container; sweep off excess with finger, knife edge, or metal spatula.

When a measuring spoon is too large to go in the container, as often happens with spices, use the wax paper technique described above.

WET INGREDIENTS

Milk, water, juices, and semi-liquid ingredients such as honey and yogurt: Use clear glass cup measures that come in sizes ranging from one cup to eight cups. With liquids, there's not the same need to use exact-size measures as there is with dry ingredients; as long as the appropriate mark is clearly visible, you can measure one-half cup water in an eight-cup measure.

To measure liquids: place cup on countertop or other level surface. Pour (or spoon) in liquid. Bend over and check measurement at eye level.

When measuring sticky ingredients such as honey or molasses, you can first lightly oil the measure (or spray with cooking spray). The honey will pour out more easily.

FATS AND OILS

Oils: Pour into glass measure, as described above, or into measuring spoons.

Butter or margarine: The wrappers of sticks or cubes of butter and margarine are usually marked in tablespoons and cups. When the wrapping machine errs and the paper isn't on straight, it is usually enough to measure by eye, keeping in mind that:

4 tablespoons (½ stick) = ½ cup (2 ounces)
8 tablespoons (1 stick) = 1 cup (4 ounces)
12 tablespoons (1½ sticks) = ¾ cup (6 ounces)
16 tablespoons (2 sticks) = 1 cup (8 ounces)

Vegetable shortening: There's no unmessy way to measure solid vegetable shortening. Press shortening into nested measuring cups with a rubber spatula and remove it the same way.

TEASPOONS, TABLESPOONS, AND CUPS: A Guide for Cooks

3 teaspoons = 1 tablespoon
4 tablespoons = ¼ cup
8 tablespoons = ½ cup
5 tablespoons plus 1 teaspoon = ⅓ cup
2 cups = 1 pint (16 fluid ounces)
4 cups (2 pints) = 1 quart (32 fluid ounces)
4 quarts = 1 gallon (16 cups, 128 fluid ounces)

ELECTRONIC SCALE EQUIVALENTS

While recipes specify the amount of some ingredients (such as meat or produce) in pounds and ounces, most stores use electronic scales, which display (and print out on labels) ounces as decimal fractions of pounds. Electronic scales are so finely tuned that a weight will seldom read any of the following figures exactly. Use them as a guide to make sure you buy what you need.

When a recipe calls for:	*A computer-printed label will show:*
4 ounces (¼ pound)	.25 pound
8 ounces (½ pound)	.50 pound
12 ounces (¾ pound)	.75 pound
1 pound (16 ounces)	1.00 pound
1¼ pounds (1 pound, 4 ounces)	1.25 pounds

To arrive at the equivalent of the decimal fraction in ounces, multiply the fraction by 16 (the number of ounces in a pound). Example: .50 × 16 = 8 (ounces).

A Few Words About Utensils

SKILLET SIZES

Most skillets are sold by the diameter, measured across the top, not the inside bottom where the food will go. For that reason, recipes in this book that call for a skillet specify the number of inches across the bottom.

DREDGERS

A dredger is like a giant pepper shaker with a handle. Keep two handy. Fill one with all-purpose flour to sprinkle on boards or countertops when you're going to roll out dough. Fill the other dredger with confectioners' sugar ready to sprinkle over unfrosted cakes or cookies for a fast, professionally finished look.

Be sure to label each dredger, or buy two very different ones (I have one shiny red one and one stainless steel).

SPRING FOR A SPRINGFORM

A springform pan is a high-sided baking utensil that comes apart. A clasp fastens the expandable sides securely in place around the removable base. Springform pans are used for hard-to-turn-out cakes such as tortes, cheesecakes, or sticky buns. After the cake is baked and cooled, you unclasp the sides and remove them. Serve the cake on the base on a pretty plate. Springform pans come in several sizes. Be sure to buy a good-quality one, or you may find that any fruit you use in a recipe, if it touches the bottom or sides, will discolor the metal and sometimes the food, too, as well as add a metallic flavor.

Breakfast Fruit

Breakfast is a time to enjoy the most delicious fruits and juices in their purest, freshest form. Whatever a menu suggests, if that particular fruit is not ripe when you go to buy it, choose another fruit.

CITRUS FRUIT

Citrus fruits—oranges and grapefruit—are the most popular breakfast fruit for eating or for juice. Citrus fruits are juiciest and most flavorful in the winter months and get sweeter as the season goes on. (I rarely buy grapefruit until late January.) When you buy citrus fruits, heft them in your hand; they should feel heavy for their size, indicating that there's plenty of juice inside.

When the season is at its height, put a basket containing several varieties of citrus—navel oranges, tangelos, tangerines, mandarins—whatever is in the market—on the breakfast table and invite guests to share several kinds.

PREPARING FAMILIAR BREAKFAST FRUITS

TO PEEL AN ORANGE OR GRAPEFRUIT:
Use a sharp or serrated-edged knife. (A laser-type edge is excellent.) Cut the skin off the top and the bottom of the orange, just down to the juicy part. Stand orange on chopping board. Cut off peel and pith in strips, cutting from top to bottom, curving the knife around the fruit, and removing as little of the juicy orange as possible.

When you've gone all around the orange, check your handiwork and cut off any pieces of pith you missed. Now the orange is ready to cut as the recipe directs. For round slices, slice crosswise; for half-moon slices, cut orange in half lengthwise before slicing crosswise.

If a recipe calls for orange or grapefruit sections, hold the peeled fruit in one hand and cut down the far side of one of the pieces of membrane that separates each section; turn the knife out and up as you get to the center, and the fruit section should come with it. Cut out remaining sections in the same way until you are left with just a handful of membrane; squeeze membrane in your hand to release as much of the remaining juice as possible.

TO PEEL A MELON:
You can peel a round or slightly oval melon such as cantaloupe or honeydew by cutting it into wedges and then cutting the rind off each individual slice.

A less tedious method, especially useful when you want to end up with melon chunks, is as follows: Cut the melon in half crosswise and scoop out the seeds. Put one half of the melon cut-side down on cutting board. With a sharp knife, work around the melon, cutting off the peel in big, thick strips from top to bottom, along with any unripe layer directly underneath the peel. Work quickly and you will find that both halves can be peeled in half the time it takes when you cut the melon into wedges and cut the rind off each wedge.

Now you can cut the melon in circles or in chunks. Or cut each half in half again from top to bottom and cut into semicircles.

TO PEEL A PINEAPPLE:
Using a large, sharp or serrated-edge knife, cut off top one inch below the leaves and about the same from the bottom of the pineapple.

Next, cut off rind in strips from top to bottom, cutting just deep enough to remove the "eyes" but not so deep you waste edible fruit.

When all the peel has been removed, halve or quarter the pineapple lengthwise and cut out the pale, chewy hard core. The fruit is now ready to slice, or to cut into chunks for serving.

TO PEEL PEACHES AND TOMATOES:
If the peach is ripe, rub it all over firmly with your fingers. The skin should then pull off easily.

If you have a gas range, you can peel a tomato by impaling it on a cooking fork and twirling it over a gas flame for a few seconds. When the skin splits and changes color in patches, pull it off.

If you don't have a gas range, or are peeling several tomatoes or hard peaches, the boiling water method is more efficient: Put enough water to cover the fruit in a saucepan (don't put the fruit in the water yet). Bring the water to a boil.

Depending on how many fruits you're peeling you can lower them into the boiling water in a strainer or with a slotted spoon. The less ripe the fruit, the longer it will need to spend in boiling water. Leave the fruit in the water for about fifteen seconds and then immediately transfer to a bowl of cold water so it doesn't go on cooking. Skins should slip or pull off easily, but if they don't you can repeat the water bath.

OTHER FRUITS

I can't think of any fruit that isn't welcome at breakfast and it is a good time to serve some of the more exotic kinds, such as papayas, mangoes, or persimmons. Instructions for preparing a few of the less common fruits follow.

PERSIMMONS:
The rich sweet flavor of persimmon is wonderful at breakfast, but be aware of the two different kinds.

Hachiya has an elongated shape and is the first persimmon on the market in fall. Select plump fruit, free of cracks or splits, and if you plan to serve it for a special breakfast, you may need to allow time for it to ripen properly. An unripe Hachiya persimmon is unbelievably astringent and will dry out your mouth. A ripe one is very soft, almost jelly-like. It can take a hard Hachiya a week or more at room temperature to ripen properly. To speed ripening, put the persimmons in a fruit-ripening bowl, or in a closed brown paper bag; putting a ripe apple or two with the unripe persimmons will help them ripen more quickly. Check once daily. As the fruits ripen, dark areas may appear on the skin; these are normal. But little round spots that look as if they penetrate the skin are little spots of rot. If they seem to be spreading, refrigerate the persimmon and take your chances with it.

To prepare Hachiya persimmons, wash the fruit, then cut off the flat green cap along with a little of the skin and fruit immediately underneath it. (Even in a ripe Hachiya, the skin immediately underneath the cap can be astringent.) Cut the fruit lengthwise in six or eight wedges; discard any black seeds you may come across. Usually the skin is soft enough to eat. If you wish to remove it, hold one wedge skin-side down on a board; hold the skin at the widest end of the wedge with fingernails and ease fruit off skin with a knife almost parallel to the board. When cut up, a very soft Hachiya persimmon may need to be served in a bowl, rather than arranged in wedges on a plate.

Fuyu persimmons are shaped more like a tomato. Although Fuyus never acquire the same intense flavor of a really ripe Hachiya, there's no need to ripen them as they taste good when still hard. Cut them into wedges, or slice thinly (crosswise) with a serrated knife and arrange slices slightly overlapping on a platter.

Persimmons come to market in early fall and are available through January, the Fuyu sometimes much longer. In parts of the south and midwest, native American persimmons grow wild, often hanging on the trees like lanterns, long after the leaves have fallen. I've only tasted a cooked purée of wild persimmon, which is used for cakes and puddings, but the small fresh ones are said to be very flavorful and sweet when properly ripened.

PAPAYAS:

With its aromatic, creamy-to-orange flesh, and dramatic, shiny black seeds, a perfectly ripe papaya is definitely a breakfast treat. Most come from Hawaii, but Florida has been producing, too. Look for papayas that are firm, without tiny soft spots. If the papayas are green, look for ones that are just showing a touch of yellow. A deep, deep green, rock-hard papaya will never ripen properly.

Do not refrigerate unripe papayas. Leave them at room temperature in a fruit-ripening bowl, if you have one, or in a paper bag with a few holes pierced in the side. When the skin is three quarters to fully yellow and the fruit "gives" when gently pressed, the papayas are ready to eat. (They may now be refrigerated for a day or two.) Cut them in half lengthwise; scoop out (or leave in, for looks) the shiny black seeds. Serve each person half a papaya to eat with a small spoon.

To serve as part of a plate of mixed fruit, peel the papaya, halve lengthwise, discard the seeds and slice the fruit either crosswise or lengthwise.

MANGOES:

Ripe mango is a luscious addition to a platter of fruit in the morning, but you may need to plan ahead; mangoes usually need time to ripen at room temperature.

Mangoes are available most of the year but the pick of the crop comes to market in late spring and summer. Depending on the variety, the fruit can be oval, kidney-shaped, or almost as round as an apple. The smooth, often freckled skin (inedible) can range in color from dark green to golden, or yellow orange with a deep red blush. While some mangoes remain green with a rose blush when ripe, most varieties turn red or yellow all over.

It is difficult to slice mango neatly. Take a sharp knife and cut the fruit in half horizontally, sliding the knife over the large, flat pit. Cut the fruit off the other side of the pit. Hold one half of fruit skin side down in hand; cut fruit into half-inch squares, cutting down to, but not through, the skin. Then pick up each half and bend it backwards so the squares flare out. Serve with a knife and fork or cut the fruit off the skin for cubes.

For slices, cut the mango halves off the pit, then cut each half lengthwise in halves or quarters. Put each piece skin side down on board, grasp skin at one end with fingertips, and with knife parallel to board, cut between skin and fruit.

Mangoes can be cut up ahead of time and refrigerated, but for fullest flavor, serve at room temperature.

PASSION FRUIT:

The size of an egg, with deep purplish brown skin, passion fruit comes from California in summer and New Zealand in winter. Fix the following in your mind: *Passion fruit is ripe when wrinkled.* Cut through the thin skin and you'll find a jelly-like mass inside. Serve a spoonful over vanilla yogurt to surprise your friends and get the day off to a great start.

LYCHEES:

Lychees are one of my favorite fruits. Put a bowlful on the breakfast table and let guests peel their own, or peel and add them to a fruit cup. Lychees are about the size of a walnut in the shell and have a thin, crackly outer skin. Break open the skin with your fingertips. Inside, find a translucent white fruit with a large brown seed in the center. Pop the fruit into your mouth and relish its perfumey sweetness. (The seed is not for eating.)

DECORATING A FRUIT PLATTER

POMEGRANATES:

With their bright red rind and painterly six-pointed blossom end, whole pomegranates add beauty to a basket of fruit on the breakfast table. The bright-red insides look like a giant raspberry run amok. Scatter the jewel-like seeds over the bowl of fruit; as you crunch them, you release their tart-sweet juice.

Pomegranates come to market in late fall and are around through January. You can keep them for at least two weeks in the refrigerator; longer in the freezer. Select pomegranates that have a firm, unbroken, bright-looking deep-red rind, and that feel heavy for their size.

When you are ready to prepare one, dress appropriately (which might be not at all); pomegranates squirt red juice that stains. Cut through the rind in quarters, from stem to blossom end. Cut off the blossom end, then pull off the rind in sections. Pull away the acrid interior pith and scoop out the seeds with a teaspoon, trying not to crush too many. You can put the seeds into a small container, cover, and refrigerate them until the next day.

FLOWERS TO EAT:

While a plate of eggs and bacon would look ridiculous garnished with rose petals, edible blossoms can be a lovely garnish for a breakfast platter of fruit. Edible flowers are now quite widely available, some even year round (check farm stands or where fresh herbs are sold in the supermarket). Here are some of my favorites:

Borage: Pink, or a most incredible blue, with black antlers and white eyes. Faint cucumber flavor. Float one or two on a glass of juice, Champagne, or iced tea; scatter over a platter of fruit.

Dandelion flowers: My mother made a dandelion wine that made fools of many who thought a flower wine innocuous. The bounty she paid us per bucket of blossoms was hard-earned, considering how many dandelion flowers it takes to fill a pail. Though dandelion leaves are more commonly eaten (young, in salads; mature, steamed and buttered), the flowers have a delicate, slightly bitter flavor. Use as an edible garnish.

Scented geraniums: Not the common red, white, or pink geraniums of summer, but a variety with very aromatic leaves. Rim a platter with the leaves before arranging sliced fruit on it; float small leaves in a glass of juice; or chop and add to muffin (or pound-cake) batter. I grow lemon-, cinnamon-, and ginger-scented geraniums in my office; it is refreshing to rub a leaf in my fingers and inhale the perfume.

Herb flowers: Purple chive or white garlic chive blossoms look beautiful on a platter of smoked fish, cheeses, or sliced tomatoes on the breakfast table, as do basil or thyme flowers. The blossoms taste good, too. In summer, when thyme and rosemary are in bloom, put two or three sprigs at each place setting for nibbling, or encourage friends to crush the flowers and inhale the aroma.

Hibiscus, honeysuckle, hollyhocks, and squash blossoms: Any of these brightly colored flowers make a dramatic garnish for a fruit platter.

Lavender: In the south of France where acres of lavender are grown for their oil, you can buy lavender-flavored ice cream, baked goods, and preserves. You can put a sprig or two at each place setting or remove the tiny flowers from the spikes and scatter them over sliced fresh melon or pineapple.

Nasturtiums: Bright, brilliant colors (yellow, orange, rust, red) and peppery, radish-like flavor make a dramatic addition to a tossed salad, a platter of fruit, or a basket of bread. For nasturtium butter, add chopped petals to soft butter. Press several more petals against the sides of a glass butter dish (or glass crock) before filling carefully with the flavored butter. (Butter will keep several days covered tightly in the refrigerator.)

Pansies, rose petals, violas, and violets: Use to garnish fruit compotes or platters.

NOTE: Not all flowers are safe to eat. Be safe; buy flowers sold as edible. If you grow flowers, be sure not to eat flowers that have been sprayed with insecticides, and only eat ones you know to be edible.

Eggs

When you think of breakfast, eggs in all their glory are perhaps the first food that comes to mind. At home, there was always a basket of fresh eggs on the pantry floor and both my mother and grandmother raised hens and sold the eggs for "pin" money. (The pin money was a pretty good deal as the farm supplied the feed and very often a good deal of labor, too.) My mother preferred to let a hired person do most of the work. My father's mother took a slightly more active role! Mid-afternoon she donned an ancient cardigan and wound an old scarf around her head. Carrying a beat-up bucket of grain in each hand, she went off down the spinney (a small wooded area) to feed her "chooks" and gather the eggs.

But enough scratching about! Time to crack the secrets of cooking eggs.

Eggs are sold by the dozen and are marketed according to size and grade standards established by the United States Department of Agriculture (USDA). The grades are AA, A, B, and C and designate the quality of the egg. You'll probably never see Grades B and C in the stores as they are most often processed into dried eggs or other egg products.

If you'd like an idea of how the grades differ, imagine that you have cracked open one each of the first three grades and dropped the contents carefully onto a countertop. If you look at them straight on, you will see that the Grade AA egg stands up tall and that there is a large proportion of thick white to thin white. A Grade A egg is very similar; the yolk is round and upstanding (as in the Grade AA egg) and there is still plenty of thick white in proportion to the thin white. The Grade B egg spreads out more than the A and AA eggs; the yolk is flattened, and there is about as much, or more, thin white as thick white.

Egg size is actually based on minimum weight per dozen. Jumbo eggs weigh a minimum of 30 ounces per carton; Extra Large, 27 ounces; Large, 24 ounces; and Medium, 21 ounces. Although any size may be used for frying, poaching, scrambling, or cooking in the shell, most recipes for baked goods, such as custards and cakes, are based on the use of Large eggs. To substitute another size for Large, use the following chart.

Large Eggs	Jumbo	Extra Large	Medium	Small	Pee Wee
1	1	1	1	1	2
2	2	2	2	3	3
3	2	3	3	4	5
4	3	4	5	5	6
5	4	4	6	7	8
6	5	5	7	8	10

STORING EGGS

I've been shocked to hear some young cooks say they've thrown out eggs after a few days because they thought they were no longer usable. Fresh eggs can be kept in the refrigerator for at least four to five weeks. Buy eggs from refrigerated cases and refrigerate them as soon as you get home. Leave them in the carton rather than storing them in the refrigerator door. Store eggs larger end up, the way they are usually packed. (Eggs will age more in one day at room temperature than in one week in the refrigerator.)

HOW TO COOK EGGS REALLY WELL

When cooking eggs, the most important thing to keep in mind is this: Use moderate heat. High heat will toughen eggs; and too-long cooking at a high temperature causes that gray-green coating on the yolks of hard-cooked eggs.

To break open an egg, hold it in one hand and firmly crack at midpoint against the edge of a bowl or the cooking pan; one crack should break the shell. Lower egg closer to surface of pan, open up shell with both hands, and let egg slide into pan. (For a funny Cordon Bleu cooking lesson on how to crack open two eggs at a time, check TV listings for an Audrey Hepburn oldie, *Sabrina*.)

FRYING

Choose a good, thick-bottomed skillet or one with a nonstick finish. (With a nonstick finish you can use very little fat or even cooking spray.) For one egg, you need a skillet about six inches across the bottom. Heat skillet over moderately-high heat, adding one tablespoon of butter (see Note). When the butter is melted and bubbly, break egg carefully into skillet. Turn heat down to moderately-low. Let the egg cook for a minute or two, until the white is the way you like it, then slide a good, wide pancake turner under the egg and lift it onto the serving plate.

Basted eggs: While the egg is frying, spoon the hot butter over the yolk. This cooks the white and yolk on top without having to turn the egg over.

Steam-basted: Add one teaspoon of water to the skillet for one or two eggs; cover the skillet for a minute or two. The water will turn into steam and baste the tops of the eggs.

Over lightly: Gently turn fried egg over with a pancake turner. Let cook a few seconds longer before removing from pan; yolks should always be creamy-soft, not hard. If yolks tend to break when

you turn the egg over, use more butter the next time.

To fry four eggs, use a larger skillet and two to three tablespoons butter.

NOTE: To check if a skillet is hot enough to fry eggs or cook French toast, flick a few drops of water into the heated pan. If the drops skitter around the pan, it is hot enough. If drops do nothing, pan is not hot enough. If water evaporates immediately, skillet is too hot; take it off the burner and let it cool for a minute or two.

POACHING

Unlike fried eggs, poached eggs can be made hours, or even a day, before you plan to serve them. Poaching requires no special equipment or gadgets, just a deep omelet pan, skillet, or saucepan.

For poaching, use very fresh, Grade AA eggs that have a higher proportion of thick white to thin white than older eggs or eggs of a lower grade. The thick white will set around the yolk, while the thin white breaks up and floats away (some people call the stragglers "angel wings").

Select a pan that is at least two to three inches deep so that it will hold enough water to cover the eggs. (A too-deep pan, however, may be difficult to lift the eggs out of.) A deep skillet about eight inches across the bottom is good for poaching two to four eggs; a ten- to twelve-inch skillet for six to eight eggs.

Poached eggs sometimes stick to the bottom of the pan. Although this is rarely a problem with a heavy-bottomed pan, you might like to grease the pan with oil, butter, or vegetable cooking spray before filling it with water.

Bring water to a gentle simmer. (Rapidly boiling water may break up the egg white as it cooks.) Use cold eggs, right from the refrigerator because the whites will stay closer to the yolk, rather than spreading out in the water. Add a pinch of salt to the water if you wish (but not vinegar, which some cooks favor, but which I dislike because the vinegary flavor it imparts to the eggs rarely enhances anything you're serving them with). Don't break eggs directly into the water. Instead, break them one at a time (or break six into a large bowl) into a custard cup, saucer, or other small dish. Hold dish close to the surface of the simmering water and gently slide the egg in.

When all eggs are in, let them cook in the water, which should be barely moving, three to five minutes, depending on how you like them done. Lift out the eggs with a slotted spoon. Touch the bottom of the slotted spoon to a paper towel to soak up the water. Trim off any ragged edges, if you wish, then put the egg onto the hash, English muffin, or whatever it is to be served on.

To prepare poached eggs ahead, slightly undercook them. Lift them from the cooking water and trim edges. Put them into a baking dish, bowl, or other container filled with cold water. The eggs don't have to be in a single layer but be sure they are covered with water. Cover dish and refrigerate. Shortly before serving, lift eggs out of the cold water with fingers or a slotted spoon and lower them into barely simmering water. Leave them for a minute or two while they heat to serving temperature and finish cooking. Lift out of the simmering water with a slotted spoon, drain, and use.

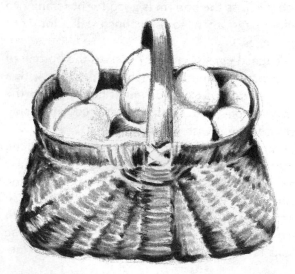

FRENCH POACHING

Once you're an experienced poacher, if you have time, you may like to try for a swirled effect. Have egg ready in custard cup or saucer and water barely simmering. Stir water round and round in a small skillet, then remove spoon. When water has slowed, but is still swirling, carefully lower egg into the middle of the whirlpool. Ideally, white should gently wrap itself around the yolk in a stylish swirl. If the water is going too fast, white may part from yolk. It's fun to try, but don't do it a first time for a party, especially since you can poach only one egg at a time.

SOFT-COOKED EGGS IN THE SHELL

Put eggs in a single layer in a saucepan that has a cover and add enough cold tap water to come at least one inch above eggs. Cover and bring to a boil over high heat. Turn off gas heat or remove pan from electric burner. Let stand one to four minutes, depending on how soft you like eggs done. Lift out eggs and rinse under cold water (for several eggs, pour off the water and replace with cold). Have serving bowl or egg cup ready. Cut shell through center with a fast slash of a sharp knife. Using a teaspoon, scoop egg into a large egg cup or small ramekin. To serve European-style, cut off large end of egg with knife or egg scissors, place egg upright in egg cup, and eat with a spoon from the shell.

There seems to be an unwritten law that whenever one prepares a soft-cooked egg for a person who insists that they be done "just so" the egg is bound to turn out either too hard to too soft in the center. Apart from inviting the fussy one to boil his or her own eggs in the future, what can be done?

If the eggs are too firm in the center, there's really no solution except to cook another batch for the particular one. (Eat the overcooked ones yourself, or save them to make into an egg salad sandwich or to chop and sprinkle over cooked broccoli.) As for the too-soft problem, I always try to anticipate that it may happen. I pour some of the boiling water into the blue pottery cup I serve soft-cooked eggs in, thus heating the cup. (It's only the first egg out of the pot that's a problem because you simply leave the second one in longer.) When I crack open the first egg, if the white is translucent and jiggly around the yolk (and if I haven't broken the yolk with the knife), I carefully lower the egg back into the saucepan and let it stand a minute or two longer. If the yolk is broken, quickly pour the boiling water out of the serving cup and scrape the egg into the cup. Cover and leave until you add the second egg. Between the heat of the cup and the heat of the second egg, the first one should cook enough to please. If it doesn't, at least it is on the bottom of the cup and you can hope the recipient will stir up both eggs and not notice.

HARD-COOKED EGGS IN THE SHELL

Follow directions for soft-cooked eggs, but leave eggs longer in the hot water: fifteen minutes for Medium eggs, seventeen minutes for Large eggs (adjust time up or down by approximately three minutes for each size larger or smaller). Immediately pour off the hot water and put pan under cold running water for one or two minutes. This will help cool eggs quickly and thoroughly, which will make them easier to peel and also prevent that unsightly dark-green surface on the yolks.

Leave the eggs in the cold water. Pick out one or two at a time to peel. Crackle the shells all over by tapping gently on sink or countertop; you may find the shells come off quickly and easily. (Peel the eggs under the cold water; it helps loosen shells and remove any tiny pieces that cling.) If shells are recalcitrant, loosen them even more by rolling the eggs gently in your palms; also, try peeling from the larger end.

If hard-cooked eggs are not to be used immediately, refrigerate them in a bowl, with or without cold water, or in a plastic bag.

Surprisingly, the fresher the egg, the harder it is to peel after it has been hard-cooked. If you know you want perfect hard-cooked eggs for a party, buy the eggs a week or two in advance so they can age (in the refrigerator, of course).

SCRAMBLED EGGS

To make scrambled eggs, mix together yolks and whites with a wire whisk, fork, rotary beater, or portable electric beater before cooking. For even color, whisk thoroughly; for a marbled effect, whisk only slightly.

For each serving, use two eggs, two tablespoons milk, and a dash of salt and pepper. Break eggs into a bowl; add milk and seasonings and beat together.

Heat skillet over moderate heat. Add from one teaspoon to one tablespoon of butter and move it around the skillet so it coats the bottom. When butter is bubbly, pour in the beaten eggs. Do not stir until you see that the egg mixture at the edge of the pan is starting to set. Then, and only then, take a pancake turner and push it gently across the bottom of the pan once or twice, allowing the still-liquid egg to flow underneath the cooked egg. Keep doing this (the whole process only takes a minute or two), until the eggs are thick, but still shiny-looking. Remove pan from heat; the eggs will keep cooking for a minute or two in their own heat. Spoon or scrape eggs onto plate and eat up.

The secrets of creamy scrambled eggs are: Use moderately-low heat; stir the eggs very little and only as described; remove eggs from heat when they are cooked a little less than you like them.

FRAZZLED EGGS

This quick method of scrambling eggs is a favorite of frazzled parents who hear the school bus coming or who are in a rush to get to work themselves.

Make one serving at a time. Don't beat the eggs. Heat skillet with butter. Break one or two eggs into skillet. Quickly stir with spoon or fork. Eggs will set almost immediately with streaks of white throughout. Serve at once. Sprinkle with salt and pepper; serve any way you like, perhaps on a toasted muffin with a spoonful of salsa or dollop of ketchup.

OMELET

The omelet is a close relative of scrambled eggs. Both start with beaten eggs; both are usually cooked in a skillet. But scrambled eggs end up in creamy clumps, while the omelet ends up more like a pancake, flat on the bottom of the pan, uneven on the surface. The omelet is also folded over before serving. Because it takes less than a minute to actually cook an omelet for one, have everything ready (plate and filling, if there is to be one) before heating the skillet.

Here's how you make an omelet for one: Break two eggs into a small bowl. Add two tablespoons water and an eighth to a quarter teaspoon salt or herb seasoning. Beat eggs with fork until well broken up.

Choose a skillet that's six to seven inches across the bottom. One with a nonstick finish works beautifully and need not be saved for omelets alone. Heat skillet over moderate to moderately-high heat, adding two teaspoons or one tablespoon butter. When a few drops of water flicked into the skillet skitter across the bottom, the pan is hot enough. Immediately pour in the egg mixture; it should set at the edges. With an inverted pancake turner, carefully draw cooked portions at edges toward center, so uncooked (still liquid) mixture can flow underneath and touch the hot pan surface. If you feel tilting the pan would be helpful, tilt it. When egg on surface looks almost set but still moist and creamy, spoon filling (if any) onto the half of the omelet farthest away from the handle. Fold half of omelet nearest handle over the filling, grab handle of pan from underneath, and either slide omelet out onto plate or tip pan upside down over the plate. As with scrambled eggs, eggs continue to cook in their own heat, so fold the omelet and get it out of the skillet while it is still slightly underdone.

If you are making omelets for a crowd, you can beat up a large batch of eggs, water, and seasoning. Have a half-cup ladle or dipper handy and dip out a full measure for each omelet.

SHIRRED EGGS

"Shirred" is a pretty, and pretty mysterious, word. Change "shirred" to "baked" and the puzzle is solved. Baked Eggs with Ham and Gruyère is an example of shirred eggs. It is a useful method of cooking that can be done in a regular oven or toaster oven. Small amounts of cooked food (asparagus, for example, or creamed spinach) can be put underneath the eggs in place of the ham.

To make one serving, heat oven to 325°F. Butter a ramekin, small shallow baking dish, or nine-and-a-half-ounce custard cup. Break two eggs into the dish; sprinkle with salt and pepper. Spoon one tablespoon light cream, half-and-half, or milk over eggs. Bake twelve to eighteen minutes, until whites are set but yolks are still soft and creamy. (If you are baking several individual portions at one time, baking time will be slightly longer.)

Breakfast Meats

Bacon, Canadian bacon, sausages, and ham are the most popular breakfast meats. Their intense, salty flavors enhance the milder flavors of other breakfast foods such as eggs, pancakes, waffles, grits, and French toast.

BACON

Bacon is cured, often smoked, pork. Most bacon is sold already sliced and with the rind removed. The rind, or skin, is a resilient layer that becomes more so when cooked. Bacon purchased from a specialty smokehouse may still have the rind attached. If it does, snip or cut it off before cooking the bacon.

Allow at least two, more likely three, slices of bacon per person. The number of slices per pound depends on how thinly the bacon is sliced, and may also vary slightly from brand to brand. As a general guide, however, count on finding the following number of slices in a pound of bacon:

Thick-sliced	12 slices
Medium-sliced	20 slices
Thinly-sliced	28 slices

Bacon is perishable. If you aren't going to use it within ten days, freeze it, unopened. Use within three months. Once opened, if you use bacon infrequently or just a few slices at a time try this way of freezing it: Tear off a long strip of plastic wrap; put a slice of bacon on one end; fold wrap over. Place another bacon strip on top of the first (which by now will be covered in plastic); fold over again. Continue putting another slice on top and folding bacon and wrap over until all the bacon is wrapped. Put the bundle of wrapped bacon in a plastic bag suitable for freezing food and squeeze out as much air as possible before closing bag tightly.

With this method, when you want a few slices of bacon you can easily unwrap as many as you wish without thawing the bacon at all.

COOKING BACON

A few slices of bacon can be cooked in a skillet. Use moderate heat, watch bacon carefully and turn slices two or three times. As soon as the bacon is an even golden brown with no white spots of soft fat, lift the strips onto a paper towel and pat them firmly with a crunched-up paper towel to remove as much fat as possible.

When you want to cook more bacon than a skillet will comfortably hold, use a microwave oven (follow directions in the manual for your oven) or a regular oven. Heat oven to 350°F. For three pounds of bacon you'll need two jelly-roll pans (or other large baking pan with sides) or you can cook the bacon in batches. Separate the bacon slices and place them, slightly overlapping, on the pans; slices will also extend up the sides but will shrink as they cook.

Bake pans of bacon fifteen to twenty minutes until bacon is really crisp (it will continue to cook briefly after it is out of the oven). While bacon is cooking, line a cookie sheet (or countertop) with a double thickness of paper towels.

Remove pans of cooked bacon from oven, being very careful not to spill the hot fat. With tongs or pancake turner, lift bacon onto paper towels, keeping slices flat. Crumple two or three pieces of paper towel in your hand and pat slices firmly to remove as much fat as possible.

The bacon may be served right away. If you want to cook it up to three hours ahead, let it cool to room temperature, then cover loosely with foil and leave at room temperature. For overnight storage, put cooled bacon in an airtight container and refrigerate.

To reheat bacon, arrange strips in a single layer on a clean jelly-roll pan or cookie sheet. Heat oven to 425°F., or heat broiler. Bake bacon three to four minutes in oven; or broil for one to two minutes, watching carefully so it does not burn.

One last word: Don't clog your drains by pouring bacon or any other fat down them. Pour the hot fat into an empty coffee can. Cover (to prevent spills) and refrigerate until hard before disposing. Before you wash the baking pans, wipe them out with paper towels.

CANADIAN BACON

Called Canadian-style bacon (because it doesn't necessarily come from Canada), this extremely lean meat is the eye of the pork loin that has been cured like ham. It has a delicious flavor and requires little cooking. In fact, because it is so lean it can quickly become hard and dry if overcooked. Cook one-ounce slices (allow two per person) in a little butter or oil in a skillet over moderately-high heat, one to one and a half minutes per side, just until edges are lightly tinged with brown.

Canadian bacon also comes in whole pieces weighing from two to four pounds. You can heat the whole piece as for ham (see below), or you can slice it and fry the slices.

SAUSAGES

There are several types of sausages including dry (chorizos, pepperoni), semi-dry (cervelat), cooked smoked (frankfurters, knockwurst, kielbasa), fresh smoked, and fresh.

Fresh sausages, made of uncured, uncooked meat, and not smoked, are the most popular for breakfast. There are flavors to suit every taste, from hot or sweet Italian sausages, to sage-scented pork sausage, and hot and spicy pork patties. Preferred seasonings will vary from one part of the country to another. Sausages come in small and large link, or in bulk packages weighing a pound or more, ready to be formed into patties. Either way, sausages can be fried, grilled, or baked.

Link sausage will be juicier if you do not prick the sausages before cooking them, because fat and moisture cannot escape. Put the links into a cold skillet; add two tablespoons of water (for eight sausages), cover the pan, and cook over moderate heat for about eight minutes. The water will turn to steam and help cook the sausages all the way through. Then uncover the pan and cook eight to ten minutes longer, turning the sausages several times, until they are browned all over.

Sausage patties can also be cooked in a skillet but do not add water. Drain sausages and patties on paper towels, pressing them lightly but firmly with another paper towel to remove as much fat as possible.

HAM

Ham is one of the most delicious and easily prepared breakfast meats and is available in many sizes, shapes, and forms.

The word "ham" properly refers to the hind leg of a hog, from pelvic bone to hock. That is why you may sometimes see in the supermarket meat labeled "fresh ham." It is fresh (uncured) meat and can also be called leg of pork. A fresh roasted ham makes a wonderful dinner, but for breakfast you want ham in the sense of pork that's been cured. When fresh pork is turned into ham, the meat may be cured in a number of different ways.

Brine-cured. This is how the vast majority of hams sold today have been cured. Raw meat is injected with a solution of water, salt, sodium nitrite and nitrates, and sugar or honey. By law, up to ten percent of weight may be added in curing liquid;

more than that and "water added" must be declared on the label. (Hams with twenty percent added water are labeled "ham and water product," and although the price per pound may seem attractive, especially compared to a true country ham, you are paying ham prices for water.)

Dry-cured. Salt, sugar, sodium nitrite and nitrates are mixed together and rubbed on the surface of the meat. This process, used to cure most "country" hams, draws out moisture (in contrast to brine-curing, which adds it) and leaves the ham with a firmer texture, and deeper, richer color and flavor. (Specialty hams such as prosciutto, Parma, and Westphalian, usually eaten "raw," are also dry-cured, some only with salt.)

Smoked. After curing, some hams are hung in a smokehouse over smoldering fires. The length of time depends on the style of the individual smokehouse. Smoking continues the aging and drying process and imparts a distinctive flavor, which can vary according to the type of wood used (beechwood, hickory, and sassafras, to mention three). Most "country" hams are smoked in a smokehouse.

Air-cured, air-dried. This is what separates real country ham from the rest. In the air-drying process, dry-cured hams are hung for six to nine months (or even longer), during which time the meat becomes more compact and much more flavorful. Some wonderful country hams are produced by small smokehouses, especially in the southern states of Tennessee, Virginia, and Arkansas. Unless you happen to live near an excellent supplier or smokehouse, look for mail order sources.

WHICH HAM TO BUY

Ham comes whole and in halves, portions, or slices; it is also bone-in, semi-boneless, or boneless. Today most ham is sold fully-cooked, ready-to-eat, but check the label to be sure.

For a quick breakfast meat, buy thinly-sliced ham; the slices need only heating in hot butter in a skillet (see Frizzled Ham, page 32).

Ham steaks or slices are also ideal for breakfast and take only a few minutes to heat (or cook). Allow three to four ounces per person, depending on the rest of the menu. Cut or snip several slashes in the fat around the edge to prevent the meat from curling. For easier serving, cut a large ham steak into three or four pieces and discard the center bone. Heat a small amount of butter or oil in a heavy skillet over moderate heat. Add ham and, depending on thickness, cook two to five minutes until lightly browned, turning once. Do not overcook, or the meat will be hard and dry; this is especially important if you are cooking slices of country ham, or Smithfield ham.

For a crowd, or a special occasion such as Easter breakfast, a fully-cooked whole or half ham is a good choice (and should leave you with leftovers for other meals). Serve the ham warm, chilled, or at room temperature. For a large crowd, order a presliced ham in advance from your market (they come boneless, or bone-in). A fully-cooked boneless ham that's been sliced and put back together can weigh from eight to ten pounds and yield thirty-two to forty servings (at four servings per pound). With scrambled eggs and hot biscuits, a delicious breakfast is in store.

Many people enjoy ham served cold, but if you want to heat a sliced ham, leave on the string that comes around it from the market. Heat oven to 325°F. Line a large roasting pan with foil (for easy cleanup). Place ham flat-side down in pan; bake one hour. Spread about half a cup of Fruit Glaze for Ham (recipe below) over top of ham. Cover loosely with foil; bake one hour more. Spread more glaze on ham; bake fifteen to twenty minutes longer, until a meat thermometer inserted in thickest part reads 140°F. Carefully lift ham to serving board or platter. Snip string and remove.

FRUIT GLAZE FOR HAM

1 cup apricot ham, plum preserves or orange marmalade
⅓ cup packed light brown sugar
¼ cup Dijon mustard

Mix all together. Makes about 1½ cups. If you have more glaze than you need for a ham, heat remaining glaze over moderate heat until sugar dissolves and serve as a sauce with the ham for another meal.

While a boneless ham is very easy to serve, a bone-in ham is more traditional and looks more handsome. Buy a whole ham, or a half. (It is better to ask the butcher to cut a ham in half for you; this way you can be sure you are getting the entire half, including the center slices.)

When you need a smaller ham, you will find many sizes in the supermarket meat counter. Not all are prepared from the hind leg of pork; turkey ham, for example, is turkey thigh cured in the same way as ham. When buying smaller hams, allow four servings to the pound and buy enough to have leftovers for a second breakfast or another meal. Try different brands—each has its own distinctive flavor, until you find the one that pleases you most.

Breakfast Beverages

There's no nicer greeting to breakfast guests than a fantastic coffee aroma. The trick is to make the flavor of the brew meet the expectations aroused by the aroma. The once-vaunted American cup of coffee has been in a weak state for a number of years, but fortunately interest in quality coffee is brewing.

COFFEE

You can buy coffee in bean or ground form from your local supermarket, by mail, or, if you're fortunate, from a local specialty store.

The ideal coffee shop roasts its own coffee beans or buys from local specialty roasters. Depending on the size of the market it serves, the store may have a small or large selection. Better a small selection and a fast turnover, than a vast selection of stale beans. (Coffee beans are basically "on hold" until roasted.)

Here's a simplified guide to coffees: When you look at roasted beans in sacks, jars, or cases, you will notice that some beans are darker in color or glossier than others. You will also notice names such as French, Italian, and Viennese. Your brain will probably remind you that coffee grows in the tropics, not in Europe. These European names refer strictly to how long the beans were roasted, until they reach the depth of flavor preferred in those countries. Italian roast, for example, is much darker than French.

The next guide to flavor are names that do in fact indicate the place the bean came from: Sulawesi, Sumatra, Colombia, Kenya, Ethiopia, and Guatemala are just some of the names you may see.

Try coffee from different countries to find out which tastes appeal to you.

Now look for words like Mocha, Arabian Mocha-Java, Copenhagen, or Scandinavian. These tell you the coffee is a blend of beans. Many good stores carry their own excellent "house" blends, including special ones for breakfast or after-dinner drinking.

Two things to beware of when shopping for coffee: blends with a high proportion of robusta beans, which are cheap but lack flavor, and "type-hype"—signs that say Java-type or Antigua-type, which are meant to lead you to believe the beans are from those countries when in fact they are not.

The only way to go is to try different coffees until you find the ones you like. (Buy only a quarter pound of each type while you're experimenting.) You may also like to do a little blending yourself. If you think a blend needs a kick, add a few Italian-roast beans. (Try adding one or two tablespoons of ground espresso coffee, available in most supermarkets, to your regular brew.) Among my personal coffee favorites are: Sulawesi-Kalossie, Bourbon Santos, Kenya, and Copenhagen (depending on the individual blend, this last sometimes needs a shot of Italian roast). A French or Viennese roast from a reliable store is always a good place to start.

CAFFÈ LATTE, CAFÉ AU LAIT, CAFÉ CON LECHE: Italian, French, and Spanish, respectively, for very strong coffee mixed with at least two-thirds as much milk and usually served in a large cup. A delicious start to the day, even with something as simple as a roll and butter, a croissant, or cinnamon toast.

Two things are essential for caffè latte: very strong coffee and very hot milk. Use a dark roast coffee and one and one-half measures of ground coffee for each six-ounce cup. Heat milk in a saucepan over moderate heat just until bubbles appear around the edge. (If you boil the milk, the flavor will be ruined.) Pour the hot milk into a pitcher. To serve with style, hold the pitcher of milk in one hand, the coffee pot in the other, and pour them simultaneously into the cup.

When next in France, you might look for the small pretty pottery bowls the French like to use to drink cafe au lait. It's great to hold the bowl in both hands and sip the steaming brew. (One slight disadvantage: The coffee tends to cool quickly.)

ESPRESSO:
Espresso in Italian (expresso in Spanish) is very dark-roast coffee preferably made in an espresso machine, which forces steam through the finely ground beans, producing a dark, strong, almost-syrupy coffee that is served in tiny cups. Well-made espresso has a thin layer of creamy foam on the surface; it's called the "crema" and is considered the best part.

Espresso isn't suitable to serve as a sipping coffee during breakfast. It's nice to offer a cup when friends arrive, or after the main course (during which regular coffee may be served).

CAPPUCCINO:
Cappuccino is similar to café con leche, except that the coffee is espresso and the milk is steamed until it is frothy and scalding hot. If you want to buy an espresso machine, be sure to select one that allows you to steam milk (a special nozzle comes out one side of the machine). Or look for a range-top steamer. It doesn't make coffee, it just steams milk.

Like espresso, well-made cappuccino has a frothy top, only much more voluminous. (Sprinkle with cinnamon or grated chocolate if you wish.) Sip it slowly. Heaven!

KAFFEE MIT SCHLAG, ESPRESSO CON PANNA:
Strong, Viennese- or Italian-roast coffee, served with whipped cream. (Whipped cream is "schlag" in German, "panna" in Italian.) Although usually served mid-morning or mid-afternoon, kaffee mit schlag can be a wonderful indulgence at the end of a delicious breakfast. Bring on the whipped cream and pour fresh hot coffee (perhaps a different, stronger brew than served with the main course). Let everyone float a spoonful of the whipped cream on top of the coffee. Don't stir the cream; sip the coffee through it.

Do not use whipped cream from a pressurized container; it lacks substance. For the real thing, buy whipping cream. Have it well chilled. Choose a deep, narrow bowl, rather than a wide, shallow one, and use metal or glass, not plastic. In very hot weather, chill the bowl, too. With a rotary or electric beater, whip the cream until soft peaks form when you lift the beaters. (Put the bowl in the sink if the cream spatters.) Watch the cream carefully and don't overbeat it, whereupon it will look separated (and eventually make butter). Unsweetened cream is best to serve with coffee, but for a group you may like to add a half teaspoon sugar to each half pint (one cup) cream when you start to beat because it will help to stabilize the cream.

Once whipped, you may cover the cream and refrigerate it for at least an hour.

COFFEE WITH CHICORY:
A longtime favorite in the south, and indelibly associated with New Orleans, coffee with chicory is now gaining a much wider audience. Chicory is made by roasting and grinding the root of the Belgian endive plant. Chicory adds a deep, robust flavor to coffee. Look in the supermarket for a ground coffee and chicory blend; or ask in a shop that specializes in coffee. It would be especially appropriate for the Mardi Gras breakfast or for Breakfast with a Southern Flair.

FLAVORED COFFEES:
Ground coffees to which have been added flavor extracts such as amaretto or Swiss chocolate have

become very popular. Each to his or her own taste, but I find coffee with flavor extracts to be a definite intrusion at breakfast.

HOW TO MAKE GOOD COFFEE:

Buy good quality coffee and have it ground to the correct specifications for your coffee maker. (Store ground coffee, in tightly closed bags, in the freezer.) Use a drip or filter coffee maker and make sure it is thoroughly clean. Use cold, freshly drawn water. Measure the coffee and water accurately. The usual measurement is one standard coffee measure or two level tablespoons of coffee to each six ounces of water. If you're serving coffee in large mugs, you'll need to increase the amount of coffee and water you use.

Serve coffee with sugar and milk or cream. (Let milk and cream come to room temperature so they don't chill the coffee.) Have sweetener on hand for guests who use it.

HOW TO MAKE GOOD ICED COFFEE:

In hot weather, a tall glass of good iced coffee is a welcome change at breakfast time. Pouring regular-strength coffee over ice cubes results in a wishy-washy drink when the ice melts. Make coffee for serving iced one and one half or even twice as strong as for serving hot. Pour hot coffee over ice cubes; or chill in a glass or ceramic container.

Serve iced coffee black. Offer sugar, sweetener, cream, and, if you wish, a bowl of whipped cream.

HOW TO MAKE COFFEE FOR A CROWD:

The easiest way to make coffee for a crowd is to use one or more automatic drip coffee makers. Borrow from friends so you can keep a steady supply of coffee going. To save time and avoid mistakes while the party is in progress, premeasure the coffee (leave it near the coffee maker so a helpful friend can get a fresh batch going).

TEA

The clean taste of tea is a wonderful way to start the day. Try serving it along with the main course,

then switching to coffee (regular or cappuccino) when you serve a coffee cake. For breakfast, choose an unfussy blend such as English or Irish Breakfast tea, Darjeeling, Assam, or Russian Caravan. Or try a rosehip and hibiscus herb tea such as Red or Lemon Zinger. Tea bags are an easy way to offer your guests a wide selection. Have boiling water handy (a stylish tea kettle on the range will do); tea does not infuse properly when a tea bag is put into a cup of water poured several minutes previously. Offer sugar, honey, and milk for those who wish to add them.

To make tea by the pot, a drip coffee maker that is also designed for making tea works well. Or put on a tea kettle or saucepan of water to boil. Shortly before it boils, pour some of the very hot water into a teapot, to warm the pot. Pour off the water; put tea bags in pot and fill with boiling water. (When you make tea this way, one tea bag is usually enough for at least two servings.) Let stand two to five minutes, then remove tea bags.

Although most English experts recommend infusing the tea for at least five minutes, for my taste, when tea is infused that long, too much of the astringent tannin is released, spoiling the flavor. Two minutes is maximum for me; but the choice is yours. Most herb teas (all herbs, not a blend of herb and black teas) can be infused for at least eight minutes without any adverse flavor developing.

When I make tea with loose tea (and I know this is heresy) I add the tea to the boiling water in the saucepan. When it has infused enough, I carefully strain the tea (through a fine strainer) into a heated teapot, taking care not to stir up the brew.

HOT CHOCOLATE

Let the children stir up instant hot chocolate mix; adults demand serious chocolate. Chocolate for grown-ups should have an intense flavor, without being overly rich. You may, of course, put a bowl of whipped cream on the table for those who wish to indulge. Other nice additions: a small shaker of ground cinnamon, a tiny bowl of grated semisweet chocolate to sprinkle on top of the whipped cream, and a small bowl of orange peel twists.

Orange is a wonderful flavor marriage with chocolate. To make twists, remove two- to three-inch long strips of peel (from a well-scrubbed orange) with a vegetable peeler. Keep strips of peel covered so they won't dry out. Twist a piece of peel over a cup of hot chocolate to release the flavorful oils and drop peel into the cup. (A small shot of orange-flavored liqueur is another delicious possibility.)

BREAKFAST HOT CHOCOLATE FOR GROWN-UPS

This hot chocolate is modest in calories because the base is made with almost-fat-free cocoa, instead of chocolate.

1½ cups Breakfast Hot Chocolate Base (recipe follows)
  6 cups whole or skim milk; or 3 cups milk and 3 cups water

Put milk and hot chocolate base into a large saucepan. Heat over moderate heat, stirring or whisking frequently, until almost boiling. Pour directly into cups or mugs; or serve in a heated pottery pitcher. *Makes 7½ cups, 6 servings.*

NOTE: For frothier hot chocolate, pour about 3 cups hot mixture into a blender and process for a few seconds; return to pot and heat again.

ICED BREAKFAST CHOCOLATE

1½ cups chilled Breakfast Hot Chocolate Base (recipe below)
  6 cups cold milk; or 3 cups milk and 3 cups water

Put chilled hot chocolate base in a blender or food processor. Add about 2 cups of the milk; process to blend. Pour into a pitcher. Rinse out blender with more of the liquid. Add to pitcher with remaining liquid; stir gently to blend. Pour into glasses and serve; or chill and serve later. *Makes 7½ cups.*

BREAKFAST HOT CHOCOLATE BASE

The better quality cocoa you use, the better the hot chocolate will be.

1 cup unsweetened cocoa powder
½ cup granulated sugar
1 cup cold water
1½ teaspoons vanilla extract
1 teaspoon instant coffee powder or granules (espresso or regular, optional)

Mix cocoa powder, sugar, and water in a heavy, medium-sized saucepan. Stir over moderate heat until smooth, thickened, and boiling. Remove from heat; stir in vanilla and coffee. Use right away; or pour into a storage container, cover, and refrigerate. The base keeps at least 2 weeks. *Makes 1½ cups.*

Index

Listings in **bold** are menu titles.

A

After the Ball, 131–133
Almond:
    Christmas Pastries, Dutch, 124–
        125
    Coffee Cake, Cherry-, 41
    Coffee Cake, Orange-, 91
    Muesli, Swiss, 60
    Puffs, Apricot, 180
Ambrosia, 138
Apples, 121
    and Apricots, Baked, 34
    Baked, Fans, 105
    Cider and Orange Juice,
        Mulled, 109
    -Cinnamon Yogurt, Fresh
        Applesauce with, 142
    Compote of Fresh and Dried
        Fruit, 145
    English Muffin Pastries, 147
    Honey-Crunch Baked, 82
    Hot, Providence, 121
    Lemon-Poached, 93
    Pick-Up Fruit with Creamy
        Banana Dip, 76
    See also Applesauce
Applesauce:
    Fresh, with Apple-Cinnamon
        Yogurt, 142
    Fresh Quince, 142
    Muffins, Milk-free, Egg-free,
        176–177
Apricots:
    Almond Puffs, 180
    Apples and, Baked, 34

Marmalade Muffins for Two, 11
Streusel Coffee Cake, 53
Artichokes: Casserole Eggs
    Sardou, 16
Avocado, Mashed, 52

B

Back-to-School Breakfast Party,
    75–77
Bacon, 195–196
    Canadian, 32, 196
    and Egg Sandwiches, 79
Bagels, 19
    Lox and, 133
Baked Apple Fans, 105
Baked Apples, Honey-Crunch, 82
Baked Apples and Apricots, 34
Baked Eggs, 35
    with Ham and Gruyère, 82
    Shirred Eggs, 194
Baked goods:
    Apricot Almond Puffs, 180
    Apricot Struesel Coffee Cake,
        53
    Baps, 129–130
    Blackberry Jam Coffee Cake, 17
    Buckwheat-Triticale Muffins,
        172
    Cherry-Almond Coffee Cake,
        41
    Cream Biscuits, 139–140
    Dutch Almond Christmas
        Pastries, 124–125
    Easter Breads, 27–28
    Easy Gingerbread People with
        Cinnamon-Honey Butter,
        123–124

Fresh Pear and Vanilla Muffins,
    83
Gingerbread Date Muffins, 23
Honey-Glazed Raisin and
    Sunflower-Seed Twist, 57–
    58
Irish Oat Bread, 68
Jim Dodge's Nutmeg Pear Pie,
    111
Lemon-Chocolate Chip Muffins,
    7–8
Lemony Brown-rice Muffins,
    179
Low-sodium, Low-cholesterol
    Corn Peaks, 177
Marmalade Muffins for Two, 11
Milk-free, Egg-free Applesauce
    Muffins, 176–177
Miniature Corn Muffins, 163
Miniature Cream Biscuits, 156–
    157
Miriam Rubin's Honey Cake, 88
Oat Date Nut Muffins, 178
Oatmeal-Raisin Breakfast
    Cookies, 80
Orange-Almond Coffee Cake,
    91
Parmesan Chive Biscuits, 36
Plum Upside-Down Coffee
    Cake, 61
Pumpkin Walnut Muffins, 107
Quick Christmas Tree Bread,
    119
Sesame Pecan Brown-rice
    Muffins, 178–179
Supersticky Cinnamon Rolls,
    99–100
Walnut Cinnamon-Chocolate
    Coffee Cake, 136

Baked Mushrooms, 118
Baked Polenta, 94
Baked Prune Plums, 90
Bananas:
    Ambrosia, 138
    Dip, Creamy, Pick-Up Fruit
        with, 76
    Papa Bear's Breakfast, 172–173
Baps, 129–130
Barley:
    Cereal, Hot Hulled, 171
    Porridge, Finnish, 117
Basil Tomatoes, 56
Basted Eggs, 191
Beef:
    Corned:
        for Hash, 97
        Hash, Homemade, 96–97
        Hash in a Hurry, 98
    Grillades, 14
    Steaks, North Dakota Breakfast,
        55
Bellinis, 50
Best-ever Oatmeal, 145–146
Beverages:
    Apple Juice, Hot Spiced, 22
    Bellinis, 50
    Café au Lait, 199–200
    Café con Leche, 199–200
    Caffè Latte, 199–200
    Cappuccino, 200
    Chocolate:
        Breakfast Hot, Base, 202
        Breakfast Hot, for Grownups,
            202
        Iced Breakfast, 202
    Coffee, 199–201
        with Chicory, 200
        Flavored, 200–201
        Iced, 201
    Espresso, 200
    Fresh Blueberries and
        Strawberries in Orange
        Juice, 55
    Highway Champagne, 79
    Kir Royale, 155
    Milk Punch, 13
    Mimosa, 155

Mulled Cider and Orange Juice,
        109
    Strawberry-Orange Juice, 6
    Tea, 201
        Cranberry-Red Zinger, 103
Biscuits:
    Cream, 139–140
    Miniature Cream, 156–157
    Miniature Ham, 156
    Miniature Smoked Turkey, 156
    Parmesan Chive, 36
Blackberry Jam Coffee Cake, 17
Black currants. See Currants
Blintz filling, 87
Blintzes, Grandmother Rubin's,
        85–87
Bloaters, 48
Blueberries:
    Farmer Cheese with, 47
    Melon and Berry Platter, 13
    and Strawberries, Fresh, in
        Orange Juice, 55
Borage, 189
Breads:
    Easter, 27–28
    Irish Oat, 68
    Low-sodium, Low-cholesterol
        Corn Peaks, 177
    Quick Christmas Tree, 119
Bread Pudding:
    Scotch, Miriam Rubin's, 127–
        128
    Ham and Cheese Breakfast, 143
Breakfast Birthday Cake, 64
Breakfast for a Crowd, 151–152
Breakfast from the Oven, 81–83
Breakfast Hot Chocolate Base, 202
Breakfast Hot Chocolate for
        Grownups, 202
Breakfast Indian Pudding, 169
A Breakfast Smorgasboard, 65–68
Breakfast with a Southern Flair,
        137–140
**Breakfast with a Southwestern
        Flavor,** 49–53
**Breakfast Treats for Pumpkin
        Pickers,** 101–103
Brown-rice Breakfast Pudding, 170

Brown-rice Muffins, Lemony, 179
Brown-rice Muffins, Sesame Pecan,
        178–179
Brown-Sugar Syrup, 7
Buckwheat-Triticale Muffins, 172
Buckwheat groats:
    Kasha, 170
    No-cholesterol Kasha, 176
Butter and Margarine, 8
Buttermilk, 68

C

Café au Lait, 199–200
Café con Leche, 199–200
Caffè Latte, 199–200
Cake:
    Breakfast Birthday, 64
    Honey, Miriam Rubin's, 88
    See also Coffee Cake
Calories-Don't-Count Granola,
        169
Campari, Grapefruit Sections with,
        127
Canadian Bacon, 32, 196
Cantaloupe, 186
    Festive Fruit Platter, 158–159
    Melon and Berry Platter, 13
    Pick-Up Fruit with Creamy
        Banana Dip, 76
Cappuccino, 200
Carambolas:
    Festive Fruit Platter, 158–159
    Stars, 159
Casserole Eggs Sardou, 16
Caviar, Srambled Eggs and, 132
Celebrate Rosh Hashanah, 84–88
Cereals:
    Barley:
        Hot Hulled, 171
        Porridge, Finnish, 117
    Granola:
        Calories-Don't-Count, 169
        Crunchy, 168–169
    Mush and Milk, 168
    Oatmeal, Best-ever, 145–146
    Papa Bear's Breakfast, 172–173
    Swiss Almond Muesli, 60

Cheddar and Parsley, Scrambled Eggs with, 122
Cheese:
    Baked Eggs with Ham and Gruyère, 82
    Cottage, with Chopped Fresh Vegetables, 67
    Danish, Detroit Fried, 58
    Farmer, with Blueberries, 47
    Grits, Garlic, 15
    Ham and, Breakfast Bread Pudding, 143
    Parmesan Chive Biscuits, 36
    Parmesan Toast, 44
    Platter of Sliced, 66–67
    Scrambled Eggs:
        with Cheddar and Parsley, 122
        with Chilies and, 51
    Soufflés, Rolled, with Spinach Filling, 160–162
    See also specific cheeses
Cherry:
    -Almond Coffee Cake, 41
    Melon, and Grape Platter, 46
Cherry Tomatoes, Sauteed, 159
Chestnut and Orange Bowl, 116
Chicken Livers, Herbed, 146–147
Chicory, Coffee with, 200
Children, recipes for:
    Cinnamon-Raisin French Toast Baked in the Oven, 31–32
    Dutch Baby, 63
    Frizzled Ham or Canadian Bacon, 32
    Parmesan Toast, 44
    Strawberry Smash, 31
Chilies and Cheese, Scrambled Eggs with, 51
Chili Pancakes, Double Corn and, 90–91
Chili Salsa, Special, 98
Chocolate:
    Chip:
        Muffins, Lemon-, 7–8
        Pancakes, 102–103
    Coffee Cake, Walnut Cinnamon-, 136

Hot, Breakfast:
    Base, 202
    for Grownups, 202
    Iced Breakfast, 202
Cholesterol, 175–176. See also Special diet dishes
Christmas Morning Feast, 120–125
Christmas Tree Bread, Quick, 119
Chunky Salsa Salad, 94
Cider and Orange Juice, Mulled, 109
Cinnamon:
    -Chocolate Coffee Cake, Walnut, 136
    -Honey Butter, Easy Gingerbread People with, 123–124
    Pineapple, 50
    -Raisin French Toast Baked in the Oven, 31–32
    Roll Dough, 100
    Rolls, Supersticky, 99–100
Citrus fruit, 186. See also specific fruits
Coffee, 199–201
    with Chicory, 200
    Flavored, 200–201
    Iced, 201
Coffee Cake:
    Apricot Streusel, 53
    Blackberry Jam, 17
    Cherry-Almond, 41
    Orange-Almond, 91
    Plum Upside-Down, 61
    Walnut Cinnamon-Chocolate, 136
Cold cereal. See Cereals
For a Cold Country Morning, 144–147
Come Help—Raise Our New Roof, Plant Bulbs, Rake Leaves, 89–91
Come See the First Blossoms, 18–20
Come Trim the Tree, 115–119
Compote of Fresh and Dried Fruit, 145

Cookies:
    Easy Gingerbread People with Cinnamon-Honey Butter, 123–124
    Oatmeal-Raisin Breakfast, 80
Corn:
    Double, and Chili Pancakes, 90–91
    Muffins, Miniature, 163
    See also Cornmeal
Corned Beef:
    for Hash, 97
    Hash, Homemade, 96–97
    Hash in a Hurry, 98
Cornmeal:
    Baked Polenta, 94
    Double, and Chili Pancakes, 90–91
    Griddle Cakes, 6
    Low-sodium, Low-cholesterol Corn Peaks, 177
    Muffins, Miniature, 163
    Mush and Milk, 168
Cottage Cheese with Chopped Fresh Vegetables, 67
Coulis, Warm Cranberry, 87
Cranberry:
    Coulis, Warm, 87
    -Poached Pears, 116–117
    -Red Zinger Tea, 103
    Cream Biscuits, 139–140
    Miniature, 156–157
Crunchy Cucumber Salad, 47
Crunchy Granola, 168–169
Cucumber Salad, Crunchy, 47
Currant Confusion, 117

D

For Dad, with Love, Too, 42–44
Dandelion flowers, 189
Danish, Detroit Fried Cheese, 58
Dates, 23
    Muffins, Gingerbread, 23
    Nut Muffins, Oat, 178
Detroit Fried Cheese Danish, 58
Devilish Egg Bunnies, 26
Double Corn and Chili Pancakes, 90–91

Dredgers, 185
Dutch Almond Christmas Pastries,
    124–125
Dutch Baby, 63

E

An Early-Morning Picnic, 21–23
Easter Breads, 27–28
Easter for Adults and Children,
    24–29
Easy Gingerbread People with
    Cinnamon-Honey Butter,
    123–124
Egg-free, Milk-free, Applesauce
    Muffins, 176–177
Eggs, 28, 190–194
    Bacon and, Sandwiches, 79
    Baked, 35, 194
        with Ham and Gruyère, 82
    Basted, 191
    Bunnies, Devilish, 26
    Frazzled, 193–194
    French Poaching, 192
    Frying, 191
    Hard-cooked, in the Shell, 193
    Omelet, 194
        Mushroom, with Dill Sour
            Cream, 10–11
    Over-lightly, 191
    Poaching, 191–192
        Kedgeree and, 128–129
    Sardou, Casserole, 16
    with Sausage, Peppers, and
        Potatoes, 40
    Scrambled, 193
        and Caviar, 132
        with Cheddar and Parsley,
            122
        with Chilies and Cheese, 51
        George Greene's Special, 175
        with Smoked Salmon and
            Potatoes, 20
    Shirred, 194
    Soft-cooked, in the Shell, 192–
        193
    Spaghetti Frittata, 43
    Steam-basted, 191

Endive Leaves, Smoked Salmon,
    157
English Muffin Pastries, Apple, 147
Espresso, 200

F

Farmer Cheese with Blueberries, 47
Festive Fruit Platter, 158–159
Finnish Barley Porridge, 117
Fish:
    Fresh Salmon Hash, 34–35
    Kedgeree and Poached Eggs,
        128–129
    Lox and Bagels, 133
    Smoked, 48
        Platter, 46
        Salmon Endive Leaves, 157
Flowers, edible, 189
Fourth of July Steak Breakfast,
    54–58
Frazzled Eggs, 193–194
French Poaching, 192
French Toast:
    Cinnamon-Raisin, Baked in the
        Oven, 31–32
    Kangaroo Pockets, 77
    Nutmeg, 70
Fresh Applesauce with Apple-
    Cinnamon Yogurt, 142
Fresh Blueberries and Strawberries
    in Orange Juice, 55
Fresh Peaches and Raspberries, 60
Fresh Pear and Vanilla Muffins, 83
Fresh Quince Applesauce, 142
Fresh Salmon Hash, 34–35
Frittata:
    Potato, No-cholesterol, 175
    Spaghetti, 43
Frizzled Ham, 32
Frozen Red and Green Grapes, 63
Frozen yogurt:
    Breakfast Birthday Cake, 64
Fruit, Breakfast, 186–188
    Compote of Fresh and Dried,
        145
    Glaze for Ham, 197–198
    Platter:
        decorating, 188–189

Festive, 158–159
    See also specific fruits
Fuyu persimmons, 187

G

Garlic Cheese Grits, 15
George Greene's Special
        Scrambled Eggs, 175
Gingerbread Date Muffins, 23
Gingerbread People with
        Cinnamon-Honey Butter,
        Easy, 123–124
Graduation Day Breakfast, 33–36
Grains, Great, 167–173. *See also*
        Breads; Muffins; specific
        grains
Grandmother Rubin's Blintzes, 85–
        87
Granola:
    Calories-Don't-Count, 169
    Crunchy, 168–169
Grapefruit, 186
    Pink, Sections with Honey, 116
    Sections with Campari, 127
Grapes:
    Ambrosia, 138
    Frozen Red and Green, 63
    Melon, Cherry, and, Platter, 46
Grating and Shredding, 15
Gravlax, 48
To Greet the Groundhog, 5–8
Grillades, 14
Grits:
    Breakfast Indian Pudding, 169
    Garlic Cheese, 15
    Perfect, 139
Gruyère, Baked Eggs with Ham
        and, 82

H

Hachiya persimmons, 187
Haddock:
    Kedgeree and Poached Eggs,
        128–129
Ham, 196–198
    Biscuits, Miniature, 156
    and Cheese Breakfast Bread
        Pudding, 143

Frizzled, 42
Fruit Glaze for, 197–198
and Gruyère, Baked Eggs with,
    82
Steaks with Hot-Pepper Jelly
    Glaze, 138–139
Happy Birthday!, 62–64
Hard-cooked Eggs in the Shell,
    193
Hash:
    Corned Beef, Homemade, 96–
        97
    Corned Beef for, 97
    Fresh Salmon, 34–35
    in a Hurry, Corned Beef, 98
**Hearty Breakfast for Columbus
    Day,** 92–94
**Hearty Fare for a Country
    Weekend,** 104–107
Herbed Chicken Livers, 146–147
Herb flowers, 189
Hibiscus, 189
Highway Champagne, 79
**Hogmanay—A Scottish New
    Year,** 126–130
Hollyhocks, 189
Home-fries, Rosemary, 118
Homemade Corned Beef Hash,
    96–97
Homemade Sage and Thyme
    Sausage Patties, 106
Homemade Vanilla Pearl Sugar, 29
Honey:
    -Baked Pears and Prunes, 96
    Butter, Cinnamon-, Easy
        Gingerbread People with,
        123–124
    Cake, Miriam Rubin's, 88
    -Crunch Baked Apples, 82
    -Glazed Raisin and Sunflower-
        Seed Twist, 57–58
    Pink Grapefruit Sections with,
        116
Honeydew melon, 186
    Festive Fruit Platter, 158–159
    Melon and Orange Bowl, 19
    Pick-Up Fruit with Creamy
        Banana Dip, 76

Honeysuckle, 189
Horseradish Sauce, Superb, 46
Hot Apples, Providence, 121
Hot cereal, *See* Cereals
Hot Chocolate, Breakfast:
    Base, 202
    for Grownups, 202
Hot Hulled Barley Cereal, 171
Hot-Pepper Jelly Glaze, Ham
        Steaks with, 138–139
Hot Spiced Apple Juice, 22

I
Ice cream:
    Breakfast Birthday Cake, 64
Iced Breakfast Chocolate, 202
Iced Coffee, 201
Ice milk:
    Breakfast Birthday Cake, 64
Indian Pudding, Breakfast, 169
Ingredients, Measuring, 183–184
In Search of Perfect Oatmeal, 146
Irish Oat Bread, 68
Irving Rubin's Pillow Potatoes, 56
Italian Sausage, Sweet or Spicy, 93

J
Jim Dodge's Nutmeg Pear Pie, 111

K
Kangaroo Pockets, 77
Kasha, 170
    No-cholesterol, 176
Kedgeree and Poached Eggs, 128–
        129
Kippers, 48
Kir Royale, 155
Kiwi fruit:
    Festive Fruit Platter, 158–159

L
Lavender, 189
Lazy August Breakfast, 69–71
Leaves, 86
Lemons:
    -Chocolate Chip Muffins, 7–8
    Lemony Brown-rice Muffins,
        179

    -Poached Apples, 93
Lemony Brown-rice Muffins, 179
Light Breakfast for a Hot Day,
        59–61
Livers, Chicken, Herbed, 146–147
Low-sodium, Low-cholesterol
        Corn Peaks, 177
Lox, 48
    and Bagels, 133
Lychees, 188

M
Make-ahead Breakfast, 141–143
Mangoes, 188
Mardi Gras, 12–17
Margarine, Butter and, 8
Marlin, smoked, 48
Marmalade Muffins for Two, 11
Mashed Avocado, 52
Measuring equivalents, 184
Measuring Ingredients, 183–184
Meats, Breakfast, 195–198. *See also*
        specific meats
Melon, 186
    and Berry Platter, 13
    Cherry, and Grape Platter, 46
    Festive Fruit Platter, 158–159
    Pick-Up Fruit with Creamy
        Banana Dip, 76
    and Orange Bowl, 19
Memorial Day, 39–41
Milk-free, Egg-free Applesauce
        Muffins, 176–177
Milk Punch, 13
Mimosa, 155
Miniature Corn Muffins, 163
Miniature Cream Biscuits, 156–
        157
Miniature Ham Biscuits, 156
Miniature Smoked Turkey Biscuits,
        156
Miriam Rubin's Honey Cake, 88
Miriam Rubin's Scotch Bread
        Pudding, 127–128
For Mother, with Love, 30–32
Muesli, Swiss Almond, 60
Muffins:
    Buckwheat-Triticale, 172

Muffins (cont.)
English, Apple, Pastries, 147
Fresh Pear and Vanilla, 83
Gingerbread Date, 23
Lemon-Chocolate Chip, 7–8
Lemony Brown-rice, 179
Low-sodium, Low-cholesterol Corn Peaks, 177
Marmalade, for Two, 11
Milk-free, Egg-free Applesauce, 176–177
Miniature Corn, 163
Oat Date Nut, 178
Pumpkin Walnut, 107
Sesame Pecan Brown-rice, 178–179
Mulled Cider and Orange Juice, 109
Mush and Milk, 168
Mushrooms:
Baked, 118
Omelet with Dill Sour Cream, 10–11

N
Nasturtiums, 189
A New England Breakfast, 95–100
No-cholesterol Kasha, 176
No-cholesterol Potato Frittata, 175
North Dakota Breakfast Steaks, 55
Nutmeg, 13
French Toast, 70
Pear Pie, Jim Dodge's, 111

O
Oat Bread, Irish, 68
Oatmeal:
Best-ever, 145–146
Hotcakes, 105–106
Papa Bear's Breakfast, 172–173
-Raisin Breakfast Cookies, 80
In Search of Perfect, 146
See also Oats
Oats:
Calories-Don't-Count Granola, 169
Crunchy Granola, 168–169
Date Nut Muffins, 178

Papa Bear's Breakfast, 172–173
Olive oil, 43
Omelet, 194
Mushroom, with Dill Sour Cream, 10–11
Orange Juice:
Fresh Blueberries and Strawberries in, 55
Mimosa, 155
Mulled Cider and, 109
Strawberry-, 6
Oranges, 186
-Almond Coffee Cake, 91
Ambrosia, 138
Bowl, Chestnut and, 116
Bowl, Melon and, 19
Festive Fruit Platter, 158–159
Marmalade Muffins for Two, 11
Wedges, 135
See also Orange Juice

P
Pancakes:
Chocolate Chip, 102–103
Cornmeal Griddle Cakes, 6
Double Corn and Chili, 90–91
Oatmeal Hotcakes, 105–106
Pansies, 189
Papa Bear's Breakfast, 172–173
Papayas, 188
Parmesan Chive Biscuits, 36
Parmesan Toast, 44
Paskha, Unorthodox, 29
Passion Fruit, 188
Pastries:
Apple English Muffin, 147
Dutch Almond Christmas, 124–125
Peaches, 187
Bellinis, 50
and Raspberries, Fresh, 60
Pearl Sugar, Vanilla, Homemade, 29
Pears:
Compote of Fresh and Dried Fruit, 145
Cranberry-Poached, 116–117
Fresh, and Vanilla Muffins, 83

Pick-Up Fruit with Creamy Banana Dip, 76
Pie, Nutmeg, Jim Dodge's, 111
and Prunes, Honey-Baked, 96
Pecan Brown-rice Muffins, Sesame, 178–179
Peeling and Coring Apples, 121
Peppers, Sausage, and Potatoes, Eggs with, 40
Perfect Grits, 139
Persimmons, 187–188
Pick-Up Fruit with Creamy Banana Dip, 76
Pie, Jim Dodge's Nutmeg Pear, 111
Pineapples, 187
Ambrosia, 138
Cinnamon, 50
Festive Fruit Platter, 158–159
Pick-Up Fruit with Creamy Banana Dip, 76
Pink Grapefruit Sections with Honey, 116
Platter of Sliced Cheeses, 68
Plums:
Prune, Baked, 90
Simmered, 71
Upside-Down Coffee Cake, 61
Poaching Eggs, 191–192
Polenta, Baked, 94
Pomegranates, 188–189
Pork Cutlet Breakfast Sandwiches, 135
Porridge, Finnish Barley, 117
Portable Breakfast for a Fall Outing, 78–80
Potatoes:
Eggs with Sausage, Peppers, and, 40
Eggs Scrambled with Smoked Salmon and, 20
Frittata, No-cholesterol, 175
Pillow, Irving Rubin's, 56
Rosemary Home-fries, 118
Sausage, Swedish, 122–123
Pre-ski Energy Input, 134–136
Providence Hot Apples, 121
Prune Plums, Baked, 90

Prunes, Pears and, Honey-Baked, 96
Pudding:
  Bread:
    Scotch, Miriam Rubin's, 127–128
    Ham and Cheese Breakfast, 143
    Brown-rice Breakfast, 170
    Indian, Breakfast, 169
Pumpkin Walnut Muffins, 107
Punch, Milk, 13

Q
Quantity cooking, 151–153
Quick Christmas Tree Bread, 119
Quince Applesauce, Fresh, 142

R
Raisin and Sunflower-Seed Twist, Honey-Glazed, 57–58
Raspberries:
  Festive Fruit Platter, 158–159
  Fresh Peaches and, 60
  Melon and Berry Platter, 13
  Sauce, 158
Red Zinger Tea, Cranberry-, 103
Rhubarb Sauce, Strawberries in, 25
Rice:
  Brown:
    Breakfast Pudding, 170
    Muffins, Lemony, 179
    Muffins, Sesame Pecan, 178–179
  Kedgeree and Poached Eggs, 128–129
  Rolled Cheese Soufflés with Spinach Filling, 160–162
Rosemary Home-fries, 118
Rose petals, 189

S
Sablefish, smoked, 48
Salad:
  Chunky Salsa, 94
  Crunchy Cucumber, 47
Salmon:
  Fresh, Hash, 34–35

Lox and Bagels, 133
  Smoked, 48
    Endive Leaves, 157
    and Potatoes, Eggs Scrambled with, 20
Salsa:
  Chunky, Salad, 94
  Cilantro, 51
  Special Chili, 98
Sandwiches:
  Bacon and Egg, 79
  Breakfast, Pork Cutlet, 135
  Kangaroo Pockets, 77
  Parmesan Toast, 44
Sauces:
  Chili Salsa, Special, 98
  Cranberry Coulis, Warm, 87
  Horseradish, Suberb, 46
  Raspberry, 158
  Salsa Cilantro, 51
  Strawberry, 64
Sausages, 196
  Eggs with, Peppers, and Potatoes, 40
  Italian, Sweet or Spicy, 93
  Patties, Homemade Sage and Thyme, 106
  Swedish Potato, 122–123
Sauteed Cherry Tomatoes, 159
Scented geraniums, 189
Scotch Bread Pudding, Miriam Rubin's, 127–128
Scrambled Eggs, 193
  and Caviar, 132
  with Cheddar and Parsley, 122
  with Chilies and Cheese, 51
  George Greene's Special, 175
  with Smoked Salmon and Potatoes, 20
Sesame Pecan Brown-rice Muffins, 178–179
Shirred Eggs, 194
Shredding, Grating and, 15
Simmered Plums, 71
Skillets, 185
Smoked Fish Platter, 46
Smoked Salmon Endive Leaves, 157

Smoked Turkey Biscuits, Miniature, 156
Soft-cooked Eggs in the Shell, 192–193
Soufflés, Rolled Cheese, with Spinach Filling, 160–162
Spaghetti Frittata, 43
Special Chili Salsa, 98
Special diet dishes, 174
  Apricot Almond Puffs, 180
  George Greene's Special Scrambled Eggs, 175
  Lemony Brown-rice Muffins, 179
  Low-sodium, Low-cholesterol Corn Peaks, 177
  Milk-free, Egg-free Applesauce Muffins, 176–177
  No-cholesterol Kasha, 176
  No-cholesterol Potato Frittata, 175
  Oat Date Nut Muffins, 178
  Sesame Pecan Brown-rice Muffins, 178–179
Spinach Filling, Rolled Cheese Soufflés with, 160–162
Springform pans, 185
Squash blossoms, 189
Squash Waffles, 110
Star fruit. See Carambolas
Steaks, Breakfast, North Dakota, 55
Steam-basted Eggs, 191
Strawberries:
  Festive Fruit Platter, 158–159
  Fresh Blueberries and, in Orange Juice, 55
  Melon and Berry Platter, 13
  -Orange Juice, 6
  in Rhubarb Sauce, 25
  Sauce, 64
  Smash, 31
Sturgeon, smoked, 48
Successful Big Bashes: Advice from a Pro, 153
Sugar:
  Brown-, Syrup, 7
  Homemade Vanilla Pearl, 29

Sunflower-Seed Twist, Honey-
    Glazed Raisin and, 57–58
Superb Horseradish Sauce, 46
Supersticky Cinnamon Rolls,
    99–100
Swedish Potato Sausage, 122–123
Sweet or Spicy Italian Sausage, 93
Swiss Almond Muesli, 60
Syrup, Brown-Sugar, 7

T
Tangerines Masquerading as
    Pumpkins, 102
Tea, 201
    Cranberry-Red Zinger, 103
Thanksgiving Day, 108–111
Thick Yogurt, 66
Toast, Parmesan, 44
Tomatoes, 187
    Basil, 56
    Cherry, Sauteed, 159
Tortillas, Warm, 52
Triticale Muffins, Buckwheat-, 172
Trout, smoked, 48

Tuna, smoked, 48
Turkey, Smoked, Biscuits,
    Miniature, 156

U
Unorthodox Paskha, 29
Upside-Down Coffee Cake, Plum,
    61
Utensils, 185

V
Valentine's Day, 9–11
Vanilla:
    Muffins, Fresh Pear and, 83
    Pearl Sugar, Homemade, 29
Vegetables, Chopped Fresh,
    Cottage Cheese with, 67.
    See also specific vegetables
Violas, 189
Violets, 189

W
Waffles, Squash, 110

Walnut:
    Cinnamon-Chocolate Coffee
        Cake, 136
    Muffins, Pumpkin, 107
Warm Cranberry Coulis, 87
Warm Tortillas, 52
A Wedding Breakfast, 154–163
Weekend Breakfast on the Porch,
    45–48
Wheat Berries, 171
    Papa Bear's Breakfast, 172–173
Whitefish, smoked, 48
Whiting, smoked, 48

Y
Yogurt:
    Apple-Cinnamon, Fresh
        Applesauce with, 142
    frozen, Breakfast Birthday Cake,
        64
    Pick-Up Fruit with Creamy
        Banana Dip, 76
    Strawberry Smash, 31
    Thick, 66